The Palace Law of Ayutthaya and the Thammasat

Cornell University

Translated and edited by Chris Baker and Pasuk Phongpaichit

The Palace Law of Ayutthaya and the Thammasat

Law and Kingship in Siam

Southeast Asia Program Publications
Southeast Asia Program
Cornell University
Ithaca, New York
2016

Cornell Southeast Asia Program Publications
640 Stewart Avenue, Ithaca, NY 14850-3857

Studies on Southeast Asia Series No. 69

Printed in the United States of America

ISBN: PB 9780877277699
ISBN: HC 9780877277996

Cover: designed by Kat Dalton

Cover image: The first folio of one manuscript volume of the 1805 Three Seals Code (National Library of Thailand mss no. 26). Courtesy of the Fine Arts Department of Thailand

TABLE OF CONTENTS

List of Tables, Illustrations, and Maps

List of Tables

List of Illustrations

List of Maps

PREFACE

Ayutthaya was capital of Siam[1] for four centuries, from the mid-fourteenth century to 1767. When Europeans arrived in the sixteenth and seventeenth centuries, some placed Siam among the great countries of Asia, along with India and China. They described Ayutthaya as a center of Asian trade, as the head of a powerful military empire, and as the capital of a resplendent monarchy—"In the Indies, there is no state that is more monarchical than Siam."[2]

One of the legacies of the Ayutthaya era is the Three Seals Code, a collection of law texts assembled in 1805 from old manuscripts. This source has been studied by several scholars, including Robert Lingat, Yoneo Ishii, and Michael Vickery. Ishii in particular laid out the extensive nature of the code, which includes twenty-seven or forty-two laws, depending on how they are counted. Yet there has been little reflection about what the existence of such an impressive corpus of law implies regarding the nature of state and society in Ayutthaya.

In this book, we present not only translations of two key laws in the Three Seals Code, but also a proposal that the role of royal-made law was a distinctive feature of the Ayutthaya state. Law was not made by legislation the way contemporary law is made, but by the accumulation of court judgments and proclamations made by the king or in his name. These were written down and preserved by royal scribes, so their effect became more than ephemeral. Once collected in codes, they were labeled as "sacred" and "royal" (*phra ratcha*) to underline their authority. In the political theory of late Ayutthaya, the king created the means for his subjects to pursue the path to *nibbana* (liberation from suffering) by protecting them from outside enemies through his military might, and by protecting them from one another through the use of law to adjudicate disputes.

The Palace Law might equally be called the Law on Kingship or the Law on Government. The core of the text is old, probably dating to the last part of the fifteenth century, a time of widespread and persistent warfare in Southeast Asia. The basis of kingship in Siam and neighboring states is often described solely in relation to sacredness and religious power through terms such as *devaraja* (god king), *thammaraja* (dhamma king), and *cakravartin* (wheel-turning emperor). The Palace Law sets out a much broader description of the meanings and underpinnings of kingship. Its major theme is hierarchy: it prescribes a top-down social order headed by the king, and establishes ways through which this order is dramatized in dress and display. It sets out an an annual cycle of ceremonies that present the king

---

[1] Siam in the Ayutthaya era expanded from a collection of cities near the gulf coast to an area roughly equivalent to the central region of present-day Thailand. Spurs that reached westward across the upper peninsula and eastward to Khorat were added in the late-sixteenth century. Some cities down the peninsula were fitful tributaries.

[2] Gervaise, *Natural and Political History*, 53.

as the patron of Buddhism, military defender of the realm, source of agricultural prosperity, fount of charity, and engineer of magical good fortune. It elaborates rules for protecting the king in person, and upholding the palace as sacred space, the large corps of royal women as a symbol of royal power, and the royal elephants as palladia of the realm. It prescribes punishments of death and disfigurement for even minor infractions of these rules. How often such punishments were served is unknown, but the contrast between the protection afforded to royalty and the vulnerability of others lays out a hierarchy of human values. This text is a constitution of its time, a constitution of royal absolutism.

Royal laws on relations between king, government, and people can be found in other South and Southeast Asian regions.[3] But such laws are only one part of the Three Seals Code. Over half of the code consists of laws relating to everyday life—marriage, theft, debt, slavery, gambling, magic, inheritance, quarreling, abuse, injury, contracts, and so on. These "social" laws are also the product of royal law-making. They originated from court judgments or proclamations made by the king or his delegates. They were preserved by the efforts of royal scribes and librarians. They were labeled as royal laws to give them authority.

When did these laws come into being, and whom did they cover? These questions are difficult to answer because of problems concerning dating the law texts and limitations in the external sources. References in the chronicles suggest royal law-making had begun by the fifteenth century. In this early period, when each city-state was largely independent, the writ of Ayutthaya laws may have been limited to the capital. Both the scale and scope of royal law-making probably expanded from the early seventeenth century, when the level of warring diminished and the society became more prosperous and more complex. Significantly, in the Three Seals Codes, these social laws are categorized as solutions to different kinds of "disputes between people." Law was a technique employed by kings to reduce conflict in a society of growing complexity. From the late-eighteenth century, there is a large amount of additional legislation with secure dates, especially on such topics as theft, debt, and management of manpower.[4] In this era, the writ of royal law was extended beyond the capital. With this expansion in the scope and reach of royal law, the number of law courts multiplied, and detailed rules on judicial procedure were developed to ensure some consistency throughout this system. By late-Ayutthaya, the extensive laws were an expression of royal power, and the elaborate judicial system was a major part of the state's infrastructure.

As part of the revival following the destruction of Ayutthaya in 1767, King Rama I took pains over the preservation of texts of three kinds: religious treatises, royal chronicles, and the laws. The laws were one of the three categories of texts that had to be rescued so that the kingdom could revive.

The importance of royal law-making has been obscured in the historiography by a tendency to assimilate Siam with a tradition descended from India through Myanmar associated with texts known as *dharmaśāstra, dhammasattha*, or *thammasat*. In this tradition, social law derives from custom or religious authority, not from the king. However, as we argue here, the evidence for the influence of this tradition in Siam is weak while the evidence for the role of royal law-making is strong. In the Three Seals Code of 1805, there is a reconciliation between the *thammasat* tradition

[3] Than Tun, *Royal Orders of Burma*; Lingat, *Classical Law of India*.

[4] See especially the Old Decrees in *KTSD*, 4 and 5.

and royal law-making. Possibly this reconciliation was a product of Buddhism's growing social role in the eighteenth century.

What is the significance of highlighting royal law-making as a defining feature of the Ayutthaya state? One is historiographical. For generations, historians of Ayutthaya have concentrated especially on commerce and warfare. Despite the existence of such an extensive textual resource as the Three Seals Code, the historical study of law has languished. Partly this is because of the technical barriers, particularly problems of dating. But these difficulties can be addressed by new methods. Analysis of the language used in the Code may help in the issue of dating. Making more of the Code available in English will allow more comparative approaches.

A reconsideration of the role of law can also add a dimension to understanding the premodern state in Siam. Studies of the state in Southeast Asia have tended to concentrate on the cultural dimensions—the role of kinship networks as the lineaments of politics, the importance of ritual as theater, and the legitimating functions of religion and cosmology[5]—or the economic dimensions, particularly the role of revenues from tax and trade.[6] While there is a growing appreciation of *protection* as a key concept of kingship in the region, little attention has been paid to how this concept is applied through the king's role as maker and enforcer of written law.

• • •

Several years ago, when he was working on a project about the Ayutthaya Palace Law, the historian Winai Pongsripian floated at us the idea of making an English translation. At the time we were busy elsewhere and doubtful we could translate such a difficult text. Only some years later did we remember Winai's suggestion, and discover that his new Thai edition of the Palace Law had made the task possible by explaining hundreds of words not found in any Thai dictionary. We are especially grateful to Acharn Winai for suggesting this translation, providing the edition that made it possible, and helping to unscramble difficulties and correct mistakes.

The idea of including the Thammasat arose later. In the course of writing the introduction on law and law-making, we realized that debates on comparative legal history in Southeast Asia had been handicapped because only small sections of the Thai Thammasat were available in English.

We have been fortunate to have help from Christian Lammerts. Our revised translation and introduction have benefited enormously from his advice and his work, especially his doctoral thesis due to appear in book form as *Buddhism and Written Law: Dhammasattha Literature and Jurisprudence in Burma, c. 1200–1850.*

We also thank two extraordinary scholars of Thai Buddhism, Peter Skilling and Justin McDaniel, for their unfailing support and readiness to answer the naïve queries of the uninitiated. We are grateful to Tamara Loos, who shares our interest in the role of law in Thai history, and who gave us some very good advice. Thapanan Nipithakul kindly shared his French translation of the Thammasat. We are grateful to the publisher's other anonymous reader, and to Niyada Lausoonthorn, Bhawan Ruangsilp, Craig Reynolds, Hiram Woodward, Kennon Breazeale, Patrick Jory,

[5] Day, *Fluid Iron*; Reynolds, "Paradigms of the Premodern State."

[6] Notably in the work of Victor Lieberman and Anthony Reid.

Barend Terwiel, Nicolas Revire, Eugénie Mérieau, Piyabutr Saengkanokkul, Somlak Charoenpot, Sriram Natrajan, Patrick Dumon, Junko Koizumi, and Fritz Goss. Thanks to Sarah Grossman and others at Cornell Southeast Asia Program Publications for their help in the process of publication.

For permission to use images of the 1805 manuscript of the Three Seals Code, we are grateful to the director-general of the Fine Arts Department of Thailand, Bovornvate Rungrujee. For help in acquiring the images, we thank Em-orn Chawsuan and Chung Dipprakhon of the National Library of Thailand.

The book is divided into three parts. The first summarizes knowledge on the making and usage of law in Ayutthaya Siam, and on the structure of the Three Seals Code of 1805. While we draw on the classic work by Robert Lingat, MR Seni Pramoj, Yoneo Ishii, and Michael Vickery, we also make use of a wave of new research in Thai occasioned by the two-hundredth anniversary of the Three Seals Code in 2005.

The second part is on the Thammasat. Since the 1920s, there has been debate on how the tradition derived ultimately from the Indian *dharmaśāstra* texts arrived in Siam. We revisit this discussion using new research, before examining in detail the role of the Thammasat in the Three Seals Code, and presenting a full English translation of the text.

The third part focuses on the Palace Law. The introduction to the translation of the text examines the physical space of the Ayutthaya palace and the making of the Palace Law, before analyzing the content of the law and what it tells us about Ayutthaya kingship. The translation shows, we believe, that this is a unique, fascinating, and important document for legal history and Southeast Asian history.

LAWMAKING AND THE THREE SEALS CODE

The Palace Law (*kot monthianban*) and Thammasat (*phra thammasat*) are two of twenty-seven legal texts compiled in 1805 on the orders of King Rama I from the stock of extant legal manuscripts. All but three of these texts are laws that survived the destruction of Ayutthaya in 1767.[1] The resulting compilation is known as the Three Seals Code. According to the code's preface, the king ordered the recompilation because of suspicion that one law (on marriage) had been falsified.[2] The king had just completed a revision of the Tipiṭaka, the Buddhist scriptures. The preface refers to this historic event, and presents the revision of the laws as a comparable task.

> In this kingdom a king who rules the realm depends on the ancient laws, the codes of written law legislated by previous kings in order that judges may decide on all cases for the populace with justice. However, these royal decrees and royal laws were very defective, faulty, and contradictory, because covetous people with no shame over sin had modified them to their own liking. Judges had thus sometimes acted unjustly on behalf of the realm.
>
> Hence the king graciously commanded that subjects with knowledge be assigned to cleanse (*chamra*) the royal decrees and laws in the Royal Library from the Thammasat onwards; ensure they are correct in every detail according to the Pali with no inconsistencies in their content; arrange them into chapters and groups; and take pains to cleanse and adjust any aberrations to accord with

1 The three texts that post-date Ayutthaya are the Law on the Monkhood, 1805; and two collection of laws and decrees dated between 1784 and 1805, titled Royal Legislation and New Royal Decrees (see numbers 16, 17, and 25 in Table 1).

2 "Nai Bunsi, a royal metalworker, presented a petition with accusations against Phra Kasem [a magistrate] and Nai Racha-at. Amdaeng Pom, wife of Nai Bunsi, had filed for divorce from Nai Bunsi. Nai Bunsi informed Phra Kasem that Amdaeng Pom had committed adultery with Nai Racha-at and then asked for a divorce, which Nai Bunsi refused. [Nai Bunsi alleged that] Phra Kasem did not investigate the testimony of Nai Bunsi, flirted with Amdaeng Pom, did not make a true and fair investigation, sided with Amdaeng Pom, and sent a selective record to the court judges, who ruled that this was a case of woman divorcing a man, and that Amdaeng Pom was thus divorced from Nai Bunsi according to law. The King graciously stated that the judges' ruling, in granting a divorce to a woman who had been unfaithful to the man, was not just or fair. The King thus ordered Chaophraya Phrakhlang to bring the laws from the court to examine against the copies in the Royal Library and Royal Bedchamber. It was found that all three copies stated that, if a woman petitions for divorce, even though the man had done no wrong, she may have it." "Prakat phraratchaprarop," *KTSD*, 1: 2–3; Lingat, "Note sur la revision," 19–20.

justice, in keeping with the king's gracious intent to be of benefit to kings who reign over the realm in the future.[3]

The recompilation of the laws was part of this king's project to revise and recompile all extant documents of importance, including the royal chronicles and religious texts.

A volume of the Three Seals Code, 1805
(courtesy of the Fine Arts Department of Thailand)

The revision of the laws was carried out by an eleven-man committee within eleven months. Each law was stamped with the seals of three ministries (Mahathai, Kalahom, and Phrakhlang), hence the name of the code. The royal preface ends with the injunction, "if any book of laws or decrees produced for consultation does not have the three seals, judicial officers will on no account pay it any attention."[4] The revised code became the law of the land until gradually replaced by Western-style lawmaking from the late-nineteenth century.[5]

Table 1 shows the contents of the Three Seals Code. Following the Royal Institute edition (2007), the laws are listed here in the order they were approved in 1805 (according to dates on the first page of each[6]) with the original titles and spelling. In the printed editions beginning with Lingat's edition in 1938–39, several changes were introduced. Law number 13 was divided into two laws, Abduction and Division of Persons; and number 22 was divided into two laws, Crimes against

[3] *KTSD*, 1: 4–5.

[4] *KTSD*, 1: 6.

[5] Loos, *Subject Siam*, 40–71.

[6] In the original manuscripts, each of the twenty-seven laws begins with a page showing the three seals; a page showing the date the law was completed in 1805, the names of those who checked the text, and the number of times they checked it; and twelve pages containing the royal announcement, called "Prakat phraratchaprarop" in the printed editions, explaining the revision (Krisda, "Nueaha khong kotmai tra sam duang").

Government and Crimes against People. Also in the printed editions, the titles of the laws on Inheritance, Military and Provincial List, and Civil List were modified by adding *Phra aiyakan laksana* to conform to the general pattern. Note that both number 5, Acceptance of Cases, and number 11, Miscellaneous Laws, are a compendium of several laws, each with its own preface and in most cases also a date. The first part of number 27, Law on Punishment, is a separate law about compensation. *Phra thammanun* is two separate laws, one on the allocation of cases to different courts and the other on the use of official seals, each with its own preface and date. Revolt and Warfare also seem to have originally been separate laws,[7] and each part has a preface and date. If these groupings are disaggregated, there are forty-two laws under twenty-seven headings (see Table 1).

There have been several exercises in categorizing the documents in the Three Seals Code according to different theories of law.[8] However, there is a classification that is internal to the code itself.

As explained below, one purpose of the Thammasat is to serve as an index to the code. The Thammasat has two lists of topics to be covered by law. The first, in section 8 of the Thammasat, contains "matters for judges and magistrates," meaning laws about judicial procedure, including, for example, the law about witnesses, but also the Tenets of Indra, a discourse on good and bad legal decisions. The second list, in section 9, contains "matters of dispute" among people, meaning all the various reasons that a case may be brought to court, including marital disputes, inheritance, debt, theft, and so on. In each of the laws covered by these two lists, the preface of the law has a back-reference to these lists in the Thammasat.[9] In the final column of Table 1, these two types are labeled as A and B, respectively.

A third category, C, includes laws directly related to the king, government, and monkhood. In the early seventeenth century, Jeremias Van Vliet noted the distinctive features of this category:

> Of all crimes, none are so heavily punished as sinning against the authority of the king, against the priests, or the temples. If anybody should try to usurp any honor due to the king secretly or in public, should act against him or his state, or should show any disrespect, should treat the priests badly, rob their properties, profane churches or idols, he or the suspected would be punished with a cruel death without trial [while other offences are submitted to court process].[10]

---

[7] After Naresuan's famous elephant duel in 1593, the nobles consulted the *Phra aiyakan suek*, the Law on Warfare, about punishment for soldiers who failed in battle (Cushman, *Royal Chronicles*, 132; Bradley, *Phraratcha phongsawadan*, 146). Presumably the amalgamation of the two laws dates after this.

[8] For example, Visanu, "Kotken kan suep ratchasombat"; and Krisda, "Khrongsang kotmai tra sam duang."

[9] In the case of the laws on procedure, this reference takes the form of a 2–3 line verse in Pali. In the case of the "dispute" laws, the reference is to a title in Pali in the Thammasat's list.

[10] *Van Vliet's Siam*, 154–55. Jeremias Van Vliet was head of Dutch East India Company's lodge at Ayutthaya from 1636 to 1642, and the most prolific writer on Siam in that era.

Table 1—Contents of the Three Seals Code

	Thai title	Transliteration	Translation	pp	type
	ประกาศพระราชปรารภ	*Prakat phraratchaprarop*	Royal Announcement (preface)	6	
1	พระทำนูน	*Phra thammanun*	Phra Thammanun	33	A
	พระทำนูน	*phra thammanun*	phra thammanun	12	
	ใช้ตราด้วยราชการ	*chai tra duai ratchakan*	use of official seals	21	
2	พระธรรมสาตร	*Phra thammasat*	Thammasat	35	
3	หลักอินทภาษ	*Lak inthaphat*	Tenets of Indra	27	A
4	วิวาทด่าตี	*Wiwat da ti*	Dispute, Abuse, Assault	24	B
5	พระไอยการลักษณรับฟ้อง	*Phra aiyakan laksana rap fong*	Law on Acceptance of Cases	41	A
	รับฟ้อง	*rap fong*	acceptance of cases	10	
	โจทกะเฉทกะ	*jotakachethaka*	dismissal of cases	7	
	ตัดสำนวน	*tat samnuan*	disqualification	6	
	ตัดพญาณ	*tat phayan*	rejection of witnesses	7	
	ประวิงความ	*prawing khwam*	delay	3	
	อัญะมัญะปฏิภาศ	*ayamayapadiphat*	substitution	8	
6	พระไอยการลักษณกู้หนี้	*Phra aiyakan laksana ku ni*	Law on Credit and Debt	35	B
7	มรดก	*Moradok*	Inheritance	38	B
8	พระไอยการลักษณอุธร	*Phra aiyakan laksana uthon*	Law on Appeal	31	B
9	พระไอยการลักษณตระลาการ	*Phra aiyakan laksana tralakan*	Law on Judges	51	A
10	พระไอยการลักษณผัวเมีย	*Phra aiyakan laksana phu mia*	Law on Husband and Wife	80	B
11	พระไอยการลักษณภญาน	*Phra aiyakan laksana phayan*	Law on Witnesses	37	A
12	พระไอยการลักษณโจร	*Phra aiyakan laksana jon*	Law on Theft	95	B
13	พระไอยการลักภาลูกเมียผู้คนท่าน บานผแนก	*Phra aiyakan lakpha luk mia phu khon than ban phanek*	Law on Abduction of Children, Wives, and Dependents, and Division of People[11]	46	B
	พระไอยการลักภาลูกเมียผู้คนท่าน	*lakpha luk mia phu khon than*	abduction of children, wives, or dependents	20	
	พระไอยการบานผแนก	*ban phanaek*	division of people	26	
14	พระไอยการทาษ	*Phra aiyakan that*	Law on Slaves	59	B

[11] This law deals with the allocation of *phrai* and the children of *phrai* to departments of government.

15	พระไอยการกระบดศึก	*Phra aiyakan krabot suek*	Law on Revolt, Warfare	49	C
	กระบด	*krabot*	revolt	17	
	ศึก	*suek*	warfare	32	
16	กฎพระสงฆ	*Kot phra song*	Law on the Monkhood	65	C
17	พระราชบัญญัติ	*Phra ratchabanyat*	Royal Legislation	35	D
18	นาทหารหัวเมือง	*Na thahan hua mueang*	Military and Provincial Lists	59	E
19	ลักษณพีสูทดำน้ำพิสูทลุยเพลิง	*Laksana phisut dam nam phisut lui phloeng*	Law on Ordeal by Water or Fire	18	A
20	กฎมณเทียรบาล	*Kot monthianban*	Palace Law	91	C
21	พระไอยการตำแหน่งนาพลเรือน	*Phra aiyakan tamnaeng phonlaruen*	Civil list	22	E
22	พระไอยการอาญาหลวง	*Phra aiyakan aya luang*	Law of Crimes against Government	114	C
	อาญาหลวง	*aya luang*	crimes against government	105	
	อาญาราษ	*aya rat*	crimes against people	9	
23	พระไอยการเบดเสรจ	*Phra aiyakan laksana bet set*	Miscellaneous Laws	90	B
	ทีบ้านที่สวน	*thi ban thi suan*	house and paddy field	20	
	เสนียดแก่กัน	*saniat kae kan*	invective and cursing	18	
	เช่า ยืม ซื้อ ขาย	*chao yuem sue khai*	rentals, lending, purchase	27	
	พนันขันต่อกัน	*phanan khun to kan*	gambling	4	
	วิวาทด้วยความสาเหตุ	*wiwat duai khwam sahet*	just cause	9	
	เวทวิทธยาคมแล กฤษติยาคุณ	*wetwithayakhom lae kruesatiyakhun*	magic and spirits	13	
24	กฎ ๓๖ ข้อ	*Kot 36 kho*	Thirty-six Laws	29	D
25	พระราชกำหนดใหม่	*Phra ratcha kamnot mai*	New Royal Decrees	179	D
26	พระราชกำหนดเก่า	*Phraratcha kamnot kao*	Old Royal Decrees	254	D
27	พระไอยการพรมศักดิ	*Phra aiyakan phrommasak*	Law on Punishment	37	A
	พิกัดกระเสียรอายุศม	*phikat krasian aiyusom*	valuation by age	12	
	พระไอยการพรมศักดิ	*phrommasak*	law on punishment	25	

Notes: The "pp" column shows the number of pages in the Khurusapha edition of the code, to give an idea of relative length. The "type" column is explained in the text.

Within this category come the laws on the Palace, Monkhood, Revolt and Warfare, and Crimes against Government.[12] Modern legal scholars have labeled this category of law as *ratchanitisat*,[13] meaning law made by the king beyond the scope of

[12] Possibly these were once not cross-referenced with the Thammasat in the same way as laws of type A and B. See below, pp. 21–24.

[13] Visanu, "Kotken kan suep ratchasombat"; Krisda, "Nueaha khong kotmai tra sam duang."

the Thammasat, but the term seems to have no historical basis. What defines type-C laws, as Van Vliet noticed, is that they deal with king, government, and monkhood—the sacred core of the realm.

A fourth type consists of recent decrees or legislation on miscellaneous matters that have not been sorted into categories. These include several decrees and laws introduced under King Rama I, and others from earlier in the eighteenth century. These are labeled D in Table 1. Type E includes the Civil List and the Military and Provincial List, which are lists of official positions with details of titles and rank.[14]

How did this impressive corpus of law come into being, and how was it used?

MAKING AND USING WRITTEN LAW IN SIAM

The foreign visitors who left the first detailed accounts of Siam in the seventeenth century noted the importance of law and particularly of the written law. Joost Schouten, a VOC (Vereenigde Ooost-Indische Compagnie, the Dutch East India Company) officer resident in Ayutthaya for six years in the 1630s, wrote:

> The King thus soveraignly disposing of all things, does notwithstanding nothing without some appearance of reason, and conformity to the Laws of the Kingdom. ... The ordinary Justice, both Criminal and Civil, is admitted through the Kingdom according to their ancient Customes and Laws, by Officers purposely appointed.[15]

Van Vliet in the 1630s commented, "In the whole kingdom there are law courts of mandarins to administer criminal and civil cases and the written laws after the old fashion."[16] Simon de la Loubère, a lawyer by training who visited Siam in the 1680s, left a long account of the organization of the judiciary in both the capital and provinces, described court process in detail, and commented on the range of punishments. While he was condescending about many aspects of Siam, he was impressed by the role of the law. He discovered there were written law codes and tried to gain access, "but so far was I from being able to get a Translation, that I could not procure a Copy thereof in Siamese."[17] The scribe of an Iranian embassy in 1685–86 left a more dismissive account of Siam's legal system, emphasizing the tendency to delay, the extraction of fees by judicial officers, and the overriding power of the king, but confirmed the general importance of the law.[18]

---

[14] Appeal is considered a form of dispute and hence is B rather than A. Ordeal by Water or Fire is an anomaly. It has no cross-referencing with the Thammasat, but does not seem to belong with others in category D.

[15] Caron and Schouten, *Mighty Kingdoms*, 126, 131.

[16] *Van Vliet's Siam*, 153.

[17] La Loubère, *New Historical Relation*, 81–88.

[18] O'Kane, *Ship of Sulaiman*, 121–27.

Making Law

The derivation of the Thai term for law, *kotmai*, means a document with a stamp, that is, with the king's authority.[19] Schouten commented on the role of the king in making law:

> The Soveraignty and Government of *Siam* is in the King ... He maketh Laws without any advice or consent of his Council, or Lords, his will being the rule he walks by, unless his goodness descend sometimes to counsel with his *Mandoryns*, them of his Council; these sometimes deliberate upon his Majesties propositions, and present their result to him by way of humble supplication which he confirms, changes, or rejects as he thinks good.[20]

The Palace Law (clause 118) specifies that the king's words become law: "If the King speaks on any government matter connected with law or custom, it is considered a ruling to be followed." Most clauses in the substantive laws in the Three Seals Code probably originated as a royal proclamation or as a judicial ruling made by the king (or his delegate) on a specific case or incident. Several are still written in a form showing this origin.[21] In the epic poem, *The Tale of Khun Chang Khun Phaen*, there is a vignette of such a ruling being made. When Khun Chang wades out into the river to present a petition to the king,

> The king then issued an edict. "Henceforth from today, should anyone on guard duty neglect their government service by allowing people into the vicinity, that person shall be liable to punishment of seven grades including execution, under this edict for the protection of the king." He disembarked and entered the palace.[22]

In the Surabha Jataka, one of the non-canonical *jataka* tales known only in Siam and nearby, a king makes a series of judicial rulings, after each of which "he orders high officials to inscribe the ruling as a royal decree for governing the realm from now on."[23]

At intervals, these collected rulings seem to have been sifted, edited into the form of a general rule rather than a specific judgment, sorted according to type (*laksana*), and written into codes with titles like *phra aiyakan laksana phua mia*, the sacred rulings of the type for husband and wife, namely the Law on Marriage. In early times, this process seems to have been rather rough and ready. In some laws that seem of early vintage, such as the Law on Marriage, clauses in different segments of the law offer contradictory rulings on virtually the same legal point. In later years, the process may have become more sophisticated. There is a trace in the preface to the Thirty-Six Laws that states that the king commanded two councils consisting of sixteen officials to review forty-eight rulings and royal orders. The councils edited these rulings and orders into thirty-six clauses issued as law.[24] This

---

19 Winai, "Khwam samkhan," 10.

20 Caron and Schouten, *Mighty Kingdoms*, 125–26.

21 For example, clause 86 of Miscellaneous Laws, *KTSD*, 3: 132–35.

22 Baker and Pasuk, *Khun Chang Khun Phaen*, 789–90.

23 *Panyat chadok*, 2: 266–382.

24 Thirty-six Laws, *KTSD*, 4: 229–30.

compilation has no date, but the content suggests the early eighteenth century.[25] In late Ayutthaya, the procedure seems to have become more sophisticated. The laws in Old Royal Decrees, which mostly date from the early to mid-eighteenth century, contain a description of the original case and ruling, followed by the decision drafted in the form of a law.

As each king had the absolute authority to make his own law, these codes theoretically lapsed at royal succession. A clause in the Three Seals Code mentions that all pending court cases lapsed "at the accident of a change of reign,"[26] and Lingat noted that "all officials ceased to be in office and had to be reappointed by [the king's] successor."[27] The new king had the authority to make his own appointments and laws. In practice, these written collections provided continuity. Successions perhaps offered an opportunity for the new king to review these codes, have the new rulings and proclamations of his predecessor sifted and sorted by type, and the codes rewritten as a single manuscript or set of manuscripts. In practice, these revisions were probably more occasional. The palm leaves and mulberry paper used for old texts can be durable if carefully stored, but will decay rapidly if exposed to heat and humidity, and are easily damaged by insects. Regular recopying was thus needed to preserve the laws. Vickery proposed that there were major revisions in the reign of Songtham (1610/11–1628) and Prasat Thong (1629–1656), but nothing between then and the 1805 code.[28] More likely there was another revision in the early eighteenth century.[29]

Dating

Most of the laws have a preface giving the date of promulgation and the titles of the king reigning at the time. The earliest of the laws appear to date from the first decade of the Ayutthaya kingdom. However, as Vickery has shown, these dates are not reliable (see below). Even so, there is plenty of evidence of written law codes in neighboring states by the fourteenth century, including an inscription of a law found in Sukhothai, possibly dated to 1397, and possibly authored by an Ayutthayan king.[30]

The written laws are first mentioned in the royal chronicles in 1548 at the accession of King Chakkraphat. This king came to power through a coup (against Si Sudachan) carried out by a group of nobles from the Northern Cities (the old Sukhothai kingdom). On the day following his consecration, the king consulted his ministers and counselors on how to reward these nobles. The "four royal

[25] The first of these laws is about the control of manpower, a focus of dispute and legislation from the late-seventeenth century onwards; see Busakorn, "Ban Phlu Luang Dynasty."

[26] "ภอเกิดอุบัติเหตุแผ่นดินกลับแล้ว," Law on Judges, clause 110, *KTSD*, 2: 179. The term for "reign" is copied from the term for "realm," *phaendin*, meaning "surface of the earth," hence a new reign is a "new surface of the earth."

[27] Lingat, "Evolution of the Conception of Law," 26.

[28] Vickery, "Prolegomena," 54.

[29] In 1687–1688, La Loubère saw a volume of laws entitled *Phraratcha kamnot* that he was told contained laws made in (perhaps, since) the King Prasat Thong reign (1629–56). In the Three Seals Code, the equivalent document, *Phraratchakmnot kao*, Old Royal Decrees, starts with a law passed in 1707 (*KTSD*, 4: 293–95), suggesting the Prasat Thong laws had been sorted into the subject codes and a new collection of new laws begun around 1700.

[30] Griswold and Prasert, "A Law Promulgated by the King of Ayudhyā in 1397." See below, pp. 17–18, for discussion of this text.

preceptors," presumably the four Brahman heads of the legal department (see below), brought out the *Phra thammanun*, which gave guidance on suitable rewards.[31] The specification of rewards for service to the king appears in the Palace Law and, in more detail, in Crimes against Government. This suggests that in 1548 the *Phra thammanun*, which by 1805 had become a law on judicial procedure, was earlier a compendium of existing laws.

From his visit in 1687–88, Simon de la Loubère reported:

> The Publick Law of *Siam* is written in three Volumes. The first is called the *Pra Tam Ra*, and contains the names, functions, and prerogatives of all the Offices. The second is intituled, *Pra Tam Non*, and is a Collection of the Enactments of the Ancient Kings; and the third is the *Pra Rajya Cammanot*, wherein are the Enactments of the now reigning King's Father.[32]

This may be a precursor of the Three Seals Code, a collection of all existing laws in a form suitable for consultation by the king and court. La Loubère failed to get access to the code and hence his description is hazy. The *Phra tamra* perhaps contained the Civil and Military Lists, or perhaps was a collection of the laws on procedure. The *Phra thammanun* seems to have contained the laws edited and classified by subject, while the *Phraratcha kamnot* contained royal decrees not yet sorted by subject. If this impression is correct, between 1685 and 1805 the *Phra thammanun* changed from being a major segment of the code into a law on the assignment of cases to various courts. This rather dramatic change, along with the expansion of the compendium from three volumes to the forty-one volumes of the Three Seals Code, suggests that there was significant development of the legal system in the last phase of the Ayutthaya kingdom.

Using the Laws

According to the conception of kingship, the king's primary duty was to maintain the peace and contentment of the people. Exercising this duty required him to decide on cases of dispute between people by making judgments guided by ethical principles. In practice, the king's power of judgment was devolved onto other officials and the king served rather like a final court of appeal. By late Ayutthaya, according to Krisda's analysis of the *Phra thammanun*, there were twenty-four courts in the capital and sixteen in a provincial center.[33] The laws existed to help the king and his delegates make just and socially acceptable judgments. In *The Tale of Khun Chang Khun Phaen*, the only realistic literary work with roots in the Ayutthaya era, there are two courtroom scenes (in chapters 22 and 34). The king as presiding judge is portrayed as acutely aware that he must be seen to act in accordance with the law, even though his power is absolute. He thinks to himself at one point, "This case

[31] Cushman, *Royal Chronicles*, 26; Bradley, *Phraratcha phongsawadan*, 37.

[32] Meaning King Prasat Thong, father of King Narai. We have slightly modified Gen's standard English translation. The French term "constitutions" is here translated as "enactments" (in place of Gen's "constitutions"), following Jacq-Hergoualc'h's gloss on the French edition of the text: "un recueil d'actes, de décret, de lois et de règlements." We have also changed "Regent" to "now reigning." La Loubère, *New Historical Relation*, 81; Jacq-Hergoualc'h, *Étude historique et critique*, 304, fn. 7.

[33] Krisda, "Nueaha khong phra thammanun," especially pp. 11–12.

must be examined by due process to get to the bottom of the competing claims and let people see who's telling the truth and who's not. That way I'll escape criticism [for showing favor]."[34]

In the court procedure described by foreign visitors, visible in the Three Seals Code, and dramatized in *Khun Chang Khun Phaen,* the roles combined under a judge or magistrate in Western tradition were split between several officers. The magistrate (*tralakan*) conducted the trial, took statements from the plaintiff and defendant, interrogated witnesses, and compiled a written report. This report was then sent to the judge (*phu phiphaksa*) who forwarded it to legal experts (*luk khun*) who consulted the written law and gave an opinion on guilt or innocence. After the judge then ruled on guilt or innocence, the magistrate called on another set of experts (*phu prap*) to determine the sentence.[35] The written law was thus a resource for consultation by legal experts.

At the highest level, these would be the two Brahmans with titles of Phra Maharatchakhru who headed a department overseeing law, astrology, and ritual. In the Civil List, each of these has a deputy who also appears to be Brahman, and several assistants who may be Thai.[36] Their role in judgment appears in a court scene in *Khun Chang Khun Phaen*:

> In the afternoon, everyone assembled including Phra Maharatchakhru, Luang Yanprakat, Luang Theprachathada, and both sentencers. All sat and listened to the record of evidence. A legal code was produced and consulted. The case was taken to be presented in royal audience ...[37]

The origins of this department are obscure. Possibly, Brahmans were first employed for royal ritual, particularly for the king-making rite of anointment (see below, pp. 70–72). The title of the second of these ministers includes the words *phraratcha prarohit,* the royal priest (*purohit*).[38] An eighteenth-century oral history of Siam states that Ramathibodi, the founder king of Ayutthaya, had eight Brahmans imported from Varanasi for his anointment as king.[39] This record may get the story right but the date wrong. According to Van Vliet's *Short History,* based on local records, "two learned brahman priests" were sent by an Indian king to serve King Ramathibodi II (1491–1529) and after that "various brahmans have come to Siam from many places, especially from Ramaradt, and have continued to be held in great esteem among the kings, princes, the royal family, and the community."[40] The fact that this king has the same name as the founder king may explain the earlier dating in the oral history.

---

[34] Baker and Pasuk, *Khun Chang Khun Phaen,* 763–64.

[35] Krisda, "Nueaha khong phra thammanun," 9; Seni, *Pathakatha.*

[36] Civil List, clause 19, *KTSD,* 1: 265–66.

[37] Baker and Pasuk, *Khun Chang Khun Phaen,* 444. Yanprakat and Theprachathada are the two deputies. The "law code" is *bot phra aiyakan.*

[38] *KTSD,* 1: 265.

[39] See *Khamhaikan chao krung kao,* 57; Tun Aung Chain, *Chronicle of Ayutthaya,* 24. This oral history was recorded in Myanmar from the nobles taken away from Ayutthaya after the city fell in 1767. The early part of the history is clearly inaccurate in many ways. See Baker and Pasuk, *Khun Chang Khun Phaen,* 882–83.

[40] *Van Vliet's Siam,* 209–12. "Ramaradt" in this account might correspond to Varanasi in the oral-history account.

It is not surprising that the Brahmans also came to oversee astrology, as royal astrology adopted the Jyotisa system from India. Their role in law is more curious. While the two Phra Maharatchakhru have the same 10,000 *sakdina* as others of ministerial rank, they had no official seal, which meant they had no executive authority.[41] Their role was to read the laws and give advice.

Who else had access to the written laws? When the Three Seals Code was completed in 1805, only four copies were made. Two were kept in the palace, and one was "placed in the royal court for judicial officers (*luk khun*)."[42] The fourth seems to have served as a backup.[43] When Mote Amatyakun and the missionary Dan Beach Bradley printed the Three Seals Code in the 1830s, King Rama III objected and had the books destroyed.[44] This incident has given the impression that the laws were hidden. In recent years, however, searches in provincial centers have found several hundred law texts, mostly dating to the nineteenth century.[45] Most of these are abstracts from the Three Seals Code. In a few cases, particularly in the south and northeast, these extracts are found alongside local laws from other sources. Jakkrit Uttho shows that some provincial heads asked for copies of parts of the code to guide their legal decisions. He also surmises that the *yokkrabat*, officers who acted as royal emissaries to the provinces from the seventeenth century onwards, may have carried parts of the laws in their toolkit. Many of the texts were found in *wat* libraries, hinting that monks and abbots acquired them to help in informal mechanisms for settling local disputes.[46]

Hence, in the nineteenth century, people involved in making judicial decisions, whether as part of official duty or as informal arbitrators, got access to the Three Seals Code to guide their decisions and to give those decisions legitimacy. There is one bit of evidence that suggests the laws had been distributed in a similar way in late Ayutthaya. In 1847, James Low published a study of Thai law based on several manuscripts he had collected in provincial Siam. One manuscript had been sent to the "Raja of Ligore for his guidance" in a year that seems to be 1740. Another had been copied for a Chaophraya Inthawong "when he went in 1596 ... as General of the Army sent against Tenasserim."[47] Low describes some of the manuscripts as "digests" with extracts from several laws, "rather confusedly jumbled," including the Tenets of Indra, Phrommasak, Acceptance of Cases, Witnesses, Slavery, and Inheritance, and "numerous cases and precedents to guide both judges and those who may come, or be brought before them." The dates, royal titles, and other aspects of these texts confirm Low's impression that these manuscripts dated to the

---

41 Vickery, "Constitution of Ayutthaya," 167.

42 *KTSD*, 1: 6.

43 Ishii, "Thai Thammasat," 144. Each of these copies consisted of forty-one *samut thai* volumes.

44 Loos, *Subject Siam*, 39. Thirty years later, King Mongkut permitted the laws to be printed.

45 Pitinai, "New Source Material"; Sarup, "Legal Manuscripts"; Pitinai, *Kotmai haeng anajak sayam*; Jakkrit, "Khwam samphan."

46 Jakkrit, "Khwam samphan," 42–49.

47 These dates are credible. In the 1590s, King Naresuan sent an army that captured Tenasserim, and subsequently appointed several officers to administer the city, including a *yokkrabat*. There is no Inthawong mentioned in the chronicles' account of the episode (Cushman, *Royal Chronicles*, 138–39). The title of Chaophraya was not in use at that time and the date of 1596, apparently in CE, is strange, suggesting Low has confused some things.

Ayutthaya era.[48] One passage tells that a king was dismayed to find that judicial officers were ignorant of the law, and thus "The King orders copies [of the laws] to be given to his officers, and it is through these officers that the people procure copies."[49]

Why then did King Rama III object to the printing? Pitinai noted that the laws found in provincial centers were mostly of types A and B (procedure and "dispute"), and only one percent were of type C, laws relating to the king and state. Pitinai proposed that the type C laws were considered secret, and thus were not allowed to be distributed or printed. Others pointed out that the extracts found in provincial centers were on subjects likely to be common matters of dispute such as marriage, inheritance, debt, and the procedure for appeal. No extracts have been found from type C laws such as the Palace Law because they would not have been of any use in adjudicating local disputes.[50] While this clearly makes sense, Pitinai may still have a point relevant to King Rama III's objection to the printing. King Rama IV authorized Bradley to print the full code in 1862–63.

Conclusion

In sum, written law in Ayutthaya was the king's law, originating from royal proclamations, royal orders, and court decisions made by the king or a judge acting on the king's behalf. By late Ayutthaya, the scope of this written law was very broad. It included laws on relations between state and subjects (type C), laws regulating disputes arising from many aspects of social and economic life (type B), and elaborate rules on judicial process (type A). While the complete code was not widely distributed, those involved in judging and arbitrating cases, either formally or informally, could secure extracts to guide and legitimate their decisions. The king's law spread throughout the land.

---

[48] See Low, "On the Law of Mu'ung Thai or Siam," 331–33. Low's first manuscript "was compiled in the year 2,155 [Anno Dom: 1614] by order of a King of Siam" whose titles Low transcribes as "Som-detcha P,hra eka t,thasong Eeso-un bárommanarot bároma báp,hecttra P,hra Chaú nay yo hoa," which might be *Somdetphra ekathat ong-issuan borommanat borom bophit phrajao yuhua*, very similar to the royal titles in the preface of eleven laws in the Three Seals Code that Vickery ("Prolegomena," table after 58) dates between 1593 and 1643. The same manuscript has an addition dated 1102, which would be 1740 if this date was CS. The second manuscript, which Low found in Mergui/Marit, has a date of 1591 and a similar royal title that is probably *Somdet ekathatsarot issuan boromma bophit phraphutthajao yuhua*. Another has the king as *Boromma chakraphat*, again a title found on several laws in the Three Seals Code. Low states that he sent the manuscripts to the Royal Society, but they seem to have been lost. Low's account of the laws is muddled up with his own observations on Siamese society and extracts from other sources, including La Loubère and the *Questions of Milinda*, but certain parts (e.g., on witnesses) clearly come from the Three Seals Code.

[49] Low, "On the Law of Mu'ung Thai or Siam," 395.

[50] This debate is summarized in Jakkrit, "Khwam samphan," 67–68.

INTRODUCTION TO THE THAMMASAT

The Thammasat stands at the head of the Three Seals Code. Many of the individual laws refer back to the Thammasat in their preface. Sometimes this reference simply quotes the Pali title of the law as it appears in the Thammasat, and sometimes it quotes a description of one or two lines. These references are in the form "there is Pali in the Thammasat as follows." The Thammasat appears to serve as a source of authority for the laws in the code.

In India, *dharmaśāstra* is an ancient genre of texts on law and ethics. Texts with names descended from *dharmaśāstra* (*thammasat*,[1] *dhammasattha*, etc.) appeared all over mainland Southeast Asia—in Myanmar, Mon, Thai, Lanna, Lao, and Khmer languages. The largest corpus of such texts is in Myanmar, where several hundred *dhammasattha* texts have been found in Mon and Myanmar languages along with Pali.

The prefatory section of the Thammasat in the Three Seals Code states:

> Throughout time, the treatise that has been of benefit to the beings of the world is that called the Thammasat, which the rishi Manosāra first expressed in the Māgadhī language [Pali], and which ancient teachers have passed down in the Ramañña [Mon] country in the Ramañña language. At this time, those who are judicial officers in the Siam country have difficulty in understanding this, hence I will compose this Thammasat in the Siam language.

Unlike most other texts in the Three Seals Code, this preface has no date and no mention of the reigning king. Since the Three Seals Code first became a focus of academic study in the 1930s, there has been debate on the origins of the Thai Thammasat and its role in the development of law in Siam. In this introduction, we revisit this issue in light of recent study of this genre of texts, and then take a close look at the contents of the Thai Thammasat. We argue that the role of the Thammasat in Thai legal history has been misunderstood.

FROM INDIA TO MON-MYANMAR

The *Manusmṛti*, or *Mānavadharmaśāstra*, known as *The Laws of Manu*, is the most famous of a genre of *dharmaśāstra* texts that emerged in India around the beginning of the Common Era. In this work, Manu is a son of the world-creating god, Brahma. He narrates to a rishi an encyclopedia of knowledge about the world, including cosmology, history, geography, and the afterlife. Most of the text consists of practical advice on what people should and should not do in everyday life. Much of this advice is framed within the fourfold Hindu *varna* (castes), but some sections on

[1] We use "*thammasat*" when referring to the genre, and "Thammasat" when referring to the text in the Three Seals Code, 1805.

topics such as sexual relations, marriage, and inheritance have more general application. One section contains advice on being a good king, covering subjects such as warfare, taxation, appointing officials, and dispensing justice. Only this section on dispensing justice resembles a law code, with details of judicial procedure and itemization of punishments for wrongdoing. The work as a whole came to be viewed as a law text because the colonial British appropriated it as a source for Hindu "native law." In reality, the *Manusmṛti* is "an encyclopedic organization of human knowledge according to certain ideal goals, a religious worldview."[2]

In ancient India, the *dharmaśāstra* texts were probably guides for judges and anyone involved in the settlement of disputes. No old copy or translation of an Indian *dharmaśāstra* has been found in Southeast Asia,[3] but the like-named texts share some of the same overall shape and purpose, as well as many similarities of detail.

The earliest reference to a *dhammasattha* in Myanmar appears in an inscription from Pagan dated 1249 CE. Following an account of the evidence in a complex inheritance case, "The king ... spoke: 'Given this testimony, take the dhammasāt and judge.'"[4]

Andrew Huxley argues that the practice of compiling *dhammasattha* developed in Pagan over the eleventh to thirteenth centuries. These texts blended elements from the Indian *dharmaśāstra* tradition with local customary law and prescriptions from the Vinaya code of monastic discipline and other Buddhist texts. With some imagination, Huxley suggests the practice of compiling these texts, particularly at the foundation of a new capital or reign, quickly spread to Mon, Myanmar, Shan, and Thai territories, reflecting a need for legal tools to manage polities of growing size and ethnic complexity.[5]

Christian Lammerts cautions that evidence on the production and use of *dhammasattha* in Myanmar prior to the seventeenth century is scant. There are several bibliographies, mostly compiled in the nineteenth century, that list many old *dhammasattha* texts by name, but few have been identified among surviving texts today. The oldest surviving manuscripts of *dhammasattha* in Myanmar language date from the mid-eighteenth century. The *Manusāra dhammasattha*, which survives in several manuscript versions, has a preface dating its original creation to 1651, with details that match other historical records. The *Dhammavilāsa dhammasattha* text may be pre-1628, but the evidence is shakier. Lammerts argues that, on current knowledge, these two may be the oldest surviving Myanmar *dhammasattha*.[6] Several other texts lay claims to much earlier origins, but these claims lack substantiation and in many cases are patently false. Earlier scholars have often accepted these claims without sufficient scrutiny.[7] Fewer texts in Mon have survived, and Nai Pan Hla suspects that only one (in two versions) dates earlier than 1757.[8]

---

[2] Doniger and Smith, *Laws of Manu*, Introduction, lxi.

[3] Until the Myanmar king had Sir William Jones' English translation of the *Laws of Manu* translated into Myanmar language in 1795; see Huxley, "Importance of the Dhammathats," 11.

[4] Lammerts, "Buddhism and Written Law," 83–94.

[5] Huxley, "Thai, Mon and Burmese Dhammathats," 88–89, 103–25.

[6] Lammerts, "Buddhism and Written Law," especially 29, 52–53.

[7] Starting with Forchammer's *King Wagaru's Manu Dhammasattham*, published in 1892.

[8] Nai Pan Hla, *Eleven Mon Dhammmasāt Texts*, xxvii.

As in India, these *dhammasattha* in Myanmar "served as a manual of instruction for those who would act as judges,"[9] including both professional judges and local wise men sought out to arbitrate disputes. The texts were not created by kings but by local figures. The preface to the *Manusāra dhammasattha* explains that the text was compiled by the "eater," or tax-lord, of a certain village with help from a "teacher" from another village, probably a famous monk, at the request of an unnamed king.[10]

Dhammasattha texts typically include a section explaining their own origin. In the *Dhammavilāsa dhammasattha*, Manusāra is a counsellor at the court of Mahāsammata, the king who, at the start of the world in this era, is appointed to rule in order to constrain the rising level of disputes and crimes; in his quest to aid the king, Manusāra finds the *dhammasattha* and other texts written on the wall of the universe, and brings them back for the good of humanity.

This origin story appears in many other *dhammasattha* texts with changes in detail. The name of the law-finder varies, but usually has some echo of the name "Manu." He is sometimes identified with King Mahāsammata, but more often is his official.[11] In some cases he is accompanied by a brother, Bhadra, and makes two visits to the wall of the universe rather than one. In Myanmar manuscripts, the texts are written on the wall of the universe in letters the size of bulls, but in Mon texts the comparison is to elephants. And so on. The same story with differences of detail.

This story establishes that the *dhammasattha* was not derived from the gods (as in the Indian version), but is a part of the universe. It is found by Manusāra somewhat akin to the way the Buddha discovers the dhamma. Its authority comes not from scripture, nor from the power of a creator, god, or king. It is simply part of nature (*thammachat, thammada*).[12]

Most *dhammasattha* texts are presented as reproductions or descendants of the original discovery, but these texts have various forms. Some interleave the original Pali with exposition, commentary, and translations. Some are digests of all or part of the document. Some claim to be purified recensions of an original. There has clearly been much cross-translation between Mon and Myanmar texts.

Besides the story of origin, many *dhammasattha* have guidance for judges. This guidance may include stories illustrating good and bad practice in making judgment; lists of principles to uphold or mistakes to avoid; advice on witnessing, including lists of those types of people who should or should not be admitted as witnesses; curses on those who make poor judgments; and promises of felicities for those who judge well.

Finally, the *dhammasattha* contain long lists of rules of conduct. Unlike in the Indian *dharmaśāstra*, these are not organized by the fourfold *varna*, though the vocabulary of *varna* may still be present. Instead, many of the texts, including all that may date prior to 1750, have a framework of eighteen "root" matters, meaning categories or subjects of law.[13] This framework has been adapted from the Indian *dharmaśāstra* tradition where there are eighteen areas of law (*vyavahārapada*). The

---

9 Lammerts, "Buddhism and Written Law," 4.

10 Ibid., 336–45.

11 Huxley, "When Manu Met Mahasammata."

12 This ontological device was challenged by clerical theorists in Myanmar in the eighteenth and nineteenth centuries; see Lammerts, "Narratives of Buddhist Legislation."

13 Lammerts, "Buddhism and Written Law," 159–60.

"root" subjects vary between manuscripts, but this example from the *Dhammavilāsa dhammasattha* text is illustrative:

> 1. debt, 2. deposit, 3. destruction of property, 4. resumption of gifts, 5. distribution of the appropriate carpenter's share, 6. wages of laborers according to their work, 7. breaking of oaths, 8. characteristics of cowherds, 9. buying and selling property, 10. demarcation of the boundaries of land, 11. slander, 12. theft, 13. assault, 14. murder, 15. duties of husband and wife, 16. slavery, 17. inheritance, 18. gambling with dice, etc.[14]

These "root" matters are often then subdivided into many more "branch" matters. The branch matters are the rules within each of these categories (sometimes with further subcategorization). These take various forms. Some are lists, such as "the five addictions among women." Some are statements of general judicial principles, such as exempting children under ten from responsibility for a death in a fight. Some are very specific rules with attendant punishments, such as "if a husband kills an adulterer outside the bed, he must pay compensation of twelve slaves."[15] In most Myanmar *dhammasattha* since the eighteenth century, these rules account for over nine-tenths of the document.[16]

In India, *dharmaśāstra* was distinguished from *rājāśāstra,* law made by a king. In Myanmar, this extensive *dhammasattha* genre existed side-by-side with codes of law handed down by kings.[17] Though further research may alter this view, there seems to be little connection or interplay between the two. The genre of *dhammasattha* seems to have flourished because local disputes were judged or negotiated by local authorities and wise men, and such persons valued these manuals of advice. As in the example of the *Manusāra dhammasattha,* cited above, kings were involved in encouraging the production of these texts, but "Dhammasattha was not seen as enacted by kings, ministers, or jurists, and was viewed as a legal tradition that developed independently of influence from the 'state' or other worldly institutions."[18]

In sum, *dhammasattha* were present in Myanmar from the mid-thirteenth century, but the manuscripts available for study today date from the seventeenth century onward. This genre is descended from the Indian *dharmaśāstra,* but has been adapted in the Southeast Asian context. The texts were manuals of advice for local judges, and hover somewhere between codes of law and codes of ethics. Typically these texts had three main sections: a story of origin that establishes a "natural" authority, practical advice on judging, and a list of rules or laws, often organized under eighteen "root" categories.

---

[14] Lammerts, "Buddhism and Written Law," 248; for comparison, see Nai Pan Hla, *Eleven Mon Dhammasāt Texts,* 540.

[15] These examples are taken from MDT 1 in Nai Pan Hla, *Eleven Mon Dhammasāt Texts.*

[16] Lammerts, "Buddhism and Written Law," 247.

[17] Than Tun, *Royal Orders of Burma.*

[18] Lammerts, "Buddhism and Written Law," 15.

FROM MON-MYANMAR TO SIAM

The opening section of the Thai Thammasat announces that the text originated from the Mon country. Robert Lingat, Prince Damrong, W. A. R. Wood, Nai Pan Hla, Andrew Huxley, Michael Vickery, and others have contributed to a debate on which text was the origin of the Thai Thammasat and when the transfer happened. Nai Pan Hla proposed that the origin must have been the Myanmar *dhammasattha* tradition because three aspects of the Thai text are found only in Myanmar texts, not Mon ones: Manosāra as the name of the Manu figure; the appearance of his brother, Bhadra, in the story; and the size of the letters inscribed on the wall of the universe being compared to elephants rather than bulls as in the Mon tradition.[19] Huxley suggested the tradition of issuing a Thammasat at the start of a reign or dynasty had reached Sukhothai by the fourteenth century.[20] Prince Damrong and W. A. R. Wood speculated that the transfer happened after the Mon victories over Ayutthaya in the 1560s.[21] Prince Dhani Nivat proposed the sixteenth century.[22] Robert Lingat speculated that the transfer may have occurred as early as the Dvaravati era, but later suggested that King Naresuan and his brother acquired the text after their victories in the Mon country at the very end of the sixteenth century.[23]

This debate has involved a great deal of imagination because the hard evidence available is scant.

The only known reference is found in Sukhothai Inscription 38, a law principally about the abduction of slaves. The dating and authorship are vexed, but it was probably inscribed around 1400.[24] The text repeatedly states that offenders against its various clauses will be punished "in accordance with the rules of the Rājāśāstra and the Dharmaśāstra,"[25] and in one place it uses the same phrase about rewarding cooperative witnesses.[26] This inscription is clear proof that the idea of a *thammasat* was known in Siam around 1400. But we should be careful not to read too much into this one reference. The repeated use of the phrase "in accordance with the rules of the Rājāśāstra and the Dharmaśāstra" seems like a formula, meaning "in accordance with law." Two other references in the law to Rājāśāstra alone give a sense of referring to a document (specifying punishments), but there is no secure sighting of a *thammasat* as a document.

---

[19] Nai Pan Hla, *Eleven Mon Dhammasāt Texts*, xxii.

[20] Huxley, "Thai, Mon, and Burmese Thammathats," 116–24.

[21] Wood, *History of Siam*, 127.

[22] Dhani, "Old Siamese Conception of the Monarchy," 97.

[23] Lingat, "Evolution of the Conception of Law," 27. Lingat hints that an entry in the chronicles for CS 957 (1595 CE) might be relevant, but dismisses it as "too vague to afford any certitude." In fact, the passage is specifically on laws concerning taxation and *kalpana* grants to monasteries, and the proper date is 1604; see: Cushman, *Royal Chronicles*, 207; Bradley, *Phraratcha phongsawadan*, 220.

[24] Griswold and Prasert argued the law was promulgated by a king of Ayutthaya in 1397. Others have suggested that the date was later, and the author was a king of Sukhothai. See: Griswold and Prasert, "Law Promulgated by the King of Ayudhyā"; Vickery, "Guide through Some Recent Sukhothai Historiography," 230–33; Terwiel, "Oldest Law Texts."

[25] ในขนาดในราชศาสตรธรรมศาสตร, *nai khanat nai ratchasat thammasat*; for Griswold and Prasert's gloss on ขนาด *khanat*, see Griswold and Prasert, "Law Promulgated by the King of Ayudhyā," 133, n. 30.

[26] Ibid., 120–45.

The preamble of the inscription states, in Griswold and Prasert's translation, that the king "desires to cleanse this region in accordance with the Manusadharrma."[27] While Griswold and Prasert translate *manutsatham* as Manusadharrma, suggesting a reference to Manu or a similarly named lawgiver, the word could equally well be translated as "human dhamma," and today means humanism or compassion.[28]

At the current state of knowledge, this is the only reference to a *thammasat* in Siam prior to its appearance at the head of the Three Seals Code in 1805. Given the large number of *dhammasattha* manuscripts found in Mon-Myanmar, and the smaller but significant caches from Lanna and Lanchang,[29] this absence is striking. Of course, there may be many reasons for this. Far fewer manuscripts of any kind have been preserved in Siam compared to Myanmar or Lanna. New material may yet be found. But recent searches for old legal texts in Thai provincial archives have failed to find any pre-Bangkok *thammasat* texts.[30]

Nor are there any indirect sightings of *thammasat* in other sources. In Siam, there is a tradition of royal panegyrics, beginning in the inscriptions of Ramkhamhaeng and Lithai of Sukhothai and continuing with poems in praise of King Trailokanath (1448–88), King Prasat Thong (1629–36), and King Narai (1656–88).[31] One standard part of these panegyrics vaunts the king's broad knowledge of many disciplines and subjects, including warfare, religion, history, and literary arts. None of these panegyrics mentions knowledge of the *thammasat*, in contrast to similar panegyrics from Cambodia, Champa, and Java.[32] The Thai royal chronicles mention revisions of several texts including the Tipiṭaka, Manual of Victorious Warfare, and *jataka* tales. If kings had ordered revisions of the *thammasat* at the start of a reign, as may have been the practice elsewhere, then these might have appeared in the

---

[27] ใครขดดพระราชศีมานีดงมนุสธรรม, *khrai khadot phraratchasima ni dong manutsatham*, Ibid., 120, 131, n. 21.

[28] It is worth noting that Griswold and Prasert make many surprising claims in this article, including that the appearance of the word *munnai* in the inscription is proof that the entire *sakdina* system was already in existence, and that U Thong possessed a Mon *dhammathat* at the time he founded Ayutthaya. Ibid., 110–11, 113.

[29] There are several texts attributed to early Lanna kings known today by titles that join the king's name with the suffix *-sat*, such as Mengraisat and Kunasat. Dating is hazy, but the contents suggest an early origin. There are many more law texts from both Lanna and Lanchang from the era of Myanmar influence from the late-sixteenth century onward. For brief summaries, see: Aroonrut, "Lanna Customary Law"; and Ishii, "Thai Thammasat," 198–99.

[30] From research in over thirty provinces, Pitinai found 683 legal manuscripts with over thirty thousand pages. Most are excerpts from the Three Seals Code, especially laws on procedure and common causes of disputes (slavery, marriage, debt). Not one is a *thammasat*. Pitinai found three copies of an abbreviated code called หลักไชย *lak chai*, attributed to an unidentified king with a date of 1125 (perhaps CE 1763). This also focuses on procedure and common disputes, and has no *thammasat*. See: Pitinai, *Kotmai haeng anajak sayam*, 125–37, 370–92; and Jakkrit, "Khwam samphan." Sarup Ritchu, "Legal Manuscripts from Southern Thailand," found the same in the south.

[31] See Griswold and Prasert, "King Lödaiya of Sukhodaya and his Contemporaries"; *Photjananukrom sap wannakhadi thai samai ayutthaya khlong yuan phai*; *Khamchan sansoen phrakiat somdet phra phutthajao luang prasat thong*.

[32] There are inscriptions dating back to 667 CE in Cambodia, 875 CE in Champa, and Java in the ninth century that vaunt the king's knowledge of *dharmaśāstra* or similar terms; see Lammerts, "Buddhism and Written Law," 189–97.

chronicles in the same way. Absence from the historical record, as currently known, proves nothing at all, especially in the case of a highly fragmentary historical record like that of Siam. Yet the absence does raise the possibility that the Thai Thammasat of 1805 was an innovation.

A second issue is the difference between the Thai Thammasat and the *dhammasattha* from Mon-Myanmar. The Thai Thammasat has an origin story, advice on judging, and a listing of "root matters," the headings for different categories for law. In these sections, the Thai Thammasat follows the structure of the Mon-Myanmar *dhammasattha*. But the Thai Thammasat presents no rules or laws under these headings at all. The material that takes up nine-tenths of the space in the *dhammasattha*, and which fulfills their purpose as a practical guide for judges, is completely missing. As a result, the Thai Thammasat differs significantly from the genre in Mon-Myanmar.

EXAMINING THE THAMMASAT

The text has four distinct parts, which vary in style and in the way these use Pali. The first part, covering section 1,[33] is a preface, telling of the document's Mon origins. The second part, covering sections 2–5, tells the story of the origin of the Thammasat, along with advice on judging, all very similar to Mon-Myanmar texts. The third part, covering sections 6–9, is a classification of law, as a prologue to the Three Seals Code. Sections 10–11 form a conclusion, defining the special nature of this descendant of the *dharmaśāstra*. Here we summarize the contents of the Thammasat, section by section, noting parallels to the available texts from Mon-Myanmar.[34]

1. Introduction.

The section opens with eight lines of Pali verse, and proceeds in *nissaya* style.[35] After a standard invocation of the Buddha, it explains that this Thammasat came from the Mon country and is here translated into Thai.

2–3. Mahāsammata

This section has no Pali. It begins with a summary of the geography of the human world from the Three Worlds cosmology, followed by a summary of the origins of society and kingship found in several Buddhist texts, especially the second part of the Aggañña Sutta.[36] These two summaries position the text in the history and geography of the Buddhist world. There is no equivalent passage in the available Mon-Myanmar texts, but there are allusions to this same, standard history and geography.

---

[33] The section numbers do not appear in the original manuscript but were supplied by Lingat for the printed edition and have been used in all subsequent editions.

[34] Note that those available in translation or summary represent only a very small proportion of the total texts.

[35] *Nissaya*, meaning "support" or "support materials," is a form of translating, glossing, and expounding a Pali text. The Pali text is followed by a translation in which individual Pali words or phrases, interspersed in the text, are glossed and expounded. *Nissaya* is a tool for teaching translation and preparing sermons. See McDaniel, *Gathering Leaves and Lifting Words*, 131–34.

[36] Collins, "Discourse on What Is Primary."

The next passage explains the expansion of human society from the four sons of King Mahāsammata to 101 countries with different customs and languages. There is an exactly similar passage in the available Mon texts, varying only slightly in the last few lines.[37]

4a. Discovery of the Thammasat

This section again has no Pali. It tells the story of the brothers, Bhadra and Manosāra, sons of Brahmādeva, finding the Thammasat written on the wall of the universe. The telling is close to the Myanmar *Manusāra dhammasattha,* though shortened. Brahmādeva is an official who goes off to become a rishi and sires two sons with a *kinnari,* a mythical bird-human hybrid. In the Myanmar version, the sons Bhadra and Manosāra make a single joint trip to the wall of the universe, where Bhadra writes down various Veda texts and Manosāra writes down the Thammasat.[38] In the Thai version, Bhadra alone makes the first trip, after which both brothers enter the service of King Mahāsammata, and only later Manosāra makes a second trip to return with the Thammasat.

4b. The Gourd Field

In between the brothers' two visits, Manosāra is employed by King Mahāsammata as a judicial official. He makes a bad judgment in a case concerning two adjacent fields of gourds. Remorse over this judgment prompts his trip to discover the Thammasat. Such tales illustrating good and bad judgments are a common feature of the Mon-Myanmar *dhammasattha.* A very similar version of the tale of the gourd field is found in the Myanmar *Dhammavilāsa dhammasattha.*[39]

4c. The Conduct of the King

The passage describes an ideal routine for part of the king's day, from evening through to audience on the following morning. Such passages can be found in the Indian *arthaśastra* texts, in the Mon-Myanmar *dhammasattha,* and in the Ayutthaya Palace Law (see below, pp. 111-12). The passage here follows one in the Myanmar *Manusāra dhammasattha,* almost clause by clause, including the distinctive teeth-cleaning, differing only toward the end. Some Mon texts also have the same passage, but with several differences in detail.[40]

5. The Four Wrong Courses

The sections opens with a four-line verse in Pali, followed by a translation with *nissaya*-style commentary.

The passage exhorts magistrates to avoid the Four Wrong Courses (*agati*), a standard prescription in the Mon-Myanmar *dhammasattha* and other Buddhist texts. Magistrates who do so will find their wealth and repute increase like the waxing

---

[37] Nai Pan Hla, *Eleven Mon Dhammasat Texts,* 593–94 (MDT IV and MDT VII).

[38] Lammerts, "A Narrative of the Origin of Buddhist Written Law," 4–9. The Mon text MDT X has the same story, with only a single visit, in an even shorter version; Nai Pan Hla, *Eleven Mon Dhammasāt Texts,* 619.

[39] Lammerts, "The Dhammavilāsa Dhammathat," 108–9. Nai Pan Hla states that this story does not appear in any Mon text, see *Eleven Mon Dhammasāt Texts,* xxii.

[40] Lammerts, "Buddhism and Written Law," 468; Nai Pan Hla, *Eleven Mon Dhammmasāt Texts,* 594–95 (MDT IV and MDT VII).

moon, while those who fail will find their wealth and repute shrink like a waning moon. This again is a common simile in *dhammasattha* and other didactic texts. The commentary adds a curse for magistrates that accept bribes. Such colorful curses are another standard element of legal and other Buddhist texts. The Myanmar *Manusāra dhammasattha* has a similar image of the bribe-taker, even when released from hell, encumbered with hands like a spade or hoe, and forced to eat his own body.[41] This section on judging is quite short compared to the attention given to the subject in some Mon-Myanmar *dhammasattha*, but the Tenets of Indra, the text that follows the Thammasat in the printed versions of the Three Seals Code, is a more extended treatise on judging, based around the Four Wrong Courses.[42]

Note that in this second part of the Thammasat, there is no Pali except in this passage on the Four Wrong Courses. This stands in contrast to the third part, which begins from here, where Pali is prominent throughout.

6. Twenty-four Concerns for Magistrates

This section lists twenty-four topics of judicial procedure, from origination of cases through to judgment, grouped under eight headings, each with three topics. The section starts with three lines of Pali verse that list the eight group headings. These headings are repeated in the body of the section, but the twenty-four topics appear only in Thai. The topics presented here are relevant to a formal, court-based process of law. There are no similar passages in the available Mon-Myanmar texts.

7. Root and Branch Matters

This short section has two pairs of Pali verses followed by translations, with no commentary. It introduces the framework of root and branch matters in the next two sections.

8. Root Matters for Judges and Magistrates

The section starts with four lines of Pali verse listing ten topics of judicial procedure. For each of the ten, there are then two or three lines of Pali verse followed by a translation.

All ten topics are covered by a law or section of a law in the Three Seals Code (see table 2). Three are covered by an individual law. Six are covered in the *Phra aiyakan laksana rap fong*, Law on the Acceptance of Cases. Each of the six has its own section of this law with its own preface, three of which have dates, all different. The topic of punishment refers to *Phra aiyakan phrommasak*. This law begins with a section on compensation, and the section on punishment follows from clause 11. For nine out of the ten topics, the preface of the respective law quotes the Pali from this Section 8 of the Thammasat. In each case, these Pali texts merely explain the scope of the law; they do not have any statement of principles. The Tenets of Indra has a different Pali verse (an invocation of the Buddha), not claimed to originate from the Thammasat.

---

[41] Lammerts, "Buddhism and Written Law," 462–63.

[42] A deity is ordered by Indra to be born as the son of a judicial official. When he succeeds his father, he invites Indra, who gives a lecture on the Four Wrong Courses, and the principles of judicial procedure (acceptance of cases, testimony, witnesses, judgment), ending with an exhortation to judges to "use the Thammasat as their two eyes, and royal decrees as Mount Meru, the secure royal pillar of the world" when making judgments. *KTSD*, 1: 42–68.

In the Three Seals Code, there are three other laws related to judicial procedure. The Law on Judges (*tralakan*) begins by quoting the Pali at the head of Section 5, above, on the Four Wrong Courses, followed by a full copy of Section 6 of the Thammasat. The Law on Ordeal by Fire and Water is not included in this list of topics, and has no Pali in its preface. The topic of appeal is considered a form of dispute rather than part of judicial procedure, and hence appears in the next section.

Table 2—Root Matters for Judges in the Thammasat

	List in Section 8 of the Thammasat	**Law or section in the Three Seals Code**	**Pali in preface compared to Pali in Thammasat**
1	Tenets of Indra	Tenets of Indra	different
2	Phra Thammanun	Phra Thammanun	same
3	witnesses	Witnesses	same
4	rejection of witnesses	Acceptance of Cases, 32 (1926)	same
5	substitution	Acceptance of Cases, 47	same
6	exclusion	Acceptance of Cases, 27	same
7	acceptance of cases	Acceptance of Cases, 1 (1899)	same
8	delay	Acceptance of Cases, 41	same
9	punishment	Phrommasak, 11	same
10	dismissal of cases	Acceptance of Cases, 21 (1591)	same

Note: On line 4, "Acceptance of Cases, 32 (1926)" means this topic begins at clause 32 of the Law on Acceptance of Cases, with a preface before this clause containing the date 1926. The right-hand column compares the Pali in the preface of the law with the Pali in Section 8 of the Thammasat.

9. Root Matters of Dispute

This section begins with a list of twenty-nine topics in Pali, and then repeats the list with a translation of each line. These "root matters" are defined as types or causes of dispute among people.

Of the twenty-nine topics, twenty-four are covered by a law or subsection of a law in the Three Seals Code (see table 3). Eighteen cite the Pali title from the section of the Thammasat in their preface, usually in this form: "There is Pali in the Thammasat as follows." In some cases two of the topics in the list are combined in one law or one subsection of the Miscellaneous Laws, and both titles appear in the preface. The topic of "valuation by age" about compensation in cases of death or injury refers to the first section of the Phrommasak. Its preface cites the Pali from this section of the Thammasat.

For two topics (4 and 6), the Pali title in the preface is claimed to come from the Thammasat, but is different from the title in this section of the Thammasat. Topic 4 probably refers to a section of the Miscellaneous Laws, which deals with return of property after divorce, and which has a preface quoting Pali "from the Thammasat," but the quote does not appear in this Thammasat.[43] The Law on Appeal, topic 29,

[43] *sinehato ca dhanaṃ dinnadhanañca bhayato saddhāya dhanaṃ tinnaṃ dhanalakkhañaṃ*; Miscellaneous Laws, clause 119, *KTSD*, 3: 152.

starts with a 6-line Pali verse not found in the Thammasat. Two other topics (7 and 20) are treated in the Miscellaneous Laws, but not in a separate section with its own preface. In all these cases, the Pali quoted in the preface as coming from the Thammasat is merely a descriptive title of the law, without any statement of principles.

The remaining three topics (2, 16, 17) are related to the king and are covered in other laws (Crimes against Government, Palace). As noted above, laws relating to king and state (Crimes against Government, Palace Law, Law on Monkhood, Revolt and Warfare) form a separate category of law, outside the root-and-branch framework. In the case of Revolt and Warfare and Crimes against Government, the topics appear in section 9 of the Thammasat, but in truth do not fit the rubric of this list as topics of "dispute among people." The Palace Law and Law on Monkhood are not mentioned in the Thammasat, and have no mention of the Thammasat in their prefaces. The preface of Crimes against Government quotes a Pali verse, claimed to be from the Thammasat, but the verse is not found there. In Revolt and Warfare, there is no mention of the Thammasat in the prefaces that look as if they existed before the two laws were amalgamated.[44]

It must be stressed that the Pali in the preface of each of these laws (except Appeal) is the title of the law alone. Lingat stated, "Siamese laws generally begin with a preamble setting forth the fundamental rules, i.e., *dhammasattham* rules, sometimes in their pali [*sic*] version, and next they give, in a succession of *mātrās* or sections, the prescriptions derived from them in course of time."[45] This is misleading. There are no rules or statements of principle in Pali in the prefaces (except Appeal). The contents of the preface, usually explaining the need for the law, are as much a part of the royal law-making as the clauses that follow.

In sum, the lists in sections 8 and 9 serve as an index to a major part of the Three Seals Code (excluding the laws on procedure and laws related to the king), but do not fit the code's contents exactly.

Table 3—Root Matters of Dispute in the Thammasat

	Pali title in Section 9 of the Thammasat	**Thai translation in Section 9 of the Thammasat**	**Linked law**	**Pali in preface compared to Pali in Thammasat**
1	*iṇṇaṃ dhanañca*	credit and debt	Debt	same
2	*raññо dhanacorahāraṃ*	misappropriation of royal property		
3	*adhammadāyajjavibhattabhāgaṃ*	partition of inheritance	Inheritance	same
4	*parassa dānaṃ gahaṇaṃ puneva*	gift and return of property	M-119	*sinehato ... suddhāya*
5	*bhattikā ca*	hired and unpaid labor	M-99	none
6	*akkhappaticāradhūtā ca*	gambling	M-132	*abbhutalakkhaña*

[44] *KTSD*, 4: 115–21, 132–33. The Pali appears on 122, which seems to have been added when the two laws were amalgamated.

[45] Lingat, "Evolution of the Conception of Law," 28.

7	*bhaṇḍañca keyyāvikayañca*	purchase and sale		
8	*avahārañca*	theft	Theft	same
9	*khettādithānañca*	house land and paddy field	M-1*	same
10	*ārāmavanādithānañca*	upland field, garden, and forest	M-1*	same
11	*dāsīdāsañca*	debt slaves and war slaves	Slavery	same
12	*paharañca khuṃsā*	assault, abuse, and insult	Assault etc.	same
13	*jāyampatīkassa vipattibhedā*	husband and wife	Marriage	same
14	*saṅgāmadosā pi ca*	warfare	Revolt and Warfare*	same
15	*rājaduṭṭhoca*	treason	Revolt and Warfare*	same
16	*rājāṇañca*	violating royal legislation		
17	*suṅkādivivādapatto ca*	royal taxes and market dues		
18	*parampaseyho pi ca atta āṇam*	threats and intimidation	Against People	same
19	*ītīyakāro*	invective and cursing	M-52	same, and more
20	*thānāvitikkamma balākarena*	trespass		
21	*puttādiādāgamanā saheva*	taking children	Abduction	same
22	*hetumpaṭicca adhikāraṅaṃ va*	just cause	M-139	same
23	*agghāpanāyū ca*	valuation by age	Phrommasak	same
24	*dhanūpanikkhā*	mortgage	M-73	same
25	*āthabbanikā pi ca*	magic and spirits	M-156	same
26	*bhaṇḍadeyyaṃ ca*	rental	M-86*	same
27	*tāvakāsīkañca*	lending and borrowing	M-86*	same
28	*gaṇīvibhāgañca*	division of subordinates	Division of People	same
29	*pañcūdarantaṃ*	appeal	Appeal	different, 6 lines

M-52 means the section of *Phra aiyakan betset* (Miscellaneous Laws) beginning at clause 52. An asterisk means two topics are combined in one law or section, with both Pali titles mentioned in its preface. For topics 4 and 6, the Pali title cited in the preface, shown in the third column, differs from that in Section 9 of the Thammasat. The Law on Appeal begins with a 6-line Pali verse, not found in the Thammasat.

10–11. Conclusion

These two sections begin with eight and eighteen lines of Pali verse, respectively, followed by *nissaya*-style translation and exposition.

In section 10, the "branch matters," which in the Mon-Myanmar *dhammasattha* means the lists of rules and principles that form the bulk of these texts, are equated with the royal law-making (*ratchasat*) accumulated over a succession of kings in the form of royal proclamations, codes of law, and royal legislation—namely, the content of the remainder of the Three Seals Code. Through this equation, the Thai Thammasat becomes totally different from the Mon-Myanmar *dhammasattha* and the Indian *dharmaśāstra*, guides for judges and arbitrators, created and used outside the scope of royal command.

Section 10 attempts to bridge the contradiction between the "natural" origin of the Thammasat and the royal origin of the laws by stating that the kings studied the Thammasat and then adapted and elaborated its content into the royal law-making. This same formulation is repeated in the preface of certain laws in the Three Seals Code.[46]

Throughout the Thammasat and similar texts, the translation and exposition in Thai often strays from the Pali at the head of the section. In this section, the divergence is greater than usual:

> Pali, translation:[47] The various divisions [of law] that go by the name of branch [laws] were established in the *dhammasattha* to serve as a measure, in conformity with wisdom, by the former king Narinda-rāmādhipati, a possessor of excellent merit who comprehended human conduct and made great effort to increase the prosperity of his kingdom.
>
> Thai: The various kinds of branch matters that go by the name of branch matters are many, namely the royal proclamations, laws, and royal legislation which are all royal law-making (*phra ratchasat*). All the branch matters described here [were created by] past kings [who] had miraculous wisdom and accumulated merit to be rulers over the populace, to have fought with enemies, and to be powerful under the splendid white umbrella[48] endowed with moral truth, honesty, good conduct with wisdom, insight, and reason, with the intention to make the city and territory within the realm prosper in happiness and joy. With the desire to support and benefit all the populace, the kings endeavored to consider matters according to the Thammasat, and to have royal legislation (*phraratcha banyat*) to adapt and elaborate [its content] as royal proclamations (*phraratcha kamnot*) and laws (*phra aiyakan*) with many articles, through a succession of reigns down to today. For this reason, learned men with the wisdom to be magistrates who examine and decide on court cases should endeavor to follow the legislation of ancient kings as laid down in these great many articles.

---

[46] For example, the *Phra aiyakan laksana rap fong*, Law on Acceptance of Cases: "Here this [the Pali quoted from the Thammasat] is elaborated as branch-matters though royal legislation [*phraratchabanyat*], which ancient kings thought out according to the Thammasat." See *KTSD*, 2: 27.

[47] With thanks to Christian Lammerts. Note that his reading of this passage is based on a conjectural reconstruction of certain Pali sequences that appear to have been miscopied in the 1805 manuscript; the translation is therefore somewhat tentative.

[48] The white umbrella is a symbol of the king's protection of his subjects.

The Thai modifies and extends the Pali in several ways. Most notably, it changes "the former king Narinda-rāmādhipati"[49] into "past kings ... through a succession of reigns," and specifically identifies the branch matters with "the royal proclamations, laws, and royal legislation which are all royal law-making." In other words, the link between the Thammasat and royal law-making is made in the Thai, not the Pali.

In 1946, Prince Dhani Nivat, who believed that the Three Seals Thammasat "might have been very old," commented on this section:

> Though appended, in the Corpus of 1805, to the *Thammasāt*, its final section should be really outside. It is obviously an interpolation for it is different to the foregoing in style as well as in matter. Whereas the Pali *Thammasāt* is written in the *sloka* metre, this last section is in the *indavajira*; whereas the grammar of the former is none too classical, that of the latter is frankly bad ...[50] In the Pali original these royal ordinances are said to have been promulgated by the ancient King Ramadhipati ... The medieval Siamese translator, however, took this in another sense. His very free rendering was '*by ancient kings in several successive periods.*' ... As has been said by scholars of legal history, the function of the king was not to legislate but to protect the people and preserve the sacred law. It might have been true in many cases that by promulgating ordinances the king could bend and entirely contravert the *Thammasat* to suit his end; and yet he could not hope to give his decisions the lasting form and authority of the latter; imposed as it was by superior agency.[51]

Prince Dhani's reaction to this section of the Thammasat highlights a problem at the heart of the historical study of law in Siam—about the roles of customary law and royal law.

Customary Law and Royal Law

Robert Lingat, the French legal scholar who edited the first academic edition of the Three Seals Code in 1938–39, had much in common with the great historian George Coèdes. Both were impressed by the impact of Indian culture on early Southeast Asia, and both sought to make sweeping region-wide generalizations about this impact. Lingat argued that there was a fundamental difference between the Western legal tradition and the Asian legal systems that were derived from India. In his view, the "positive law" in the West was created by political authority, universal in application, and susceptible to modification. He went on:

---

[49] Several possibilities: 1. A reference to the founder of Ayutthaya (a claim to antiquity); 2. "Rama the ruler," meaning Rama, king of Ayodhya in the Ramayana, and by allusion any king of Ayutthaya; 3. King Prasat Thong, who, according to the *Khamhaikan* documents, took the name Ramathibet รามาธิเบศร at his enthronement (*Khamhaikan khun luang ha wat*, 24; *Khamhaikan chao krung kao*, 97).

[50] King Chulalongkorn noted that the author "did not know Pali very well, like a monk who has studied Pali a little in the course of religion." From *Nanatham wijarini*, quoted in Channarong, "Phra Thammasat," 110. Lammerts cautions that the faults in the Pali may have arisen during copying (personal communication, July 2015).

[51] Dhani, "Old Siamese Conception of the Monarchy," 98–99.

> This notion of law is entirely foreign to the traditions of the peoples in the Far East. In the past, their law was based solely upon custom, and the binding force of custom was not considered as originating from a supposed silent common assent to it, but from its mysterious origin and the veneration people naturally feel for long observed traditions ... A ruler had no power to enact law. He was born to maintain order and peace and to protect his subjects from dangers coming from inside as well as from outside the territory. His first task was to punish people contravening custom and to settle disputes between his subjects. He was therefore supreme judge and arbitrator. As he was invested with absolute power, his judgments were final, but they were mere orders, namely personal and accidental injuctions [*sic*], having nothing of a general and permanent rule such as our law has.[52]

According to Lingat, this tradition of immutable customary law was relayed from India to Myanmar and through the Mon people to Siam, possibly as early as the Dvaravati era, through the texts descended from the *dharmaśāstra*. Because of the dominance of this tradition, "Burmese kings left no legislation." In Siam, however, the tradition was partially modified:

> Siamese kings were advised to verify their [laws'] conformity with the rules of the *dhammasattham* ... Decisions of kings became henceforward permanent rules, not because they emanated from kings, but because they were illustrations of the Eternal Law, and partaking of its authority ... By means of the system just described, Siamese kings were very near to becoming legislators. As a matter of fact, they could legislate on condition they would follow, or at least would not deviate from, the dictates of the *dhammasattham* as well as the derivative rules ascertained by their predecessors.[53]

In the lecture quoted above, which counts as the foundation text of the new form of kingship in the Bangkok ninth reign, Dhani proposed that the Siamese ruler was by tradition a "King of Righteousness" because he conformed to various moral codes including the Ten Virtues of Kingship, the description of a wheel-rolling emperor in the Three Worlds cosmology, and the customary law represented by the *thammasat*. As part of his argument, Dhani replicated Lingat's argument on the origins and nature of Siam's India-derived legal tradition,[54] and quoted extensively from the Thammasat in the Three Seals Code.

In sum, according to Lingat and Dhani, Thai kings could not make laws, meaning universal and permanent rules, unless these rules conformed to moral, customary law, represented by the *thammasat*. Owing to the status of Lingat and Prince Dhani, their view carried great weight. Yet Lingat's contrast between Western and Asian legal systems was misleading. There has been no unified

---

[52] Lingat, "Evolution of the Conception of Law," 9. The similarity of phrasing suggests that Prince Dhani, in the passage quoted above, was referring to Lingat. This Lingat article did not appear until 1951, after Dhani's piece, yet may have existed earlier but been delayed in publication because of the war. Lingat worked in Siam from 1926 until 1940, when he left during Siam's rift with France and spent the remainder of his career until 1955 mostly in Saigon and Hanoi. See Drago, "Robert Lingat."

[53] Lingat, "Evolution of the Conception of Law," 27–29.

[54] Dhani cited Lingat, "L'influence indoue."

Western tradition. Throughout history, there has been debate and struggle among those who argued law was based on custom, on moral authority derived from religion or philosophy, or on the will of a ruler.[55] As a result, the mix of custom, moral authority, and political will differs in the legal systems of various Western countries. Equally, Lingat's assumption of a single tradition in Indian-influenced Asia was exaggerated.[56] Legal systems everywhere evolve through struggle among different social forces and different philosophies. The assumption that Siam conformed to a regional pattern has restricted the exploration of the historical role of law in Siam.

As shown above, the evidence for a tradition of customary law in Siam, akin to the well-documented example from Mon-Myanmar, is weak. By contrast, the volume of written law is considerable, and these written laws are labelled as *phraratcha banyat*, royal legislation, and *phraratcha kamnot*, royal decrees, to emphasize that they originate from the king and derive their authority from the king. Efforts were clearly made to preserve these written laws across changes of reign and dynasty, and to encourage people to use the royal courts that enforced these laws. In contradiction to Lingat's theorizing, royal law-making seems to have been an important aspect of the Ayutthaya state.

Discussion

The second part of the Thammasat, including sections 2 to 4, is similar to the Mon-Myanmar texts. Indeed, most passages have close parallels in the Mon-Myanmar texts. None of the available Mon-Myanmar texts can be identified as the single origin of the Thai Thammasat, but then few of the hundreds of known texts have been translated or described to enable comparison. Lammerts notes that some Myanmar texts seem to have been assembled from earlier sources by bricolage.[57] This first part may have been assembled in this form on either side of the Tanaosi Range.

The third part, sections 5 to 9, departs from the Mon-Myanmar tradition. It still uses the framework of root and branch matters, but fills that framework differently. The number of root matters is not the standard eighteen, but thirty-nine. The topics overlap only partially with those in the Mon-Myanmar lists. The first ten of the Thai root matters are topics of judicial procedure. Some of these, particularly on witnesses, are found in the Mon-Myanmar texts, but the list as a whole reflects a court-based judicial system rather than less formal processes of arbitration. The full list of thirty-nine root matters is rather like an annotated table of contents or executive summary of the Three Seals Code as a whole. The branch matters, which occupy the largest amount of space in the Mon-Myanmar texts, are here equated with the accumulated body of royal law-making—in short, the contents of the Three Seals Code.

---

[55] Lingat's description of the India-derived tradition of customary law is very similar to the description of old Germanic law in Fritz Kern's *Kingship and Law in the Middle Ages*, a work published in German in 1914 and translated into English in 1939.

[56] Within the *dharmaśāstra* literature in India, there are different conceptions of the role of custom, moral authority, and political will. See Drekmeier, *Kingship and Community in Early India*.

[57] Lammerts, "Buddhism and Written Law," 290.

There are signs that there has been a process of editing to coordinate the prefaces of the individual laws with section 9 of the Thammasat. This is most evident in the section of Miscellaneous Laws, which includes seven topical sections that might have been individual laws. Each has its own preface and Pali title referring to Section 9 of the Thammasat. Although the dates on some of these sections are different, they mostly have a similar format for the Pali reference.[58]

The fourth part of the Thammasat, sections 10 and 11, attempts to justify this assimilation of the concept of a *thammasat* (a natural part of the universe) with *ratchasat* (the product of royal law-making). The contradiction is self-evident. Prince Dhani's suggestion that this part is a late intrusion does not overcome the problem. Lingat dealt with this issue by insisting that the kings "could legislate on condition they would follow, or at least would not deviate from, the dictates of the *dhammasattham*," and this condition was ensured by the procedure under which royal commands were filtered and redrafted by a judicial commission before becoming part of the law. However, he admitted that "it may be assumed that, under stable and strong dynasties, the process of identifying royal orders with *dhammasattham* precepts was but a formal ceremony."[59]

Modern Thai legal scholars have tried to resolve this problem by arguing that royal law-making acquired legitimacy only if it was consistent with the Thammasat. Channarong Bunnun argued it this way:

> The Thammasat in the Three Seals Code allowed the king freedom to draft royal laws [*ratchasat*] to a limited extent; that is, in drafting legislation the king had to "think according to the Thammasat" ... Kings [of Ayutthaya] did not confuse their royal power with the sacred power of law. A king had the absolute power to do whatever he liked, but a king's rulings remained mere royal orders; they could not change the law that Manu revealed and could not gain permanence as immortal law.[60]

But there is no historical evidence of royal rulings failing to become law.

Royal Law-making and the Thammasat

It is difficult to imagine that the third and fourth parts of the Thammasat came from the Mon country since they are clearly related to the kind of judicial system that existed in Ayutthaya Siam.

It is possible that in the past, around the time a *thammasat* is mentioned in Sukhothai Inscription 38, there were systems of local arbitration in Siam that created a demand for manuals to guide judges and arbitrators. However, the failure to locate any such manuscripts, in contrast to the hundreds found in Mon-Myanmar and significant numbers in Lanna, suggest that such a tradition did not flourish in Siam.

---

[58] In this form: on this topic, "cases of dispute have arisen according to the Pali in the Thammasat [Pali title of topic] and thus there are branch-matters [Pali form *saka khadi*], namely branch-matters [Thai form *king khwam*] established by royal legislation [*phraratcha banyat*] that ancient kings set down in the clauses that follow. See, for example, Miscellaneous Laws, clause 86, *KTSD*, 3: 132.

[59] Lingat, "Evolution of the Concept of Law," 28–29.

[60] Channarong, "Phra Thammasat," 91, 93.

Why that was so may be detected elsewhere in the laws. At several places in the Three Seals Code, there are clauses requiring people to use the official system of courts for settling disputes. For example, Crimes against Government states: "From this time forward," in cases of theft or abduction, "do not take revenge but bring charges at the appropriate court of the city governor"; and in cases of theft of animals, "make a complaint at the court"; and in cases over debt and slavery, "make a complaint, bring charges, or make petition at the appropriate department to be examined by the magistrate. Anyone not following this law, but taking the case into his own hands," faced punishment by caning.[61] There is a similar passage in the Law on Theft demanding that aggrieved parties bring cases to court and prescribing penalties for those who seek restitution through force.[62] There are similar instructions in the *Phra thammanun*.

As several visitors to Ayutthaya noticed, especially La Loubère, the role of the king as law-giver and as chief judge seems to have been important to the practice of kingship. Through these roles the king fulfilled his duty as a Buddhist ruler to ensure his subjects enjoyed peace and happiness. By late Ayutthaya, royal legislation had become extensive, covering many aspects of social life, and the system of courts had become complex (hence the *Phra thammanun*). Of course, monks and local leaders still might arbitrate local disputes, but without the royal encouragement for compiling *thammasat* found in Myanmar, and with pressure to bring settlement of disputes within the courts, a *thammasat* tradition could not survive. Instead, abstracts and summaries of the royal laws took the place of these manuals, as seen clearly by Low's discoveries and recent research on legal texts found in provincial Thailand.

When and why was a *thammasat* invoked as authority for royal law-making? In 1931, a Thai legal scholar, Phraya Vinaisunthorn, suggested that the Thammasat appeared for the first time in the Three Seals Code in 1805. In response, Robert Lingat pointed out that the Pali excerpts at the head of various laws do not always match the Pali in the Thammasat, suggesting there was more than one *thammasat* by 1805.[63] The variation is true, but, as shown above, the match is quite close. Possibly the adoption happened a little earlier than 1805. The Law on Slavery has clear signs of being updated around the turn of the eighteenth century with quotations from a *thammasat* but not the 1805 Thammasat. In the early eighteenth century, as Busakorn and Saichol have shown, kings felt constrained to show that their actions were consistent with the principles of Buddhism.[64] The idea of invoking a *thammasat* to add authority to royal law may date from this era.

Conclusion

Robert Lingat set the history of Thai law into a regional perspective.[65] This allowed him to recruit the history of the *dhammasattha* in Myanmar as background to

[61] *Phra aiyakan aya luang*, clause 102, *KTSD*, 4: 75–76.

[62] *Phra aiyakan lakkhana jon*, clause 66, *KTSD*, 3: 253–54; see also Phra Thammanun, clause 1, *KTSD*, 1: 161.

[63] Lingat, "Review of *Commentaire des lois sur les epoux*," 219.

[64] Busakorn, "Ban Phlu Luang Dynasty," 135–37; Saichol, *Phutthasasana*, chapters 1 and 2.

[65] In his history of Thai law, Lingat assumes all documents on Thai legal history from the Ayutthaya era were destroyed in 1767; see *Prawatisat kotmai thai*, 16–19.

the Thai Thammasat of 1805, and to portray the Thammasat as the cornerstone of a legal tradition grounded in custom and morality. Prince Dhani drew on Lingat to argue that in Siamese tradition, the rulers were "Kings of Righteousness" because they operated within moral codes, including the Thammasat. Dhani's portrayal of traditional kingship became a foundation text of the ninth reign. This view of the Thammasat and its place in Thai legal history has faced little challenge.[66] Scholars of Thai jurisprudence have generally welcomed the notion of some philosophical grounding for law in the past, and have been reluctant to challenge such authoritative figures as Lingat and Prince Dhani. No study has discussed the special characteristics of the 1805 Thammasat, or wondered about the absence of sources to substantiate the history of the *thammasat* in Siam.

Siam had a tradition of royal law-making stretching back at least to the fifteenth century. This tradition is visible in the Three Seals Code, and confirmed by all the major foreign accounts of Siam from the seventeenth century onward. The scope of royal law-making was not limited to matters of direct interest to the state, but extended to all aspects of social relations. This tradition of royal law-making seems to have expanded greatly from the early seventeenth century onward. Law-making was a key strategy in the management of a more prosperous, complex, and often disorderly society.

The Thai Thammasat of 1805 has two distinct parts. The first, on the origins of law and guidance for judges, is directly descended from the Mon-Myanmar tradition of *dhammasattha*. The second is totally different from that tradition. The lists of rules and principles that form nine-tenths of most Mon-Myanmar *dhammasattha* are completely missing. Instead, there is an attempt to build a bridge between the idea of a *thammasat* and the reality of royal law-making accumulated over several centuries. The formula for this bridge building is that royal law-making must have conformed to the principles of the *thammasat*, even though those principles are missing.

There is no evidence to show when this bridge-building began. Possibly it dates to the early to mid-eighteenth century when there was a movement to draw on Buddhism both to reform the state and to justify its power. This movement was disrupted by the fall of Ayutthaya in 1767, but resumed and strengthened under King Rama I, progenitor of the Three Seals Code of 1805.

NOTE ON THE TRANSLATION

The translation is based on พระธรรมศาตร, "Phra Thammasat," in Royal Institute, *Kotmai tra sam duang: chabap ratchabanditsathan* (Three Seals Code: Royal Institute Edition, 2007), volume 1, pp. 121–66; and Royal Institute, *Kotmai tra sam duang: phra thammasat lae lak inthaphat* (Three Seals Code: Thammasat and Tenets of Indra, 2015).

[66] The exception is Michael Vickery ("Constitution of Ayutthaya," 142): "Too much weight should not be given to the evocation of *Dharmásāstra* / *dharrmasatr* / *dhammasatham* in the *Three Seals* as evidence of foreign influence on Thai laws ... the laws of the *Three Seals*, especially those concerning administration, are not a *Dharmásāstra*. They are texts concerning practical matters arising in the cultures of the Menam [Chaophraya] Basin. Within *Three Seals* the *dharmasatr*, much abbreviated compared to Indian or Mon versions, had become simply an apparatus for classification which bears no evidence for external influences on the matters classified."

The Pali has been converted character-by-character from Thai transcription to Roman transcription with no attempt to correct mistakes or other editing. Sections 1 and 5–11 are in the style of *nissaya,* with some words from the Pali text at the head of the section interspersed in the Thai. The Pali words interspersed in the text have been omitted as they are repetitions and including them would make the translation difficult to read. The Thai translation and exposition of the Pali passages is, in many cases, quite embellished and does not closely match the Pali. This is common in such texts.

In the original manuscript, there are no paragraph breaks. Editors introduced paragraph breaks in the printed versions. In this translation we have not always followed these breaks, and have introduced several new paragraph breaks to facilitate reading. The division into numbered sections is not present in the original, and here follows the division used in all modern printed editions.

Thai extracts reproduced in the footnotes follow the spelling in the 1805 text, which often differs from modern spelling.

Where the original uses a Pali term transcribed into Thai and the term is not in general use (i.e., not in the Royal Institute dictionary), we give the standard Pali form in the translation, and an explanation in a footnote.

Where there is a note on a Thai term derived from Pali and in general use, the note gives the Thai version, followed by English transcription in italics, followed by Pali transcription in roman, for example: อริยสัจ, *ariyasat,* ariyasacca.

The Thammasat

1

natvā buddhaṃ lokādiccaṃ dhammañcādiccamaṇḍalaṃ
cakkhumā purisaṃ saṃghantarāyaṃ tena ghāṭayiṃ
vighātitantarāyassa sotthi me hotu sabbadā
yañ ca lokahitaṃ satthaṃ dhammasatthan ti pākaṭaṃ
bhāsitaṃ manusārena mūlabhāsāya ādito
paramparābhataṃ dāni rāmaññesu patiṭṭhitaṃ
rāmaññassa ca bhāsāya duggāḷhaṃ puriseniha
tasmā taṃ sāmabhāsāya racissan taṃ suṇātha me ti

Meaning. Having paid my respects[1] to the Lord Buddha, who discerned the Four Noble Truths,[2] which make the Three Worlds[3] bright as the sun that shines on the earth; and to the Nine Supramundane Teachings,[4] or Ten with Pariyatti,[5] which have a domain of virtue like the domain of the sun; and to the Eight Noble Monks,[6] the Sangha community,[7] and noble and good persons[8] of wisdom and insight; I have removed the hindrances through the power from worshipping the Three Jewels. May we receive sacred blessings for having removed the hindrances by worshipping the Three Jewels.

Throughout time, the treatise that has been of benefit to the beings of the world is that called the Thammasat, which the rishi Manosāra first expressed in the

---

[1] Homage to the Three Jewels or Triple Gem, meaning the Buddha, the Dhamma (teaching), and the Sangha (monkhood).

[2] อริยสัจ, *ariyasat,* ariyasacca, explained by the Buddha in his first teaching after attaining enlightenment: the truth of suffering, the truth of the cause of suffering, the truth of freedom from suffering, and the truth of the way to eliminate suffering.

[3] Meaning "the world of sensual desire … the world with only a remnant of material factors .. the world without material factors" (Reynolds and Reynolds, *Three* Worlds, 49), but often interpreted as the hells, the human world, and the world of the gods.

[4] โลกุตรธรรท, *lokudaratham,* lokuttara dhamma, often called the supramundane states; the nine include the four paths (stream-entry, once returner, never returner, arahant), their four fruits, and nibbana.

[5] พระบริยัติ, *phra pariyati,* pariyatti, meaning learning Buddhism in theory, as opposed to practicing it (paṭipatti), and by extension possibly meaning the Tipiṭaka, the scriptures.

[6] พระอัษฎาริยสงฆ, *phra atsadariyasong,* asṭāriyasaṃgha, monks who have attained the four paths and four fruits, who are classified into eight levels.

[7] สมมุติสงฆ, *sommutisong;* sammutisaṅgha, the sangha in convention, those monks who have not yet entered the path. *Sommutisong* does not appear in the Pali above.

[8] อาริยสัปรุษย, *ariyasapparut,* ariyasapparusaya, where *sapparut* means a good or moral person, used often for lay persons who devotedly take part in Buddhist worship.

Māgadhī language,[9] and which ancient teachers have passed down in the Ramañña country[10] in the Ramañña language. At this time, those who are judicial officers[11] in the Siam country have difficulty in understanding this, hence I[12] will compose this Thammasat in the Siam language. All of you please listen to this Thammasat from our order.[13]

2

The account will proceed from the beginning in sequence.

Learned men who adjudicate on cases should know the content of the Thammasat under the points stated here.

As has been known from the first era of the world,[14] there is a wall of the universe, great Mount Meru, seven mountain ranges,[15] four large continents, two thousand small continents, four great oceans, and seven great presiding trees, namely: the Sirisa[16] tree presiding in the Pubbavideha[17] Continent; the Kadamba tree[18] presiding in the Aparagoyāna[19] Continent; the Kapparukkha tree[20] presiding in the Uttarakuru Continent; the Jambolan[21] tree presiding in the Jambu Continent;[22] the snake tree[23] presiding in the world of the Asura;[24] the bombax[25] tree presiding in the realm of Lord Garuda;[26] and the Parikachat tree[27] presiding in the Tāvatiṃsa heaven.

---

9 มคธภาษา, *makhottha phasa*, the language of Magadha, the state where the Buddha lived (now in northern India, Uttar Pradesh and Bihar). This was the old name of the language known since the eleventh or twelfth century CE as Pali (Crosby, *Theravada Buddhism*, 89–90).

10 รามัญประเทษ, *raman prathet*, the country of the Mon.

11 วินิจฉัยอำมาตย, *winitchai ammat*, (high) officials who judge.

12 ข้า, *kha*, here as in the opening phrase, a first-person pronoun.

13 สำนัก, *samnak*, a grouping or place, perhaps a chapter of monks.

14 This is a summary of the geography of the human world in Buddhist cosmology; see Reynolds and Reynolds, *Three Worlds*, 124–35, 275–89.

15 สัตะปะริภัณ, *sattapariphan*, often portrayed as concentric circles around Mount Meru.

16 ศิริศะ, sometimes known as siris; *Albizia lebbeck* or closely related trees.

17 บุพวิเท่หะ, *buphawitheha*.

18 กระทุ่ม, *krathum*, *Anthocephalus chinensis*.

19 อะมระโคญานะ, *amarakhoyana*.

20 กรรมพฤกษ, *kammaphruek*, usually now กัลปพฤกษ์, *kalapaphruek*; a *kalpa* tree, named because it lasts a *kalpa*; in the Three Worlds, a tree of plenty that provides anything desired.

21 หว้า, *wa*, *Syzygium cumini*.

22 ชมพูทวีป, *chomphu thawip*, the roseapple continent, location of human habitation.

23 แคฝอย, *khae foi*, *Sterospermum fimbriatum*.

24 อสูระพิภพ, *asura phiphop*, a netherworld below Mount Meru, between the human world and the various hells.

25 งิ้ว, *ngio*, *Bombax ceiba*, etc.

26 สุบรรณราชพิภพ, *subannarat phiphop*, subānna bhava, the realm of Lord Garuda, meaning the lesser continents, sometimes collectively called the Yupara Continent; see Reynolds and Reynolds, *Three Worlds*, 289–90.

27 ปาริกะชาติ, *parikachat*, a wishing tree; see Ibid., 233–34.

In the first era, there appeared a lotus with five flowers, an omen that five Lord Buddhas[28] would gain enlightenment in this *bhadda* era.[29]

All the brahmas,[30] scenting the earth, came down to eat the good-tasting earth.[31] After a time, the celestial food lost its former taste and their celestial appearance deteriorated. The brahmas did not retain their fine character as brahmas. After a time, they began to eat grain.[32] Their qualities and powers as brahmas declined and disappeared. They became males and females. Lust[33] arose and immoral practice.[34] Children and grandchildren were born, generation after generation. Settlements were established in all directions of the various countries.

3

At that time, a Lord Bodhisatta was born as a great man at the start of this era. After a time, disputes arose, and nobody could be found to control them. Everyone came together in a meeting and appointed this great man to be the ruler[35] with the name King Mahāsammata,[36] equipped with the seven gem attributes,[37] and spanning all four continents.

After a time, four royal sons were born. The elder ruled in the Jambu Continent, one in Uttarakuru, one in Aparagoyāna, and one in Pubbavideha. All four princes flew to attend on their royal father every day.

After a time, the father passed away. The four princes, who lived in separate places, would travel back and forth to meet together in friendship. After a time, each went only occasionally, and their familial friendship gradually disappeared, down to today.

The elder son ruling the Jambu Continent had ten sons, and divided the Jambu Continent into eleven parts, one where he lived, and the other ten given to each of his sons. The elder son[38] was the Great Prince.[39] After a time, the father passed

---

28 At the beginning of each kalpa, a lotus appears on which the number of flowers predicts the number of Buddhas to appear in that era, maximum five. In the current era, they are: Kakusandha, Koṇāgamana, Kassapa, Gautama (the historical Buddha), and Maitreya (the future Buddha); see Ibid., 311–14.

29 พัทกัลป, *pathakalapa*, bhadda kappa, an era in which one or more Buddhas appear.

30 In the cosmology of the Three Worlds, above the worlds of desire, which include hells, the human world, and heavens, there are twenty realms inhabited by brahmas, divine beings of diminishing materiality. When the world is destroyed at the end of an era, those beings who have attained these levels survive. See Ibid., 358. This account of the origin of human society and kingship, in this and the next paragraph, appears in many texts, especially the second part of the Aggañña Sutta; see Collins, "Discourse on What Is Primary."

31 พะสุธารศ, *phasutha rot*, vasudhā rasa, the (good) taste of the earth.

32 ษาลี, *sali*, often meaning wheat, but also grain more generally, or rice.

33 ฉรรทราค, *chantharak*, chandarāga.

34 อัศธรรม, *atsatham*, a-saddhamma, the negation of the true dhamma.

35 อธิบดี, *athibodi*, the big person.

36 พระเจ้ามหาสมมุติราช, *phrajao mahasommutirat*, often translated as the Great Elect.

37 สัตะพิธรัตน, *sattaphitharattana*, sattabidharattana; the seven attributes of a great king or emperor: gem wheel, gem elephant, gem horse, gem woman, gem treasurer, gem son, and gem jewel; see Reynolds and Reynolds, *Three Worlds*, 137–70.

38 พระราชกุมารผู้ใหญ่, *phraratchakuman phu yai*, the senior royal son.

away, and the lord Great Prince ruled in his stead. The ten princes visited one another regularly. After a time, they no longer visited one another and lived separately. After a time, the ten sons[40] of King Mahāsammata each had ten sons, and the eldest was appointed the Great Prince, and each arranged the rule in his country. After a time, the fathers passed away and the Great Princes were anointed[41] as primary rulers in place of their fathers, and still went back and forth to visit one another regularly. All these 101 kings were related in the same royal solar lineage.

After a time, all entered old age, and could not go back and forth to visit each other. Each employed a senior official to go back and forth to maintain friendship and family relations. The senior officials who once used to go back and forth reached the age of decrepitude. Places they once had visited every seven days, they now visited once a year, and eventually could not go at all. Thus the sons and grandsons who continued the line no longer knew they were part of the same royal solar lineage. Each lived in his own country. Their royal articles[42] were different. All 101 had a different language and customs,[43] resulting in the 101 languages known today. When the solar lineage of King Mahāsammata was first established, the age of humanity was one *asankya*.[44]

4

At that time a great brahma lord called Brahmadeva transferred[45] from the brahma world and came down to be reborn in the family of a great official who was a servant of King Mahāsammata. On reaching the age of fifteen years, he replaced his father. After a time, he saw that all beings were suffering as a result of disputes that gave rise to various calamities. He wished for King Mahāsammata to follow the excellent Ten Royal Virtues,[46] so he resigned and went out[47] to be a rishi in the Himavanta Country near a mountain cave. He concentrated on meditation, and

---

39 มหาอุปราช, *maha upparat*, great-secondary-king, a title of precedence, sometimes translated as viceroy.

40 The text has นัดดา, *nadda*, grandson.

41 มุรธาภิเศก, *murathaphisek*, muradhābhiseka, "head anointment," conferring power by pouring water on the head, an adaptation of the ancient Indian ceremony of *abhisheka*.

42 ศิริราชราชูประโภค, *siriratcharatchupraphok*, fine articles of royal use, possibly meaning regalia. The Mon "Dhammasāt of the Hermit Manu" tells this same story of the expansion from four royal sons to 101 countries almost word for word, but in this last portion states "the people forgot they were kinfolk" resulting in their language and costumes becoming different. See Nai Pan Hla, *Eleven Mon Dhammasāt Texts*, 593–94.

43 วิไสยเพศภาษา, *wisai phet phasa*, language and other differentiating factors.

44 อะสงไขย, *asongkhai*; an *asankya-kalpa* is one quarter of a *maha-kalpa*, a great era, at the end of which everything is destroyed.

45 จุติ, *juti*, cuti, a verb applied to gods when moving from one realm to another, such as from the heavens to the human world.

46 ทศพิธราชธรรม, *thotsaphit ratchatham*, dasarājadhamma, a code of conduct for kings. The virtues are: munificence, moral living, sacrifice, honesty, gentleness, self-restraint or austerity, non-hatred, non-violence or not causing harm, patience or tolerance, and non-oppressiveness. According to the Thai version of their origin, a royal minister who had become an ascetic found this code inscribed on a hillside; see Ishii, *State, Sangha, and Society*, 44–45. The history of the concept is not known, see Skilling, "King, *Sangha*, and Brahmans," 195–96.

47 บวด, *buat*, pabbajjā, to leave a house, thus to cease being a householder, to renounce. The word is now used for the ordination of monks.

attained the Five Mental Powers[48] and Eight Attainments.[49] He ate fruit as food. As retinue, he had divine *kinnara, kinnari, gandharva, garuda, paksi, vasuki,* and *naga,*[50] who regularly came to serve the rishi with heavenly music.

One day there arose a great storm with heavy rain falling. All the divine boys and girls, *kinnara* and *kinnari* fled away and disappeared. Only one heavenly *gandharva-kinnari* came close to the dwelling of the Brahmadeva rishi. He fell in love with her. She became pregnant and had a son of beautiful appearance called Bhadra.[51] After a time, the divine *gandharva-kinnari* was pregnant and had another son called Manosāra. Both sons were intelligent. Their father and mother taught them to be rishi and to attain the Five Mental Powers and Eight Attainments. They took care of their father and mother until both the parents died.

One day the rishi Bhadra flew to the boundary of the universe, and wrote down the letters of the treatises of the Vedāṅga[52] and verses of the Veda.[53] On return, he took his younger brother, rishi Manosāra, to the court of King Mahāsammata and presented the treatise of the Vedāṅga and verses of the Veda. Bhadra renounced being a rishi and became a royal priest,[54] teaching King Mahāsammata. Manosāra rishi followed his brother and became a royal servant. The King appointed Manosāra to be in charge of court cases for all humans. Manosāra executed this command justly. All the gods scattered gold, silver, popped rice, and flowers as worshipful offerings to Manosāra the official.

After a time,[55] two men were cultivating adjacent fields of gourds. When planting the gourds, they made a path between the fields with earth. The gourd plants spread across the path and mingled together. When the gourds were ripe and both men harvested them, a dispute arose. Manosāra went to judge the case. Manosāra ruled that, as there was a road in the middle, any gourd belonged to the owner of the field where the gourd lay. But Manosāra's ruling was not just. One of

---

48 อะภิญญา, *aphinya,* abhiññā; five or sometimes six mental powers acquired by the Buddha: divine eyesight; divine hearing; supernatural ability (iddhi); insight into others' minds; and recall of former lives.

49 อรรฐสมาบัติ, *atta samapati,* aṭṭha samāpatti, the meditative attainments of the Buddha, sometimes called "absorptions," comprising the four jhānas or meditative states plus the realm of the infinity of space, realm of the infinity of consciousness, realm of nothingness, and realm of neither consciousness nor unconsciousness.

50 All are mythical creatures that appear in the Himavanta Forest and elsewhere in Buddhist mythology. *Kinnara* and *kinnari* are male and female versions of a half-bird half-human; *gandharva* is a musician; *paksi* is a large bird; *garuda* is based on a bird of prey; *vasuki* and *naga* are snakes.

51 ภัทธะระ, *Phathara,* "auspicious one."

52 The original has เภทางคประกร, which is probably เวทางคปกรณ, meaning vedāṅgap(r)akarana, treatise of vedāṅga, the limbs of the Vedas, the six auxiliary disciplines for understanding the Vedas, namely: ritual rules, grammar, etymology, phonetics, prosody, and astronomy. In Myanmar, vedāṅga may also include alchemy, yantra, and mantra, and in modern usage the term refers to astrology and supernaturalism in general, similar to the modern usage of *akhom wet* in Thai (see next note). See the discussion of the parallel passage in the *Manusāra dhammasattha* in Lammerts, "Buddhism and Written Law," especially 413–14.

53 อาคมเวท, *akhom wet,* āgama veda. In Thai usage, this phrase is also a general term for supernaturalism, particularly the use of mantra and yantra.

54 ราชปโรหิต, *ratcha parohit.*

55 The same story of the gourd field, differently told, appears in the *Dhammavilāsa dhammathat* from Myanmar; see Lammerts, "Dhammavilāsa Dhammathat," 108–9.

the men was dissatisfied, and took the case to the King, who delegated an official to examine the gourd plants that crossed the path. The official lifted the plants to find the shoot then traced the way back to the root of the plant. The two men praised King Mahāsammata for making a just ruling.

Everybody criticized Manosāra the official for showing the Four Wrong Courses[56] and not judging the case justly. The gods no longer made worshipful offerings as before because Manosāra had wrong thinking.[57] Manosāra thus reflected, "I have a bad character full of delusion."[58] After pondering thus, he felt ashamed and weary of the human world, and fled away to become a rishi. Through meditation, he attained the Five Mental Powers and Eight Attainments, and understood the human mind completely. For this reason, everyone was happy with Manosāra.

Manosāra the rishi was concerned to make the King follow the Ten Royal Virtues, so he flew to the wall of the universe and saw the Pali treatise of the Thammasat inscribed on the wall of the universe in letters as large as elephants. Manosāra the rishi committed the Pali firmly to memory, returned, and composed the treatise of the Thammasat. Hence, the Thammasat is [the work of] the chief official of justice[59] named Manosāra.

Manosāra the rishi taught King Mahāsammata, who followed the Ten Royal Virtues, the Five Precepts as normal practice, and the Eight Precepts as practice on holy days, with compassion and goodwill towards all beings.

The King endeavors[60] to respect the treatise of the Thammasat at all times, and act according to the Four Principles of Justice,[61] namely: to examine the right or wrong of any person's actions that benefit or do not benefit the King; to support those who act with moral truth; to acquire royal wealth justly; and to maintain the happiness and contentment of the territory through justice. He upholds royal traditions without fail.

In the evening,[62] the King listens to music; then at the first watch,[63] he listens to ancient tales of royal tradition; then at the middle watch he listens to traditions[64] of

---

[56] อะคติ, *akhati*, agati; see section 5 below.

[57] อกุศลจิตร, *akusonlajit*, akusalacitta, unwholesome or demeritorious thinking.

[58] โมหาคติ, *mohakhati*, mohāgāti, one of the Four Wrong Courses, alternatively translated as illusion or ignorance.

[59] สมุหบดีธรรม, *samuhabodi tham*, samuhapati dhamma. This passage is ambiguous and possibly defective. This phrase may refer to the Thammasat rather than to Manosāra, in which case the sentence reads: Hence, the Thammasat is a master (pati) collection (samuha) of the dhamma [under the] name of Manosāra.

[60] Here the text becomes a model for kings to follow, rather than a description of King Mahāsammata, so the tense is here switched to the present.

[61] ธรรม ๔ ปรการ, *tham 4 prakan*, four points of dhamma; perhaps วุฑฒิธรรม, *wutthitam*, vuḍḍhidhamma, principles of wisdom and prosperity, adapted for a king.

[62] This passage on the three watches, the tooth cleaning, and attendance at the law court appears with slight variation in the *Manusāra dhammasattha*, see Lammerts, "Buddhism and Written Law," 468–69, and in the Mon version of the same text, Nai Pan Hla, *Eleven Mon Dhammasāt Texts*, 594–95.

[63] ยาม, *yam*, here a period of four hours, with the first beginning at 6 PM.

[64] Here and in the two previous lines, the term used is ประเพนี, *prapheni*, defined in the Royal Institute dictionary as "something practiced regularly and passed on so that it becomes a custom or tradition."

justice; then at the last watch, he enters the royal bedroom and sleeps comfortably for an appropriate time; when rising from the bed and washing the royal teeth, he turns his face to the east, refrains from giving instructions to royal servants on any matter, takes a tooth-polishing stick about twelve fingertips[65] long of a type with thorns and sap, and cleans the royal teeth; when the teeth cleaning is done, the royal teeth-cleaning stick is put in a pristine place.

Having washed his face, he goes to pay respects to the Three Jewels, the powerful divine being,[66] and his royal father and mother; is dressed in royal ornaments and splendid bright clothing; opens his mouth and laughs happily;[67] is seated on the excellent royal throne; and sees four groups of people—doctors, astrologers, the solar lineage,[68] and scholars with wisdom. After conversing with these four groups as befitting, he proceeds to the hall of judgment[69] along with high officials,[70] poets, royal priests, [and] astrologers, those upholding moral truth, to concentrate on hearing cases being examined by magistrates as justly as [with] a crystal circle,[71] and uses the Thammasat as his eyes to see the affairs of state[72] appropriately. Then he takes his right arm, namely[73] his wisdom and insight, holding the gem short sword,[74] namely his skill in evaluation and judgment, to give decisions on all cases of the populace with justice.

Here ends this short account of the royal chronicle of King Mahāsammata and the origin of the treatise of the Thammasat.

---

65 องคุลี, *ongkhuli*, aṅgulī, a unit of length equal to the last joint of the middle finger.

66 เทพยุดาผู้วิเศศ, *thepayuda phu wiset*; in section 11 below, this phrase explicitly means Manosāra.

67 The original has บริหาร, *borihan*, administer, probably an error for บริหาศ, *borihat*, to laugh, from Pali parihasati. In the Myanmar *Manusāra dhammasattha*, which has this same passage, the king appears smiling and making a good face (hasanaṃ katvā ... sumukhaṃ katvā); Christian Lammerts, personal communication.

68 Meaning those of the royal family.

69 The original has สาระพินิจฉัย, *sara phinitchai*, matters of judgment, probably in error for *sala*, hall, as in the same sequence in the *Manusāra dhammasattha*.

70 มุกขมนตรี, *mukkhamontri*, important officials, those who attend in audience.

71 แว่นแก้ว, *waen kaeo*, a glass circle, a magnifying glass, meaning as clearly as if seen with a magnifying glass.

72 เทศกาลบ้านเมือง, *thesakan ban mueang*, the time-and-place of the village-and-city, a conventional phrase.

73 The two uses here of คือ, *khue*, meaning "namely" or "that is," have the sense of "representing."

74 พระขรรคแก้ว, *phra khan kaeo*. The *phra khan* is a short sword that is part of royal regalia.

5

Here will be described the nature of those who are magistrates,[75] as the Pali of the Thammasat states:

chandā dosā bhayā mohā yo dhammaṃ ativattati
nihiyati tasasa yaso kālapakkhe va candimā
chandā dosā bhayā mohā yo dhammaṃ nātivattati
abhivaḍaḍhati tasasa yaso sukkapakkhe va candimā ti

Translation. If any person who is a magistrate violates justice through the Four Wrong Courses, namely love, anger, fear, and delusion, and examines a case differently from the Thammasat, and is biased toward either the plaintiff or the defendant, the standing and wealth of that magistrate will decline and disappear like the moon in the waning phase, creating great difficulties. If any person who is a magistrate does not violate justice through the aforesaid Four Wrong Courses, upholds moral truth, and examines all cases for the populace in a correct way according to the aforesaid Thammasat, the standing and wealth of this magistrate will prosper and increase by the day like the moon in its waxing phase.

Explanation. When both parties to a case have arrived, do not examine and rule on the case with envy and dishonesty, but have compassion toward both parties with an even mind, and make that case a matter of personal concern. If any magistrate encourages the party at fault to offer a bribe to achieve a ruling that does not follow the Thammasat, when that magistrate dies, he will go to burn in the realms of woe[76] and suffer for eternity as a suffering ghost,[77] with fingernails as big as hoe blades, licked by powerful flames, scooping out his own flesh and blood to eat; and when he passes from the realms of woe to be born as a human, a remnant of sin[78] will still be attached, and his organs will be deformed, such as smelly breath, for many lifetimes.

Here ends the brief description of the Four Wrong Courses of magistrates examining cases.

6

Here will be described the twenty-four matters of concern for magistrates according to the Pali in the Thammasat as follows:

timūlato tithānato tiatthato tinālasyato
tidaḷhato tiissaro tidhammato timaggato

---

[75] กระลาการ, *kralakan*, kralakāra, usually *tralakan*. Note that this officer conducts the case but does not pass judgment or decide on punishment; see the description of court procedure on p. 10, above.

[76] อบายภูม, *abayaphum*, apāyabhūmi, the four realms below the human world containing hells and netherworlds.

[77] เปรต, *pret*, peta, a category of spirits who live in the netherworlds between the human world and the various hells, who suffer constantly (e.g., from hunger), and who can sometimes return to the human world in frightful forms.

[78] ปาปะกาวะเศศ, *papakawaset*, pāpaka avasesa, still with some deficit of karma.

catuvīsati hetuyo manosārena kittita

Meaning. The twenty-four matters of concern for magistrates stated by the teacher Manosāra are as follows: origination of cases, three points; status of cases, three points; negotiation of cases, three points; avoiding delay, three points; accuracy, three points; authority, three points; just adjudication, three points; method of judgment, three points; in total, eight subjects covering twenty-four matters of concern for magistrates.

Here will be described the details classified by eight subjects according to the Pali in the Thammasat, as follows.[79]

timūlato Origination of cases, three points are: the plaint and [the defendant's] testimony [conforming with law]; the person accepting the plaint and testimony [having standing in law]; plaintiff and defendant not being incompetent.[80]

tithānato Status of cases, three points are: plaintiff and defendant reaching an agreement [on the truth] in the court record; plaintiff and defendant not reaching agreement and submitting to ordeal; plaintiff and defendant not reaching agreement and calling witnesses.[81]

tiatthato Negotiation of cases, three points are: negotiating to achieve a compromise; using words that the parties to the case should pay heed to; using words to force [the parties] to comply.[82]

tinālasyato Avoiding delay, three points are: if judges stray from the court record, paying heed and drawing attention; questioning within seven days; magistrates completing the examination of statements speedily in accordance with the royal ordinance.

tidaḷhato Accuracy, three points are: [ensuring] accuracy in selecting what is written into the court record; ensuring accuracy in the wording of the court record; tying[83] the court record and then keeping safely.

tiissaro Authority,[84] three points are: magistrates establishing themselves in authority; granting the plaintiff and defendant [equal] authority in the case; paying heed only to words in the court record of the plaintiff and defendant that have authority in the case.[85]

---

[79] The Thai in the remainder of this section is abbreviated and clumsy. Rather than smoothing it out, we have inserted just enough bracketed insertions for readability, and put some interpretation in the footnotes.

[80] Before a case can be accepted, the documents must be in order, the judge must have standing, and the two parties must be competent.

[81] After the case is accepted, there are three possibilities: the parties come to an agreement based on the written submissions; there are no witnesses, so a decision is made by ordeal (by fire or water); witnesses are called.

[82] Judges should first try to achieve a compromise and, failing, must use verbal authority to control the case.

[83] The written court record was folded flat, pierced with a hole, threaded, and tied with string, and the knots sealed with clay and marked with a fingernail. When the site of the inner court at Ayutthaya was excavated in the early twentieth century, many fingernail-marked clay seals were found, baked hard by fire. They are kept in the Ayutthaya museum.

[84] อิศรภาพ, *itsaraphap*, being big, being in charge.

[85] The judge must have authority, meaning he is not under the authority of anyone else that may bias the result; he must grant equal standing to the two parties; and he must not allow extraneous matters to interfere.

tidhammato Just adjudication, three points are: adjudicating the case according to truth following the Thammasat; adjudicating the case honestly according to the Thammasat; adjudicating the case even-handedly according to the Thammasat.

timaggato Method of judgment, three points are: following the great way, namely the method of adjudicating according to the Thammasat; avoiding the wrong way, namely the method of adjudicating without thinking of worldly temptations;[86] studying the great way, namely studying the Thammasat to be expert.

The twenty-four matters of concern for magistrates end with the points described here.

7

Here will be explained about root matters and branch matters,[87] according to the Pali in the treatise of the Thammasat as follows.

tattha atthā dvidhā vuttā mūlasākhappabhedato
mūlatthā dvidhā vuttā sākhatthā ca anekadhā

Meaning. As for the various matters, the teacher Manosāra in the treatise of the Thammasat divided them into the categories of root matters and branch matters. The teacher Manosāra described two types of root matter, and several types of branch matter. On the two types of root matter, there is Pali as follows.

akkhadassā dasañceva vivādā ekuṇatiṃsa
dubbidhā pī ca mūlatthā ācariyena kittitā

Translation. Root matters are of two types: root matters for magistrates and judges, of which there are ten; and root matters on disputes between people, of which there are twenty-nine. The teacher Manosāra described them as follows.

8

The ten root matters for judges and magistrates appear in Pali in the Thammasat as follows.

indabhāso dhammānuñño sakkhi ca sakkhichedako
aññamaññapaṭibhāso paṭibhāṇañca chedako
aṭṭagāho aṭṭakūṭo daṇḍo codakachedako
akkhadassā dasañceva ete mūlā pakittita

Translation. The root matters for magistrates and judges are ten in number: Tenets of Indra;[88] Phra Thammanun;[89] law on witnesses; law on excluding

---

[86] โลกามิศ, *lokamit*, loka āmisa, things the world desires; probably meaning bribery.

[87] มูลคดี, *munlakhadi*, สาขะคดี, *sakhakhadi*. See pp. 21–24.

[88] หลักอินทภาษ, *lak inthaphat*, the principles of the words of Indra; a text that appears in the Three Seals Code immediately following the Thammasat, consisting of instructions for judges and other judicial officials handed down by the god Indra, focusing on the Four Wrong Courses.

witnesses;[90] law on substitution; law on disqualification; law on accepting cases; law on avoiding delay; law on punishment;[91] law on dismissal of cases; as the teacher Manosāra stated.

On the law titled the Tenets of Indra, there is Pali as follows.

indovāde pi viññūnaṃ ṭhitānaṃ saccasīlasmiṃ
tulānaṃ majjhabhūtānaṃ agatānampi aggatiṃ
lakkhaṇo akkhadassānaṃ indabhāso ti vuccare

Translation. All judges and magistrates should know the advice of Lord Indra, king of the gods: uphold the truth and the precepts, five and eight; be absolutely straight like scales or a ruler; have a neutral mind and take the middle way; avoid the Four Wrong Courses; as the teacher Manosāra stated under the title, the Tenets of Indra.

On the law titled Phra Thammanun, there is Pali as follows.

yo kiñcāpi vicāraṇo dhammānurūpalañcanaṃ
avahārāduyatthānaṃ so dhammānuñño ti vuccare

Translation. In any situation, consider carefully the placement of the case according to the type,[92] and send it accordingly, for instance, to the ministry of the capital, ensuring that the placement by type is fair; as the teacher Manosāra stated under the title, Phra Thammanun.

On the law titled on witnesses, there is Pali as follows.

yo cāyaṃ pi saccabhūto yutto sakkhī ti nāmako
so pi dhammo vivādānaṃ kaṅkhachindanidassano

Translation. Among various situations, the situation where someone hears or sees for real and can describe matters without doubt with respect to persons who are in dispute is called a situation where the witness is appropriate.

On the law titled on *sakkhichedaka,*[93] there is Pali as follows.

vimhāpanādiko dhammo sakkhichinno ti kittito
paṭipakkhasabhāvo so sakkhino pi vidhaṃsano

---

[89] พระธรรมนูญ, a law in the Three Seals Code on the classification of court cases and their assignment to various courts.

[90] ตัดพญาณ, *tat phayan*, "cutting witnesses."

[91] กรมศักดิ์, *krommasak*, usually *phrommasak*, a code for calculating fines and other punishments according to *sakdina*.

[92] ตระทรวง, usually กระทรวง, *krasuang*, originally meaning grouping or type, and later evolving to its modern usage as "ministry."

[93] สักขีเฉทก, *sakkhi chethaka*, "cutting" or rejecting a witness (or witnesses).

Translation. Among various situations, there are situations, for example, where witnesses are startled, alarmed, and confused. The teacher Manosāra described this under the title, witness rejection; such persons are truly dangerous as witnesses, and should be excluded.

On the law titled on *aññamaññapaṭibhāso,*[94] there is Pali as follows.

yo patīkathanasīlo paṭivacanavaccano
aññamaññapaṭibhāso pitāputtādiko ca so

Translation. Any persons, such as a father and son, who by nature may launch a case or defend a case in place of each other, such persons are called substitutes.

On the law titled on *paṭibhāṇachedaka,*[95] there is Pali as follows.

yaṃ cocudakavacanaṃ paṭivākyassa chindanaṃ
tampi yeva paṭibhāṇachedako ti pakittitaṃ

Translation. On deciding whether any words exchanged between the plaintiff and defendant should be excluded from the court record, even if those words are truthful, Manosāra the teacher describes under the title of matters for exclusion.

On the law titled on *aṭṭagāho,*[96] there is Pali as follows.

mūlatthappatigāho yo yuttāyuttajānako
so gahitatthamūlo aṭṭagāho ti vuccare

Translation. Any person usually knows what should and should not be accepted as a case. Whether that person has a case that can and should be accepted, Manosāra the teacher explains in the law titled on the acceptance of cases.

On the law titled on *aṭṭakūṭo,*[97] meaning delay, there is Pali as follows.

yo cāyaṃ akkhapravatto aṭṭameva pravattaye
so naro aṭṭapravatto aṭṭakūṭo ti vuccare

Translation. Any person who delays a case, or delays [emergence of] content that is true, [the fact that] such a person intentionally causes delay, Manosāra the teacher explains under the title *atthakut.*

On the law titled on punishment, there is Pali as follows.

daṇḍābhipattikāraṇaṃ yaṃ sabbesaṃ parājīnaṃ

---

[94] อัญมัญญะปฏิภาษ, *anmanyapatiphat,* (can be) compared to each other; substitutes.

[95] ปฏิภาณเฉทก, *patiphan chethaka,* "cutting" or excluding statements.

[96] อรรฐคาหะ, *attakaha,* acceptance or admissibility of legal cases.

[97] อรรฎกูฏ, *atthakut,* Pali aṭṭakūṭo, false or fraudulent legal cases. This seems to be a mistake. The law referred to here is about delay.

tampi patitadaṇḍaṃ daṇḍo nāmā ti kittitaṃ

Translation. The application of punishments including any fines and compensation[98] for anyone who loses a case are stated by Manosāra the teacher under the title of punishment.

On the law titled on *codakachedaka,*[99] there is Pali as follows.

parihāravacanaṃ yaṃ codakānamukkoṭikaṃ
sabbantaṃ dhammasātena codacchedakamuddise

Translation. Concerning the words of a defendant that may result in the dismissal of the plaintiff's case, Manosāra the teacher has explained about these words under the title of dismissal of the plaint in the Thammasat.

This brief account of the ten root matters for judges and magistrates ends here.

9

Here will be described the twenty-nine *ekunadueng*[100] root matters of dispute, according to the Pali in the Thammasat, as follows.

iṇañca rañño dhanacorahāraṃ
adhammadāyajjavibhattabhāgaṃ
parassa dānaṃ gahaṇaṃ puneva
bhattikka akkhappaticāradhūtā
bhaṇḍañca keyyāvikayāvahāraṃ
khettādi ārāmavanādithānaṃ
dāsī ca dāsaṃ paharañca khuṃsa
jāyampatīkassa vipattibhedā
saṅgāmadosā pi ca rājaduṭṭho
rājāṇsuṅkādivivādapatto
parampaseyho pi ca atta āṇam
ītīyakāro vividho paresam
thānāvitikkammabalākarena
puttādi ādāgamanā saheva
hetumpaṭicca adhikāraṇaṃ vā
agghāpanāyū ca dhanūpanikkhā
āthabbanikā pi ca bhaṇḍadeyyaṃ
te tāvakālīka gaṇīvibhāgaṃ
pañcūdarantaṃ tu vivādamūlā
ekuṇatiṃsādividhā pi vuttā
porākavīnā varadhammasātthe ti

---

[98] สินไหม, *sinmai,* sums paid to the wronged party as compensation, and พิไนย, *phinai,* fines remitted to the treasury.

[99] โจทะกะเฉทะกะ, *jothakachethaka*; spelled โจทกะเฉท in the second appearance, below; Pali codakachedaka, meaning "cutting" or dismissing a plaintiff.

[100] เอกุณะดึงษ, a Thai rendering of the Pali for thirty-minus-one, ekūnatiṁsa.

Translation. The root matters of disputes that arise are twenty-nine in number:

iṇnaṃ dhanañca namely, disputes of the type about credit and debt;

rañño dhanacorahāraṃ namely, disputes of the type about misappropriation and alteration of royal property;

adhammadāyajjavibhattabhāgaṃ namely, disputes of the type about unfair partition of inheritance;

parassa dānaṃ gahaṇaṃ puneva namely, disputes of the type about gift and return of property;

bhattikā ca namely, disputes of the type about hired and unpaid labor;

akkhappaticāradhūtā ca namely, disputes of the type about gambling, for instance, on cowries or *ska;*[101]

bhaṇḍañca keyyāvikayañca namely, disputes of the type about purchase and sale;

avahārañca namely, disputes of the type about theft;

khettādithānañca namely, disputes of the type about house land and paddy field;

ārāmavanādithānañca namely, disputes of the type about upland field, garden, and productive forest;[102]

dāsīdāsañca namely, disputes of the type about debt slaves[103] and war slaves, male and female;

paharañca khuṃsā namely, disputes of the type about assault, abuse, and insult;

jāyampatīkassa vipattibhedā namely, disputes of the type about matters of husband and wife;

saṅgāmadosā pi ca namely, disputes of the type about warfare;

rājaduṭṭhoca namely, disputes of the type about revolt against the realm;

rājāṇañca namely, disputes of the type about violating royal legislation;

suṅkādivivādapatto ca namely, disputes of the type about royal wealth such as taxes and market dues;

parampaseyho pi ca atta āṇam namely, disputes of the type about threats and intimidation;

ītīyakāro namely, disputes of the type about invective and cursing;[104]

thānāvitikkammabalākarena namely, disputes of the type about trespass;

puttādiādāgamanā saheva namely, disputes of the type about abduction of children;

hetumpaṭicca adhikāraṇaṃ vā namely, disputes of the type about just cause;

agghāpanāyū ca namely, disputes of the type over valuation by age, male and female;[105]

dhanūpanikkhā namely, disputes of the type about mortgage;

āthabbanikā pi ca namely, disputes of the type about supernatural methods[106] such as *chamop* and *jakla;*[107]

---

[101] สะกา, *saka*, usually สกา, a game similar to backgammon.

[102] ป่าพึ่ง, *pa phueng*, forest that can be relied upon.

[103] ทาสสินไถ่, *that sin thai*, persons who have sold themselves into slavery and can redeem themselves by repayment.

[104] กระหนาบคาบเกี่ยวให้เป็นเสนียดแก่กัน, *kranap khap kieo hai pen saniat kae kan*; roughly, to press in on both sides (i.e., be overbearing) and wish evil upon.

[105] This refers to a section of the Phrommasak about the calculation of compensation in cases of death, injury, or disablement; *KTSD* 1: 197–207.

bhaṇḍadeyyaṃ ca namely, disputes of the type about rental;
tāvakālīkañca namely, disputes of the type about lending and borrowing;
gaṇīvibhāgañca namely, disputes of the type about division of people into groups;[108]
pañcūdarantaṃ namely, disputes of the type about reviving cases for appeal.

As learned men in the past stated in the Thammasat that is excellent and true.
The brief account of the twenty-nine root matters of disputes ends here.

10

Here will be described the many branch matters according to the Pali as follows.

sākhatthanāmena pabhedabhinnā
anekadhā sā varapuññavante
nācāravīcāraṇasampajaññe
na raṭṭhavaḍḍhena hitatthinā vā
porāṇarājena narindarāmā
dhipattiyenābhiparakkamena
ñāṇānusārena pi dhammasātthaṃ
mātrābhidhayyena patiṭṭhitā te

Translation. The various kinds of branch matters that go by the name of branch matters are many, namely the royal proclamations, laws, and royal legislation that are all royal law-making.[109]

All the branch matters described here [were created by] past kings [who] had miraculous wisdom and accumulated merit to be rulers over the populace, to have fought with enemies, and to be powerful under the splendid white umbrella, endowed with moral truth, honesty, good conduct with wisdom, insight, and reason, with the intention to make the city and territory within the realm prosper in happiness and joy. With the desire to support and benefit all the populace, the kings endeavored to consider matters according to the Thammasat, and to have royal legislation to adapt and elaborate [its content] as royal proclamations and laws with many articles, through a succession of reigns, down to today. For this reason, learned men with the wisdom to be magistrates who examine and decide on court cases should endeavor to follow the royal legislation of ancient kings as laid down in these great many articles.

The branch matters are briefly described thus according to the Pali in the Thammasat.

---

106 กฤติยาคม, *kridiyakhom*, one of many terms for supernaturalism, lore, especially when used for malicious purpose.

107 ชะมบ จะกละ, *chamop*, the spirit of a woman who died in a forest and appears as a shadow; and *jakla*, a spirit in the form of a cat that adepts can use to do harm to others.

108 This refers to the law titled *phra aiyakan ban phanek*, Division of People, about registration and control over *phrai* and slaves (*KTSD* 2: 1–26).

109 พระราชสาตร, *phra ratchasat*.

11

ye momūhena tamena channā
lobhādhimuttā hinavīriyā ca
gaṇṭhaṃ imaṃ dhammasatthābhidheyyaṃ
loke pure aggatilakkabhūtaṃ
patiṭṭhathambhaṃ ratanāmayaṃ va
asikkhayantā paguṇaṃ dhuvaṃ ca
aṭṭaṃ janānaṃ pi vinicchayanti
ajānamānā phalathānupatti
mohanti tamhi bhaṇane pi sabbe
andhāva gajjā vicarāvane te
nāsaṃ gatā se idha jātumohā
tasmā hi poso kusalo matīmā
rañño bhaṭo pākaṭanāmadheyyo
sacce patiṭṭhāya mahākulajjo
saddho tu sīlo paramettacittaṃ
pavattayanto sakalo pi niccaṃ
sikkheyyamīmaṃ mahatā guṇena
upetarūpaṃ dhammasātthavhayanti

Translation. Persons of any group who act as the special crystal circle[110] in place of the eyes of the great king to adjudicate on cases of the populace, namely as judges and magistrates, [if they are][111] mired in darkness and delusion, have no wisdom and reason, [then] their insight is blocked, they cannot see benefit in this world and the after-world,[112] the benefit for themselves and for others, such as their lord [the king]; they have minds controlled by desire for praise[113] and worldly temptations of various kinds, and do not adjudicate cases according to traditions of justice following the Thammasat; they are under the sway of the Four Wrong Courses, such as the wrong course of love, as described above, and make no effort to study the Thammasat, that offers wisdom and insight, the supreme treatise, most celebrated in the world, like a gem that the exceptional divine being, namely Phra Manosāra the rishi, had the compassion to first bring back from the boundary of the universe to be established for the benefit of all peoples for whom the root matters of dispute of various kinds arise.

For this reason, those who are magistrates who have not studied the twenty-four matters of concern; the ten root matters for magistrates, such as the Tenets of Indra, or the *phromathan,*[114] that is the Krommasak code on final[115] punishment; the twenty-four root matters on the various disputes that give rise to court cases among people; and the branch matters that ancient kings, following the Thammasat,

[110] See note 71, above.

[111] The grammar in the original of this rambling sentence is difficult to follow. The insertions in square brackets allow the sentence to make sense, but other fixes are possible.

[112] อิทโลกย์ ปะระโลกย, *ithalok paralokaya,* idhalok paralokiya.

[113] สิดหลก, usually โศลก, *slok,* siloka, praise, fame, reputation.

[114] พรหมธรรม์, possibly distorted from พรหมทัณฑ์, *phrommathan,* the rod or staff of Brahma, a metaphor for punishment (Doniger and Smith, *Laws of Manu,* 129).

[115] ปริโยสาร, *pariyosan.*

legislated as chapters of articles in great numbers, to become expert in both knowing and speaking, they will not know the reasons, primary and secondary, for good and bad, what should and should not be, then their rulings in cases for the people will be wrapped in darkness and delusion, and will not have insight, reason, and wisdom. All such people who are magistrates, even though they live to a hundred years old, and even though they have enough eloquence for bad people to respect them, will not be praised by learned men because their judgments will be as confused as blind elephants wandering in the forest until the time they meet final disaster through the wrong course of delusion.

For this reason, learned men born in noble lineages who are servants of the royal foot with standing and recognition in the King's court, should prepare themselves to gain the King's trust to serve as his eyes and ears by having an honest character, upholding the five and eight precepts, being honest in words, having fear and shame about sin, *pen hiri-ottappa*,[116] the fine teaching that governs the world,[117] and having faith in the fruits of the precepts, the fruits of goodness, and the virtue of the Three Jewels. They should set their mind to be compassionate leaders for all beings, and to show gratitude and loyalty to the King who is their lord, and who is working towards enlightenment.[118] When they are disposed to think of the virtue of the King in this way, they should endeavor to study the Thammasat thoroughly and follow its contents so that they may have the special quality to be the eyes of the King, able to decide cases for the populace within the territory of the realm, without encountering difficulties like stumps, thorns, and splinters, so that cases of dispute among crooked people of dishonest character are brought to a productive conclusion, removing the root of the dispute and suffering, and bringing about happiness and joy at all times.

---

116 เปนหิริโอตับ, *pen hiri-ottappa*, fear and shame about sin, a Pali-derived version of the preceding phrase in Thai.

117 ธรรมโลกยยบาลราศรี, *thammalokyaban rasi*, usually *lokabantham*, a gloss meaning that fear and shame about wrongdoing guide mankind to good actions.

118 ทรงบำเพญผลโพทธิญาณ, *song bamphen phon photthiyan*, meaning he is a bodhisatta, a future Buddha.

Introduction to the Palace Law

The Palace Law was *the* law on government in early Ayutthaya, "like a constitution" according to Seni Pramoj.[1] It addresses several subjects that are dealt with in greater detail in other laws on government in the Three Seals Code—Crimes against Government, Revolt, and Warfare. Probably these laws were separated at a later date, when the code became more complex.

The word for the palace in the title of the law, *monthianban*, comes from Pali roots, *mandira pāla*, meaning to govern or guard a holy building or palace. In Thai, *mandira* translates as *ruean luang*, which has the double meaning of a royal building or a royal body.[2] In one sense, the Palace Law is about the physical space of the palace and its day-to-day operations. But in another sense, the law is more generally about the government of Siam because of the central role of the king in the polity. The palace was not only the residence of the king and his family, but also the seat of government. This centrality of the palace can also be seen from the numbers of officials. The early government of Siam had four divisions known as the "four pillars": palace, land, city, and treasury. Sometime before the late fifteenth century, two others, Mahatthai and Kalahom, were added to manage the expanding territories beyond the capital and its immediate region. Kalahom subsequently developed into the ministry of the military. The relative importance of these ministries can be roughly gauged from the Civil List and Military List, the listing of the personnel of each ministry in the Three Seals Code. The number of pages occupied by each ministry is as follows:[3]

Palace	46
Land	2
City	2
treasury	4
Mahatthai	4
Kalahom	41

Almost half of all personnel in these lists came under the palace.

[1] Seni, "Pathakatha," 69. Webster defines a constitution as "the mode in which a state or society is organized, especially the manner in which sovereign power is distributed ... a written instrument embodying the rules of a political or social organization."

[2] Winai, "Khwam samkhan," 25.

[3] Each page contains the names of twenty to thirty posts. The palace count includes five pages on the entourage of the royal family as well as those listed under the palace ministry. The Kalahom count excludes the governors of upcountry cities. Woraphon ("Kan borihan ratchakan krom wang," 47) argues that the titles used in the palace listing show that the list is old, certainly before the mid-seventeenth century, and excludes many divisions of the palace that appear in other sources and were presumably added later.

The departments under the palace ministry can be categorized into several types. First, some looked after the physical fabric and the day-to-day life of the king and his family. These included departments to manage the buildings and gardens; the corps of pages and the royal chamberlain who attended on the king; units that took care of clothing, regalia, and ceremonial artifacts; various craft units that produced articles for everyday and ceremonial use in the palace; units that looked after the women's section of the inner palace along with the royal children and grandchildren; and the palace-rear unit that attended to several unpleasant duties, including jailing offenders and removing corpses.

Second, there were departments to look after the realm's resources of people, wealth, and other goods. The department of rolls oversaw the recruitment of people for military and other labor services. The main treasury and many subsidiary treasuries came under the palace, and several were located inside the palace confines. Third, there were military units, including the department of elephants, department of horse, and several guard units. Fourth, there were specialist departments headed by Brahmans in charge of law, medicine, ritual, and astrological prediction. Finally, there were units of scribes and scholars for copying documents, recording history, and drafting royal orders.[4]

The Palace Law reflects both the narrower aspect of the physical space of the palace and its day-to-day life, as well as the larger aspect of the palace as the focus of many different functions of government.

The Grand Palace of Ayutthaya

The palace complex housed royal residences, audience and throne halls, working space for ministers and officials, treasuries, workshops, stables for elephants and horses, barracks for guards, shrines, gardens, a jail, and a parade ground. Joost Schouten, the VOC officer resident in Ayutthaya in the 1630s, recorded: "The Kings Palace is seated upon the River, resembling a little Town apart, great and magnificent, many of its Buildings and Towers being entirely gilded."[5] The design of the palace was closely related to its function as both a stage set for the theater of power and working space for day-to-day administration. This design evolved over the four centuries of the Ayutthaya era, in five main phases of construction.[6]

Phase 1. The palace of King U Thong (Ramathibodi I, 1351–69) may have been built of wood, including a surrounding palisade, so no traces remain. The chronicles state that the palace site was later occupied by Wat Phra Si Sanphet, but it is unknown whether the palace occupied the same area as the *wat*. Possibly it extended further south and Wat Phra Ram was built opposite its frontage. This site was chosen because the ground here was slightly elevated. The main palace building may have become the principal preaching hall (*wihan luang*) at the eastern end of the *wat*, as digging showed this building has very deep foundations.[7] The *Description of Ayutthaya*, an eighteenth-century text, states that three buildings, which date from this early phase and which are named in the chronicles, were still in existence and

[4] Woraphon, "Kan borihan ratchakan krom wang."

[5] Caron and Schouten, *Mighty Kingdoms*, 125.

[6] This account depends heavily on Prathip, "Phraratchawang boran," 211–15.

[7] Piriya Krairiksh ("A Revised Dating of Ayudhya Architecture," 14–15) argues that this *wihan* dates from the seventeenth century, yet it still could have been built on old foundations.

used for votive purposes.[8] Perhaps these had become ancillary buildings within the *wat*, but cannot now be identified.

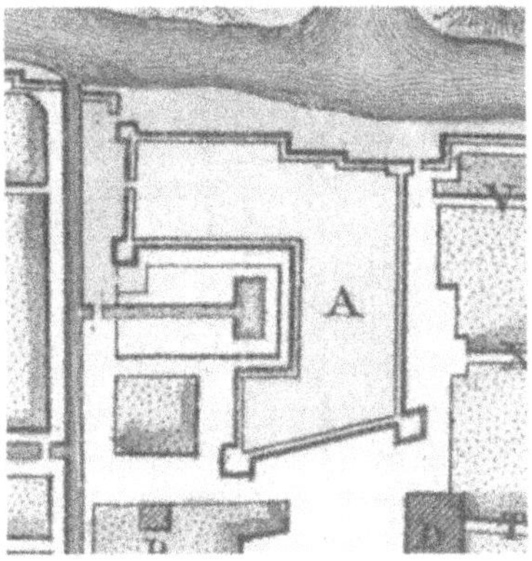

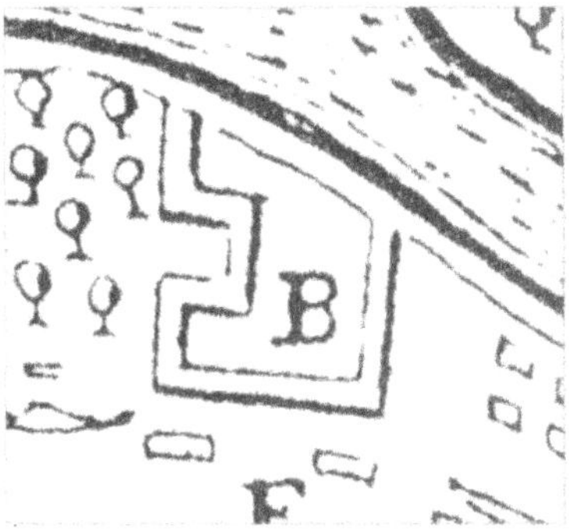

On the left: Grand Palace on map by La Mare, 1687;
on the right: Grand Palace on map in La Loubère's *New Historical Relation*, 1691

Phase 2. After two fires late in the previous reign in 1440 and 1441, King Trailokanat (1448–88) built Wat Phra Si Sanphet on the old palace site,[9] and founded a new palace farther to the north toward the river, but not on its bank. Here the ground was lower than that of the old site, partly underwater, and needed to be raised. Wat Phra Si Sanphet, which served as the *wat* of the palace and became a reliquary for the remains of successive kings, was situated outside the walls of this new palace complex. So was the palace garden and the parade ground used for royal rites and spectacles.

Phase 3. In a year given in the chronicles as 1632, King Prasat Thong (1629–56) built a new hall, the Jakrawat Phaichayon, outside the palace to the southeast, probably to overlook the parade ground.[10] Beginning four years later, he massively expanded the palace in three directions. First, he enclosed the space to the north between the palace and the city wall, relocating a Brahmin temple that had occupied the site. Sometime later, he built a new wall to the east to enclose the parade ground, and walled the Phaichayon Benjarat Garden, thus enclosing the space between the palace complex and Wat Phra Si Sanphet. The result was a distinctive shape, indented on the west where the Grape Garden and Crystal Pond areas were not enclosed, as shown on the maps, below, by La Mare and La Loubère from the 1680–90s.

Phase 4. King Narai (1656–88) made significant changes to the palace complex, but surprisingly little detail appears in either Thai or Western sources. Perhaps the spur was, as before, a major fire that occurred in the year before his accession.[11] To the west of the palace complex in an area that had probably been part of the women's quarters, he dug ponds, used the earth to raise the land around them, and then built a new principal palace for residence and audience, the Banyong Rattanat.

[8] Baker, "Grand Palace," 100–101.

[9] Cushman, *Royal Chronicles*, 15–16.

[10] Ibid., 220.

[11] Ibid., 226–27; Heeck, *Traveller in Siam*, 39.

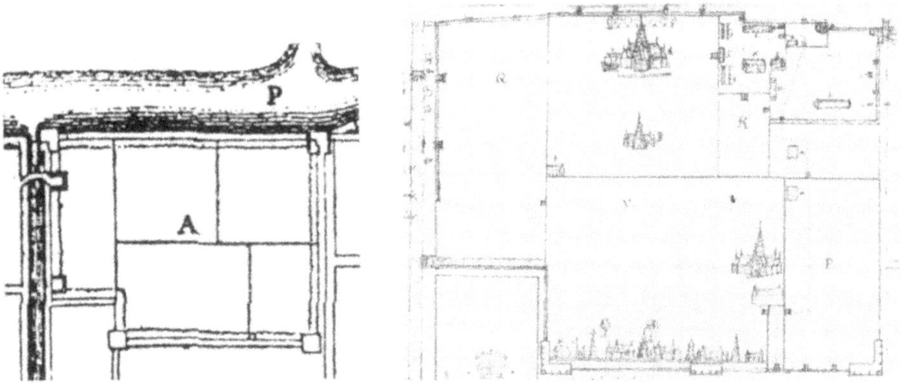

On the left: Grand Palace on Printed Version of Kaempfer's Map;
on the right: Grand Palace on Kaempfer's Original Sketch, 1690

In the chronicles, this building is dated to the start of the reign of King Phetracha, Narai's successor, but clearly existed earlier, as the Banyong Rattanat is described by French visitors in 1687 and its distinctive shape and orientation appears on the VOC's Judea painting and the Vingboons' map, both created in the 1660s. The flamboyant conception of the building matches with Narai's development of Lopburi. Narai also built a new residence for his queen and daughter nearby.[12]

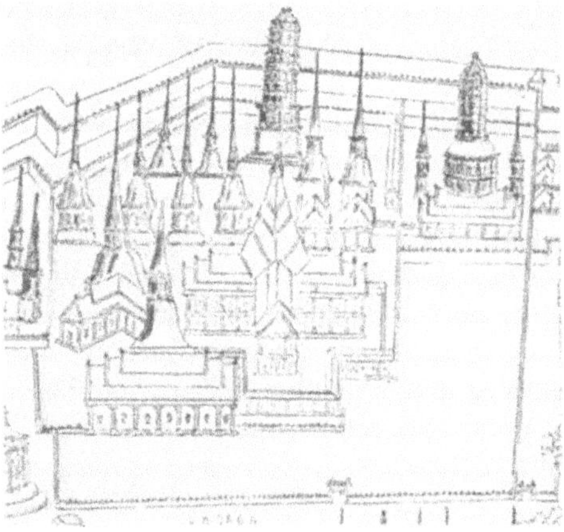

Grand Palace on Vingboons Map, 1665

At some time not known, the *sala luk khun nai*, the principal administrative building of the "front" section, was transferred to this area of the palace along with many other administrative buildings, and the "inner" women's section was confined to the northwest corner. An additional wall was built on the western side, enclosing the areas known as the Grape Garden and Crystal Pond, and giving the whole palace complex a roughly oblong outline, visible on Kaempfer's map from 1690.

[12] Piriya ("A Revised Dating of Ayudhya Architecture," 13) argues that Narai also made major alterations to Wat Phra Si Sanphet.

Phase 5. King Borommakot (1732–58) further extended the palace area by enclosing the Rabbit Garden on the southwest corner. The area occupied by the Grand Palace (not including Wat Phra Si Sanphet) thus expanded from around 40 hectares in the first phase, to 95 hectares in Trailokanat's rebuilding, 165 hectares after Prasat Thong's expansion, and 220 hectares after the additions during the Narai and Borommakot reigns.

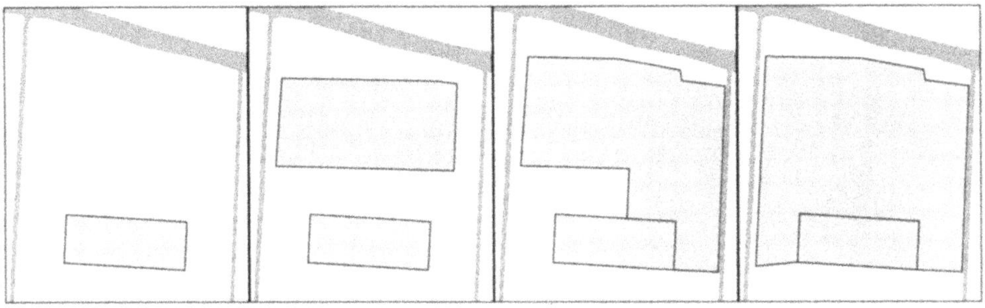

Development of the Grand Palace: Phases 1, 2, 3, 5

Internal Design

The first two phases of the whole palace complex and all the early major buildings that have survived were aligned roughly east–west, but each is aligned differently and none exactly to the compass. They may have been aligned to the river, a common practice in Thai settlements.[13] Internally, the palace was divided into three zones, progressing from public to private. The "front," to the east, devoted to government administration, included buildings used by officials, storehouses for various goods, stables for horses and elephants, and a parade ground for public display. This area was accessed through gates at the northeast corner, and extended to the front of the audience halls (see illustration on p. 56). The central part housed the audience halls, residences of the king and other major royal family members, and the main treasury. The "inside" included the women's quarters and private gardens. In Trailokanat's new palace, these three zones were arrayed from east to west in a block design, separated by north–south dividing walls. This use of space seems to have been the main factor determining the elongated rectangular shape found in the first two phases of construction.

The audience halls at the core of the palace were organized with a similar tripartite division of zones along an east–west axis,[14] from public to private, and with a similar elongated rectangular shape. On the eastern end was an open portico used for everyday audiences. In the center was a closed area for major audiences, such as with foreign emissaries. To the west was a section used for residence and dining.

---

[13] Stuart-Fox and Reeve, "Symbolism in City Planning," especially 122–25.

[14] An east–west axis is the preferred orientation of ordinary dwellings in Siam, to catch the wind's north–south flow.

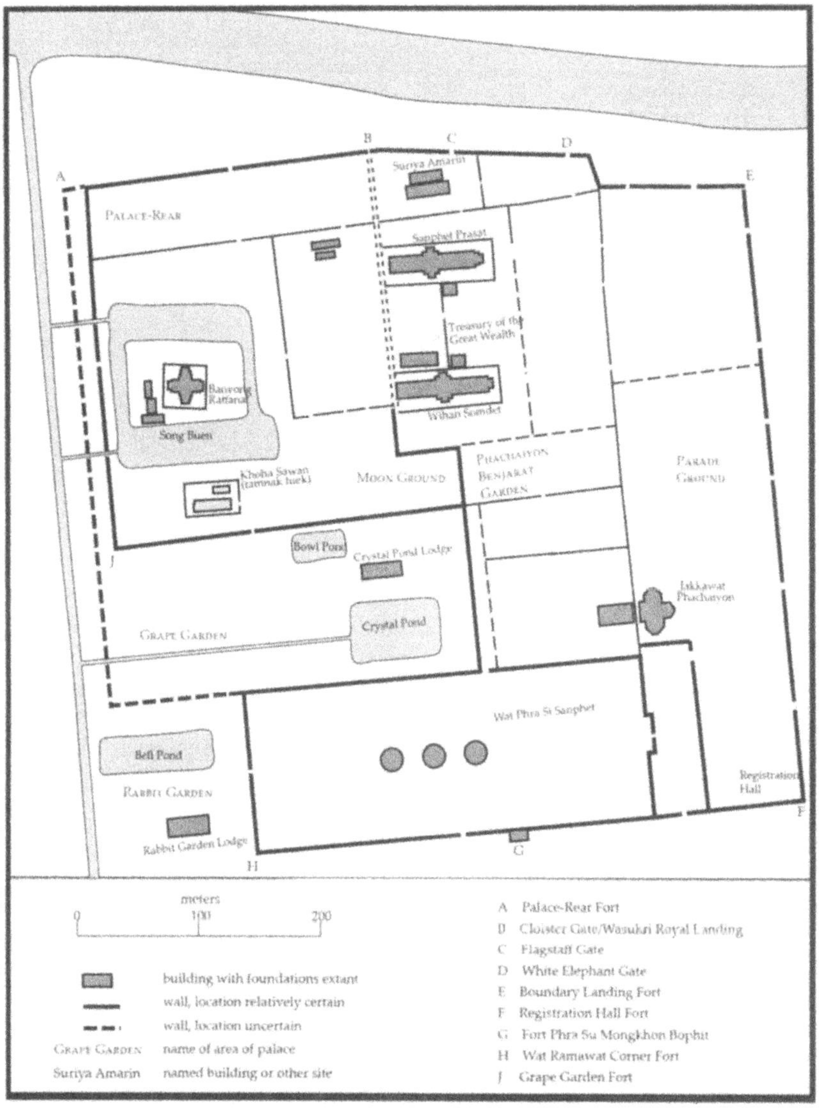

The Grand Palace in Late Ayutthaya

Sources: This map was drawn by laying the latest (1989) Fine Arts Department of Thailand map of the archaeology of the palace and Sumet Jumsai's map of Ayutthaya over an image from Google Earth, and plotting data from the *Description of Ayutthaya*. Also used were a Fine Arts Department map from 1966, Kaempfer's sketch of the palace from 1690, research by Patrick Dumon, and some legwork.

Although Prasat Thong's expansion obscured any overall design in the palace complex, it retained the east–west progression from public to private in the palace layout and in the principal audience halls. Narai's construction of the Banyong Rattanat, however, disrupted everything. The building was placed on the western side of the palace, at the heart of the old "inside," resulting in many administrative buildings migrating to this area. The Banyong Rattanat abandoned the long rectangular shape of earlier audience halls in favor of a cruciform design. Even though this design strongly recalls a mandala, the building was set about 10 degrees askew from the compass and not obviously aligned to the river or any natural feature.

Making the Palace Law

Dating the Palace Law

Dating the law is difficult. As Michael Vickery has shown, the dates given in the prefaces of many Three Seals laws, including the Palace Law, were "corrected" in later revisions and can no longer be known for certain.[15] In addition, the names of kings mentioned in these prefaces have to be considered with care. During their reigns, Ayutthaya kings were known by various kingly epithets (king of kings, great ruler, refuge of the three worlds, etc.), and only later appeared in chronicles with a more precise name that has been adopted by posterity. The names in the law prefaces are the epithets used during the reign, and these cannot be used with certainty to identify a specific king. However, Vickery shows that the choice of epithets did change across eras, which allows for some bracketing of the date. The controversy over the dating of the Palace Law is summarized in footnote 2 of the translation (below p. 77). In brief, the date can be adjusted with some logic, but no certainty, to correspond to 1468 CE in the reign of the king conventionally known as Trailokanat. Vickery agrees that this date is possible, but cautions that the law might date from an earlier reign. Besides, because of the cumulative nature of law-making at Ayutthaya, some clauses may have originated before the dated promulgation, and some have clearly been added after (see below). Winai Pongsripian suggests that there may have been a Palace Law from the earliest stage of the Ayutthaya kingdom and that the date in this preface may mark a major revision.[16]

Evidence found in the text of the law suggests that parts of the law date from early Ayutthaya and have not been substantially changed. The early part up to clause 78, with the exception of clause 2 (see below), and the segment on palace administration in clauses 100–127, appear to date to early Ayutthaya. Several place names (gates, landings, palace buildings) mentioned in this part are not found in the detailed descriptions of the palace and city from late Ayutthaya, and do not appear among the many place names mentioned in the elaborate accounts in the chronicles from the late sixteenth century onward, suggesting that these are old place names that were already lost and forgotten.[17] In certain clauses (e.g., c.21 and c.22), it is clear that the part of the palace around Crystal Pond is not enclosed, showing that these clauses predate the major modification of the palace during the Prasat Thong reign (1629–56; see above). There is no mention of the multiple audience halls that existed by the early seventeenth century. In the provisions for guarding the king, firearms are not mentioned. Most of all, several clauses suggest a striking simplicity: this is a palace where the king has to be woken up in the middle

[15] Vickery, "Prolegomena" and "Constitution of Ayutthaya."

[16] Personal communication.

[17] For example, the Gate Showing Ram in clause 15, Jao Sai shrine in clause 17, Palace of the Night in clause 28, and Uthokkaratsot shrine in clauses 187–88.

of the night should a buffalo wander in: "In the event of a fire, enemy attack, or a tiger, cow, buffalo, or elephant on the rampage, or bandits brawling, if the King is sleeping, wake him to manage the matter" (c.124).

The segments on royal activities and ceremonies in clauses 150 to 196 also seem largely from early Ayutthaya. The vocabulary, including proper names, is similar to the opening section of the law. Three of the royal ceremonies described at length as part of the annual royal calendar had been lost by late Ayutthaya. The only building mentioned is the Mangkhalaphisek audience hall that was destroyed by fire in the early seventeenth century. However, as noted below, there are also signs of updating in this segment.

The segment on discipline in clauses 79 to 99, and the clauses from 197 to the end, seem to be later additions. The clauses on punishment of royal family members and palace staff reflect the intense internal conflict that marked the Ban Phlu Luang dynasty (1688–1767) and especially the reign of King Borommakot (1733–58). The arrangements for exile to the provincial cities (c.199–200) recall the story of the exile of the court poet, Si Prat, to Nakhon Si Thammarat in the 1680s.[18] The clauses on precedence, forms of address, and regalia reflect the intense concern over hierarchy in this era.[19]

As noted below, the list of cities and tributaries in clause 2 must have been compiled in late Ayutthaya and clumsily inserted near the beginning of the law. The segment on the inner palace in clauses 128 to 149 may have clauses accumulated from several different eras.

The 1805 Revision

How far can we assume that the law compiled in 1805 represents the law from the Ayutthaya era? The revision in 1805 was not done to preserve historical manuscripts but to produce a new code for use in the courts of the day. Robert Lingat, the French legal scholar who made the first modern edition of the Three Seals Code in 1938–39, warned that we cannot be sure how much was changed because the manuscripts used in the revision are lost—they were almost certainly destroyed to ensure the new code was unique.[20]

There are some reasons to suggest that any revision in this law was minor, however. The committee of eleven scholars completed the massive task in fewer than eleven months.[21] There was clearly pressure of time. Almost a quarter of the new code consists of royal proclamations from late Ayutthaya and early Bangkok; in earlier revisions, such recent laws were sorted under the thematic laws, but in 1805 this was not done. Lingat notes that some 80 to 90 percent of the extant manuscripts found in the archives in 1805 were excluded from the revision.[22] There are other signs of haste, including duplication of clauses and segments. Although the king ordered the committee to ensure the laws were "correct in every detail according to the Pali" and to "adjust any aberrations to accord with justice," the

---

[18] The figure of Si Prat may be a romantic invention, but exile for sexual misadventure in the palace was still a reality; see the introduction in Winai, *Kamsuan samut*.

[19] Busakorn, "Ban Phlu Luang Dynasty," especially 156–59.

[20] Lingat, "Note sur la revision," 21–22.

[21] The committee comprised four scribes, three judges, and four royal scholars; see *KTSD* 1: 5.

[22] Lingat, "Note sur la revision," 23; Lingat, *Prawatisat kotmai thai* 1: 17.

time constraint probably precluded any deep appraisal of the content.[23] In the case of the Palace Law, the last few clauses seem to be new rulings, including some redrafts of the same clause, not yet rearranged into any thematic order, suggesting the work of sifting and sorting was skipped. There are no obvious signs of "weeding," such as removal of ceremonies that had lapsed or other outdated practices. Clause 2 is the only evident insertion, possibly made at this revision. The king may have made some alterations on the committee's draft, but nothing was recorded. In sum, this document is most likely the Palace Law from the Ayutthaya era with little addition or amendment, but perhaps with some invisible omissions.

CONTENTS OF THE PALACE LAW

Hierarchy

The major theme of the Ayutthaya Palace Law is announced in the first clause: hierarchy and precedence. The opening passage, probably the original core of the law, describes precedence within the royal family. In all, some 30 of the 211 clauses are devoted to hierarchy. These rules are designed not only to enforce discipline within the family, but to *publicize* the importance of hierarchy as a social principle. The palace is the stage set for the theater of power. The law starts with the dramatization of royalty.

For determining precedence in the royal family, two principles are on display. First, queens are ranked quite elaborately through titles and regalia, and this ranking affects the precedence of their sons. Second, specific sons are given precedence, identified by the grant of titles. In effect this is a two-stage system of nomination. The hierarchy continues down to children and grandchildren. These clauses also lay down various ways this hierarchy is dramatized and displayed for others to see through differentiation of dress, height and splendor of throne, regalia carried, conveyances for traveling, and number of servants in an entourage.

Later clauses reinforce this royal hierarchy by detailing how family members will appear at ceremonial events when members of the nobility are present. These clauses provide stage directions for postioning family members to display their order of precedence, and rules prescribing hierarchical details, such as headgear that will be easily visible. Other clauses extend the same principles to travel, again concentrating on easily visible details, such as distinctions in the roofs of boats. Often these instructions are finely detailed; in attendance at one ceremony, royal consorts sit "with a curtain tied to posts as a back-rest, only chest-high" (c.182).

Other clauses extend the same principles, but with much less detail to senior members of the court. These rules concentrate on dress, insignia carried, horse tack, and number of people in their entourage. They prescribe instant punishments for anyone overstepping his station.

---

[23] *KTSD* 1: 5. The meaning of "correct according to the Pali" is open to debate. Did it mean that the laws should follow the principles of the Thammasat? Or did it reflect the colloquial use of this phrase, derived from the time when monks read from Pali texts but spoke in Thai (as when chanting the Mahachat), meaning "correct as in the original"? See the discussion in Lammerts, "Narratives of Buddhist Legislation," 143–44.

Security

The second most prominent theme of the law, both in terms of the number of clauses and their position within the law, is the security of the palace and the king.

There are three deployments for guarding the palace and the city. One allocates units to guard the perimeter of the palace (c.18); the second allocates units for a zone that is probably around half a kilometer deep around the palace (c.15); and the third covers the whole moated city, divided into four quadrants (c.17). Other clauses have specific penalties for abusing the gates, climbing the walls, bringing weapons into the palace, and actions that might be either dangerous or insolent, such as flying kites or throwing articles over the walls.

A much larger batch of clauses is devoted to protecting the king in person. Guarding arrangements are specified when the king visits various areas of the palace (c.27–28), and more detailed arrangements for when he travels outside the palace. Specific measures are prescribed when the king travels by boat (c.23–24), rides an elephant (c.37–39), goes on elephant hunts (c.40–42), and plays polo (c.32–33). The punishments for failing to guard the king are severe, in most cases summary execution for the offender or his whole clan. A handful of clauses seem designed to guard the king against any threat from his major sons. The number of men who may accompany such sons inside the palace is strictly limited. If they appear when the king is traveling outside the palace, the king's guards are placed on high alert (e.g., c.24). Protection of other members of the royal family is scarcely addressed, except for two clauses on security for the primary queen when traveling by boat (c.25).

Security extends also to the supernatural protection of the city. Harsh punishments are prescribed for anyone who threatens the sacred aura of the city (c.76). One striking clause (c.149) prescribes rites to purify the palace after an inauspicious event. The clause cites only two such events, but it hints at a much broader concern for safeguarding the palace as sacred space. The first type of inauspicious event cited is any kind of bloodletting inside the palace as a result of fighting. This is a common taboo. The second type of event, a birth or abortion by a servant woman, is more complex and arcane. The problem is created by a birth or abortion, in other words, the appearance of a new child, whether alive or dead. Female blood is often seen as dangerous and powerful, but this clause adds an extra element: the problem arises only if the mother is "a servant woman who is a slave or freeman,"[24] in other words, not of noble rank. Blood that is both female and of commoner status appears to be especially threatening to the sacred aura of the palace.

In the mandated ceremony of purification, Buddhist monks circle the palace with sacred thread and chant, while Hindu priests make offerings. These are standard rites of purification. But there is a third element: at each of four main gates, two chickens are the focus of rowdy ceremonies, after which they are released "outside the city to take the inauspiciousness, evil, danger, and misfortune out beyond the King's capital." Chickens have a prominent role in ancient Tai rituals, such as those recorded among the Zhuang and Ahom,[25] but have virtually no place in Brahman, Buddhist, or spirit ceremonies among the Siamese as known today. Is this an early Tai survival?

---

[24] ทาสไท, *that thai*, the only appearance of this phrase in the law.

[25] Ghosh, *Tai Cultural Heritage in Northeast India*.

The law imposes a range of punishments including demotion, jail, fines, beating, disfigurement, and execution. Some have a metaphorical relation to the offense, including cutting off a hand for theft, disfiguring the mouth for an offense of speech, or pouring hot liquor into the mouth of an illicit drinker. As a rule, these punishments are not dissimilar to those prevalent in Europe in the same era. What is striking, however, is the imposition of summary execution, including execution of the offender's "whole clan,"[26] for even relatively minor infractions involving the protection of the king and royalty, including failures on guard duty, misbehavior with royal women, or damage to the protective aura of the palace or city. How often such punishments were inflicted is not known, yet in the epic poem *Khun Chang Khun Phaen* the hero's father is summarily executed for a slip in organizing a royal hunt, and his wife is executed ostensibly for fomenting disorder.[27] Besides, these punishments have an ideological purpose. The contrast between the efforts expended in protection of the king and other royal things, on the one hand, and the low threshold for the death sentence, on the other, maps a steep hierarchy in the value of human life. This, too, is part of the law's emphasis on hierarchy.

Audience

The next theme, in terms of weight and sequence, concerns the royal audience. This was the central institution of royal government, with both a practical function as a mechanism of decision-making and a symbolic function as a daily dramatization of royal power.

The Palace Law contains a program of the king's daily activities, which includes specific times for audiences with royal family members, palace insiders, and various outside groups (c.157). Small gatherings were held inside an audience hall, while for large events the king appeared on a portico at the end of the hall and attendees gathered in the courtyard below. The design of the palace was in large part shaped by this central institution. The inputs and outputs of the royal audience were managed in the "front" zone of the palace to the east of the audience halls. At the *sala luk khun nai*, the most senior nobles met with one another and with petitioners bringing matters to government prior to audience, and executed royal decisions in the aftermath. Several buildings known as "swordstores" (*thim dap*) were scattered around the front for other officials' work, along with a Translation Hall and Scribes Hall for handling documents.

The Palace Law's clauses on audiences enforce strict discipline, starting from how courtiers arrive, and including details of route, dress, regalia, and permitted entourage (c.12–14). During the audience, strict silence is required (c.50–57). Other sources describe how courtiers had to remain on their knees, not raising their heads.[28] A special vocabulary is required when addressing the king. When outsiders

---

[26] Meaning all living relatives. Other laws in the Three Seals Code specify execution for "seven generations" of the offender's clan, meaning the offender's own generation plus three up and three down.

[27] Baker and Pasuk, *Khun Chang Khun Phaen*.

[28] "The most respectful, or to say better, the most humble posture, is that in which they do all keep themselves continually before their King ... They keep themselves prostrate, on their knees and elbows, with their hands joined at the top of their foreheads, and their body rested on their heels; to the end that they may lean less on their elbows, and that it may be possible (without assisting themselves with their hands but keeping them still joined to the top of their forehead) to raise themselves on their knees, and fall again upon their elbows, as they

attend, such as provincial governors and diplomatic missions, they have to be formally announced (c.28–29). Penalties are prescribed for skipping an audience, speaking or whispering with colleagues, wearing improper dress, and other infringements.

The audience is designed to dramatize royal supremacy. Only the king has freedom to act or to initiate actions, while all others are constrained by strict rules. His spoken words immediately have the force of law, though there are provisions for appeal (c.118). Several clauses attempt to restrict transactions outside the audience (c.79–84). Courtiers and royal family members are not allowed to raise issues with the king in private. Provincial governors are not allowed to visit each other. Officials of senior and medium rank are forbidden from socializing together, talking to each other in private, or meeting with members of the royal family. While such measures were probably impossible to enforce, they asserted the principle that every person of importance, from both royalty and officialdom, had to transact individually with the king in the framework of the royal audience.

Inner Palace

Siamese kings accumulated large numbers of wives and consorts for several purposes. They helped to ensure continuity of the royal line. They acted as political linkages with other states and important families. But most of all, they served as a symbolic statement of royal power.[29] Protecting the royal women is another major section of the Palace Law.

The number and hierarchy of royal wives undoubtedly changed from reign to reign. The configuration that appears in the opening clauses and in some descriptions of ceremonies perhaps dates to the fifteenth century, but is based on principles that held more generally. There are four major queens with specific titles. Following the principle of counterbalance, these are divided into two pairs on the left and the right. The leading queen of the right pair is the primary queen (*akkaramahesi*). In certain clauses, these four seem to be identified with the four major provincial cities at the cardinal directions. Below these four comes a rank translated as head mother, which may refer to consorts who have given birth, especially those who bear the king a son. Within the royal palace there are also consorts, "governesses" who look after the administration and were often senior members of royal-related lineages, various categories of servant, and female guards ("sentinelles").

There are also eunuchs, categorized into Chinese and "Western," meaning from India or the Middle East. They act as guards in situations where the presence of men may be threatening, such as when royal women travel by boat (c.27), and also have roles in administration and ritual (c.113, c.159, c.183, c.188). Little is known about them. There is also fleeting reference to the presence of hunchbacks and dwarfs (c.143, c.159), a focus of fascination for royalty across cultures.

Naturally enough, the protection of the royal women is most stringent in the case of the primary queen. One clause dramatizes this. She may not be touched,

---

do thrice together, as often as they would speak to their King." La Loubère, *New Historical Relation*, 57.

[29] Loos, "Sex in the Inner City," especially 889–97.

even to rescue her from drowning (c.25).[30] Palace officials who disobey this rule face the death penalty. Other people who do not touch her but only attempt to save her nevertheless face death for their whole clan. This one dramatic example establishes a principle of protection that presumably applies, with diminution down the hierarchy, to other senior royal women.

The protection of royal women in general is specified in one of the most succinct statements in the whole law (c.130): "Anyone who is lover with a court lady or royal consort is executed to die over three days, and the woman is executed also." The penalty of a lingering death is perhaps the most brutal in this whole law. This clause is supplemented by several others imposing punishments on royal consorts who escape from the palace or have sexual relations with other women, and on people who abduct consorts or abet any of these activities (c.128–49).

The law, however, goes beyond protecting the actual and potential sexual partners of the king. Clause 130, the execution clause cited above, applies not only to consorts, but also to *chamae*, translated as "court ladies," a term that may mean members of the royal lineage working in the palace. Other clauses penalize men who form liaisons with female servants working in the inner palace, and condemn the woman to the same death penalty as applied to a consort if she is found to be complicit. Execution is the punishment for a man who "brings books of poetry into the palace to seduce palace maids and inner palace servants" (c.142).

Several other clauses outlaw any sexual liaison within the palace including between male and female palace servants, between a man and any woman visitor to the palace, and between any man and woman (c.139). While these liaisons may be offences against the sacred space of the palace, the fact that these clauses appear in the section on the inner palace, interleaved with clauses protecting the consorts, indicate that they are rules on *royal* women. Though the level of protection diminishes from the primary queen down through the hierarchy, it appears that all women inside the palace to some extent count as "royal women" to be protected.

Royal Service

Several clauses give general instructions on the conduct of officials. The broadest and most remarkable (c.20) instructs officials to appropriate any "animate being or inanimate thing" that will "nourish the capital" and "enhance the wealth of the realm." More specifically, officials are enjoined to be loyal and honest, to know their job, and to stand down if they are incompetent or incapacitated by sickness.

All officials are required to swear the water oath of loyalty (c.85–87). This old oath calls on a long list of gods and spirits to bring down terrible retribution on anyone who acts disloyally. The solemnity of the oath is magnified by a ritual in which the official drinks a full cup of sacred water and upends the cup over his head

[30] In 1880, Queen Sunandha Kumariratana, a daughter of King Mongkut and one of the four queens of King Chulalongkorn, drowned along with her own daughter when her boat capsized in the Chaophraya River. A myth arose that her entourage gave no assistance in accordance with this law, but the king's diary records that boatmen dived into the water, pulled the queen and her daughter from the entangling curtains, and carried them to another boat, where attendants worked in vain to resuscitate them. See Chulalongkorn, *Chotmaihet phraratchakit raiwan*, Vol. 9, 123–24. Chulalongkorn created a memorial at Bang Pa-in with an epitaph in English: "This memorial is erected by Chulalongkorn Rex, Her Bereaved Husband, whose suffering from so cruel an endurance through these trying hours made death seem so near and yet preferable. 1881." See Tri, *Official Guide to Ayutthaya*, 57.

as proof. The Palace Law imposes the death penalty on anyone failing to take the oath, and lesser penalties on anyone trying to evade the oath by feigning sickness, covertly avoiding drinking the water, or failing to perform other parts of the ceremony.

Several clauses enjoin officials not only to act properly, but also to spy on their colleagues and members of the royal family and report instances of wrongdoing.

Conduct in the Palace

Prior to the Prasat Thong reign in the early seventeenth century, the palace was not enclosed within a continuous wall. An open area among the palace buildings was accessible from the west, and the parade ground was not walled on the east. The open area to the west seems to have been popular as a sort of park, as two clauses (c.17, c.21) forbid people from using the area for fishing, boating, romancing, playing music, or other entertainments. Another clause (c.22) suggests that foreigners were prone to wandering unawares onto the parade ground or into the palace-rear.

Several clauses scattered through the law regulate behavior within the palace precincts. Guards are to apprehend any man entering wearing perfume or dressed in a flashy way, perhaps on grounds of decorum, but more likely because such persons were likely to be intent on seduction. Other clauses ban arguing, fighting, gambling, cockfighting, and drinking liquor. Several impose penalties for stealing. There is special concern over the area around the royal horse stables (c.36, c.125). In later Ayutthaya, the stables were on the east side of the palace, in front of the audience halls. Officials are warned against riding horses "provocatively close" to these stables, and their wives are forbidden from opening umbrellas in the vicinity.

Several clauses specify procedures for handling crises inside the palace. In case of a fire (many of which are recorded in the chronicles), guards are deployed immediately (perhaps to prevent looting), and priority is given to removing the horses and elephants (c.125).

Warfare

As noted above, warfare is dealt with more extensively in other laws, and the few clauses in the Palace Law may date before those other laws were compiled. These clauses deal entirely with rewards and punishments for performance on the field of battle (c.44–49).

Rewards are given for "taking" (which might mean killing or capturing) the enemy. The rewards are graded, with the highest prize being for taking an enemy "lord" (*thaophya*), followed by an elephant, horse, man, and weaponry. The lowest prize is for simply surviving to return alive and hence be available to fight again. A special category of rewards is offered to those who win an elephant duel, the dramatic focus of early warfare. Harsh penalties are specified for any form of retreat, and for allowing the enemy to come close enough to threaten the king. In battles, soldiers collected heads to claim these rewards. In the martial poem *Yuan Phai*, dated to the 1470s, "Ten men against a massive thousand Lao, they lop off heads and lug them back to give the king."[31]

These clauses suggest an era of hand-to-hand warfare where success or failure depended on individual talent, and where success in war was the route to wealth

[31] Baker and Pasuk, *Yuan Phai*, stanza 280. See also Cushman *Royal Chronicles*, 31, 61, 62.

and social advancement. An ordinary soldier who took an enemy lord was rewarded with "good gold, good silver, appointment to eat [i.e., govern] a city, and a royally presented wife" (c.46)—in short, a complete life transformation.

Elephants

Elephants were royal mounts for military and ceremonial purposes, as well as symbols of kingly power. The use of elephants in warfare increased in the late-fifteenth century. The first report of an Ayutthaya king leading an elephant hunt is dated to 1483/84,[32] and the reports increase in frequency from then onward. The discovery of so many "white" elephants in the early sixteenth century was a result of the increased scale of elephant hunting. In late Ayutthaya, the king kept several elephants either inside the palace or nearby in the city.

Seven clauses deal with royal elephants (c.37–43). These specify the kitting of a royal mount, procedures for the safety of the king when he rehearses for an elephant duel or goes on an elephant hunt, and rewards for anyone who helps the king to acquire an "important elephant," meaning one considered auspicious because of physical characteristics defined in elephant manuals, including the white elephants.

The Reach of Ayutthaya

Clause 2 lists the eight principal cities of the kingdom outside the capital, and another thirty places claimed as tributaries. Historians have used the clause to gauge the extent of Ayutthaya's reach. This clause probably did not appear in the early versions of the law. It has clearly been inserted later, as it disrupts the account of the royal family that begins in clause 1 and continues in clause 3. This position was presumably chosen to give the clause prominence.

The list of eight major provincial cities is similar to the classification of first-class cities in the Civil List in the Three Seals Code and comparable lists.[33] It dates after the late-sixteenth century, when Ayutthaya took control of Khorat to the east and the Mon coastline to the west.

The list of tributaries is more problematic. It includes places where Ayutthaya exercised some influence in its early years, but not later (such as Johore and Melaka); places where Ayutthaya exercised some influence in later years, but not earlier (such as Hsenwi); places that appear fleetingly in Thai history (such as Chiang Krai and Chiang Kran); and some that are difficult to identify (such as Reo Kaeo, usually the term for the Ryukyu Islands, but here classified among places to the north). Perhaps this is a list of places that are recorded as sending the gold and silver flowers of allegiance *at some time* in Ayutthaya's history, but were never all permanently under the capital's sway. Vickery suggests that the list may represent the aspirations of Bangkok at the time the Three Seals Code was compiled in 1805.[34]

Royal Timetable

Clause 157 presents an hour-by-hour program of the king's activities throughout the day. Similar programs are found in early Indian texts on kingship.[35]

---

32 Cushman, *Royal Chronicles*, 18.

33 Compared to the list in the Palace Law, the Civil List includes Phetchaburi, omits Tawai, and uses the name Sawankhalok rather than Satchanalai (*KTSD* 1: 317–21).

34 Vickery, "Constitution of Ayutthaya," 189.

35 Wales, *Siamese State Ceremonies*, 44.

Succession

Neither in this document nor in any other historical source is there any trace of rules for royal succession, the principal focus of the current Palace Law in Thailand and elsewhere. Several foreign visitors to Ayutthaya reasoned that there must have been such rules and sought to discover what they were, without success. Seni Pramoj argued that such rules were not recorded because it would have been inauspicious to imagine the demise of the current king.[36] More likely, such rules did not exist as rules. After reviewing the history, Visanu Kreu-ngam concluded that "The Thai rules of succession in the past were not systematized until 1886."[37]

Schouten and Van Vliet argued that a younger brother of a deceased king had precedence.[38] Given that many kings died before their sons had matured, succession by a younger brother was practical, but there is no evidence that this practicality was enshrined in a rule.

In practice, the majority of successions at Ayutthaya were coups or contests (see Table 4). In the early years, these were struggles among the ruling houses of the prominent cities. As a major role of the king in this era was to lead the army to war, succession by armed struggle could be construed as pragmatic and efficient. Perhaps this law introduced or confirmed the practice of the king designating someone with a title as prospective successor. From around 1600, the level of warring dropped, prosperity rose, and the king never again led an army to war. In this era, the first two successions were peaceful affairs, to son and then to brother, but from then until the fall of Ayutthaya in 1767, eight of the nine successions were coups or contests, some lasting months or even years and involving high bloodshed.

Two features of these later coups and contests are worth noting. First, the contestants were all somehow related to or associated with the previous king. Sons and brothers were the most common. The future kings Prasat Thong and Phetracha were members of the royal circle, but not close relatives. Second, victors in these contests made a point of marrying women from the former king's line. This can be construed in several ways. Perhaps these women brought with them some royal legitimacy through the principle of cognatic kinship (descent from both male and female). Perhaps they were a type of hostage, providing safety against revenge by their kin. Perhaps both.

In the various theories of kingship that prevailed in early Ayutthaya, the king becomes king because he is the person of highest merit. There are at least three theories that consider merit. First, in the Aggañña Sutta, people select the most meritorious man to become the first ruler to constrain the growth of crime and social disorder, and future kings are the metaphorical descendants of this *sommutithep* "as-if god" or *mahasommut* "Great Elect."[39] Second, in the *jataka* stories and other texts, the king is a bodhisatta, an exceptional individual in the process of accumulating the merit to become a Buddha in the future. Third, in the theory that appears in the poem *Yuan Phai* and at the enthronement of King Ekathotsarot in 1606,

---

[36] Seni, *Pathakatha*, 69.

[37] Visanu, "Kotken kan suep ratchasombat," 11. An alternative explanation would be that King Rama I removed this part of the law as his own succession could not have complied with it. The absence of any other reference to succession rules in the sources, however, suggest that such rules simply did not exist.

[38] *Van Vliet's Siam*, 256–57.

[39] Collins, "The Discourse on What is Primary."

Table 4—Royal Succession at Ayutthaya

King	Reign dates	Relationship to predecessors	Succession
Ramathibodi I	1351–1369		
Boromracha I	1370–1388	none	coup
Ramesuan	1388–1395	son of Ramathibodi I	coup
Ramaracha	1395–1409	son	nomination
Intharacha	1409–1424	grandson of Boromracha I	coup
Boromracha II	1424–1448	son	contest
Trailokanat	1448–1488	son	nomination
Ramathibodi II	1491–1529	grandson	nomination
Boromracha IV	1529–1533	son	nomination
Chairacha	1534–1547	younger brother	coup
Chakkraphat	1548–1569	younger brother	contest
Thammaracha	1569–1590	son-in-law	contest
Naresuan	1590–1605	son	nomination
Ekathotsarot	1605–1610	younger brother	nomination
Songtham	1610–1628	son by consort	coup
Prasat Thong	1629–1656	uncertain	contest
Narai	1656–1688	son	contest
Phetracha	1688–1703	son of wet-nurse	coup
Sua	1703–1709	son	coup
Thai Sa	1709–1733	son	nomination
Borommakot	1733–1758	brother	contest
Uthumphon	1758, (1767)	elder son	contest
Ekathat	1758–1767	brother	coup

Notes. "Nomination" means the king nominated his successor, or there was no contest to an obvious succession. "Coup" means a seizure of power that overrode such nomination, and "contest" means a seizure that was contested and fought over by at least two contenders. In contested successions, kings who ruled for only a short time (such as during the successions of 1628–29 and 1656) are not shown in this table.

eleven gods cooperate to instill their divinity into the king.[40] This latter theory is dramatized in the ceremony of installing a king when a human is transformed into king by the conferment of godly powers by anointment. In all these theories, the king is king because of his individual quality, his personal stock of merit. Each reign is thus discreet. As noted above, all laws, court cases, and official appointments theoretically became void "at the accident of a change of reign."

In European conceptions of kingship, royalty is passed down in the blood. Succession laws map this flow. But in Siamese theory, merit does not flow in the blood but is individually attained. Being (re)born in a royal lineage, however, may be

[40] Cushman, *Royal Chronicles*, 199; see "Theory of Kingship" section at http://en.wikipedia.org/wiki/Yuan_Phai, accessed March 1, 2015; compare Doniger and Smith, *Laws of Manu*, 128.

evidence of merit accumulated in past lives.[41] Those who contest for the succession, then, may simply believe they have greater merit than any opponent. In some contests, the initial nominee was a child or juvenile and the challenger was an older man. The future kings Prasat Thong and Phetracha seem to have had enormous confidence in their own abilities. And of course, once a contestant had secured the kingship, that victory in itself was proof that he possessed greater merit than his rival(s)—the principle of "the best man won." Although European and Chinese commentary on these successions talks about "usurpers," this vocabulary is absent from the Thai sources.[42]

Ceremonies

The clauses on ceremonies occupy over a quarter of the total length (by number of pages) of the Palace Law. Most of the ceremonies form part of an annual cycle, usually titled the Royal Ceremonies of the Twelve Months. This is an old tradition. There are allusions to the cycle in a fifteenth-century poem;[43] a complete cycle embedded in the account of the Borommakot reign (1732–58) in *Khamhaikan khun luang ha wat*;[44] several manuscripts dating from the early Bangkok era, probably recording late Ayutthaya practice;[45] and a famous recasting by King Chulalongkorn. The cycle clearly changed over time, and the version in this law differs significantly from King Chulalongkorn's account (Table 5).

A summary list of the annual cycle appears in clause 156. Possibly this clause is a late addition, since the detailed accounts in later clauses do not match this clause. Some ceremonies are described in later clauses as if they are part of the cycle, yet do not appear in the list. Some from the list are missing from the detailed accounts, while others are brief, garbled, or confusing.

This cycle of ceremonies makes the king central to achieving the well-being of the kingdom in five different ways: through military might to defend and expand the kingdom; by nourishing Buddhism for advancing the spiritual well-being of the population; by achieving an abundant harvest from agriculture; by offering charity; and by attracting general good fortune through the good offices of several deities, including those of the Hindu pantheon and various spirits.

In this version of the cycle, the treatment of Buddhist ceremonies is conspicuously light. In clause 156, the only Buddhist ceremonies are *Wisakha pucha*, *Sat*, and the beginning of the rains retreat (or Buddhist Lent), and there is no

---

[41] In several of the "Fifty Jatakas," the non-canonical stories of the Buddha's past lives, one of the rewards of accumulating merit in this life is a guarantee of being born in a high rather than a low family in future lives. A high family is often defined as the family of an emperor or king. So being born into the king's family, or even perhaps a slightly wider circle, is proof of merit. See *Panyat chadok*.

[42] For instance, from the *Khamhaikan* documents, which include the interpretation of late Ayutthaya history by nobles swept away to Burma in 1767; and from "Sangkhitiyawong," the chronicle composed in the *wat*.

[43] *Thawatotsommat khlong chan*, a love poem built around a theme of the twelve months, with mention of some of the ceremonies. See http://www.reurnthai.com/wiki/โคลงทวาทศมาส, accessed March 1, 2015.

[44] *Khamhaikan khun luang ha wat*, 103–7.

[45] For example, *Tamra baep thamniyom nai ratchasamnak* and *Tamra phraratchaphithi kao*. Both of these are reprints of old texts kept in the Wachirayan Library.

detailed description of any of these in the later clauses. There is no mention of the *kathin* ceremonies that figure prominently in foreign accounts of the Narai reign. Perhaps this is because this account of the cycle comes from the library of the court Brahmans, or perhaps Buddhist ceremonies were less prominent in the early part of the Ayutthaya era.

Table 5—Royal Ceremonies of the Twelve Months

Month	Palace Law	Borommakot reign	King Chulalongkorn
5	*Phadetsok* (solar new year)	*Thaloengsok* (solar new year)	*Si satja pankan* (water oath) *Thot chueak* (elephant noose) *Songkran* (solar new year)
6	*Wisakha pucha* *Jarot phraratchangkhan* (plowing)	*Jarot phranangkhan* (plowing)	*Phitmongkhon* (plowing) *Wisakha pucha*
7	*Thun nam lang phrabat* (washing the royal feet)	*Tulaphan* (weighing for alms)	*Khenkathingchang* (elephant) *Thun nam lang phrabat* (washing the royal feet)
8	*Khao phrawasa* (entering Buddhist Lent)	*Awasat* (ordination)	*Khao phansa* (entering Buddhist Lent)
9	*Tulaphan* (weighing for alms)	*Narai prathomsin* (bathing)	*Tulaphan* (weighing for alms) *Phirunsat* (rain)
10	*Phatharabot* (Brahman) *Sat* (merit-making)	*Phatharabot* (Brahman)	*Sat* (merit-making) *Kuan khao thip* (merit making) *Chaloem phrachon phansa* (royal birthday)
11	*Asayut* (boat race)	*Asayut* (boat race)	*Khaeng ruea* (boat race)
12	*Jongpriang* (lantern)	*Jongpriang* (lantern)	*Jongpriang* (lantern)
1	*Lai ruea* (boat) *Triyampawai* (swinging)	*Khlaeng* (kite)	*Lai ruea* (boat)
2	*Butsayaphisek* (bathing) *Chawian phra kho* (cow)	*Butsayaphisek* (bathing)	*Butsayaphisek* (bathing) *Triyamphawai* (swinging)
3	*Thanyatho* (alms)	*Thanyatho* (alms)	*Thanyatho* (alms) *Siwaratri*
4	*Samphatcharachin* (guardian spirits)	*Samphatcharachin* (guardian spirits)	*Rot jaet* (calendar) *Samphatcharachin* (guardian spirits)

Source: *Khamhaikan khun luang ha wat,* 103–7; Chulalongkorn, *Phraratchaphithi sipsong duean.*

Military Parade

The military parade is not mentioned in the twelve-month list of ceremonies in clause 156, but the description is introduced in the form used for such calendric events ("On the fifth waxing day of the fifth month ..."), suggesting that it was once part of the cycle. To this day, many states hold an annual military parade, but its scale and prominence differ greatly depending on what role militarism plays in the purpose and ideological justification of the state. Early Ayutthaya, up to the mid-sixteenth century, was a highly militarized state.[46] The prominence given to the military parade in this account of the ceremonial cycle reflects that era. Later, the military parade was dropped from the cycle; it does not appear in the Borommakot or Chulalongkorn lists.

The detailed account of the parade falls into three parts (c.170–71; c.172–73; c.174). The first two parts seem to describe a single event that extends over two days. The vocabulary describing the royal family is similar to the opening clauses of the Palace Law, suggesting this description may date to early Ayutthaya. The third part may be a third day of the same event, but more likely is a full description dating from a later era.

In the first part, the sequence is as follows. Many units of troops appear in parade as a show of force, with a prominent role for elephants. In a nice practical touch, the ground afterward has to be cleared of elephant dung before the next stage can begin. There are then displays that seem to be re-enactments of battlefield maneuvers, followed by demonstrations of various martial sports, followed by presentations to the king. On the second day, there is again a procession, this time in front of the extended royal family and staff arrayed to display the hierarchy by virtue of position and various forms of regalia. This audience then observes musical performances, military maneuvers, martial sports, and various contests and races.

In the third part, "the parade ground is closed to prevent people entering." Sometime after 1632, King Prasat Thong had a wall built enclosing the parade ground. Before that, it had been open. This third part may be a description of the military parade at a later era, after this enclosure was built, and it has suggestive differences. The big show of military force and the re-enactment of military maneuvers have both disappeared. The display appears to be only for the king and royal family. Martial sports and contests remain in the program, but include more music and dancing. Perhaps this account reflects the transition from militarism to trade in the seventeenth century, along with the concealment of the king's body in the same era.[47]

Bathing Ceremonies

Abhisheka is a Sanskrit term for ceremonies in which anointment with some substance (oil, water, milk, paste) signifies the conferral of power. Ceremonies that make kings are one form of *abhisheka*. The Thai coronation can still be traced to a form of *rajya-abhisheka* in old Indian texts. The ceremony today is based on a form recreated by King Rama I from memories of the practice in late Ayutthaya.

In the Indian original, the subject is first purified with water and then anointed with divine power through the medium of oil. In the Thai version, the oil has disappeared, and the two functions of purification and unction have been fused,

---

[46] Baker, "Ayutthaya Rising."

[47] Baker, "Grand Palace," 79–84.

with sacralized water acting as the medium to transfer divine power to the king.[48] In the Chakri-era ceremony, after the anointment, senior officials present the newly created king with all the property of his realm, including the populace, officialdom, military forces, tax revenues, and so on, and the king returns each of these to the officials to administer.

Bathing with sacred water forms part of several ceremonies in the Three Seals Code. Clause 167 lists nineteen (though miscounts them as seventeen). Five of them have *phisek* (*abhisheka*) as part of their title and bathing as a major element, including the king-making ceremony and another for conferring titles on court Brahmans. Three others are ceremonies that mark stages in the lifecycle of the king. Eight are part of the twelve-month cycle; in many of these, bathing is an incidental part of the ceremony. The full description of the king-making rite has been lost, but clause 168 is possibly a fragment describing the bathing element in that ceremony. Water from thirty-two flasks is poured into a bath and then fed through a "thousand streams," a nozzle.

One *phisek* ceremony is part of the twelve-month cycle. *Butsayaphisek* (c.183) is a symbolic re-enactment of the king-making ceremony, an annual reaffirmation of the king's divine power. This ceremony, under the same Pali-Sanskrit name, appears in a tenth-century Angkor inscription.[49] The ceremony takes place in the main throne hall in the presence of the royal family and senior officials. The Brahmans offer sacralized water to the king in what is perhaps a reduced symbolic version of the original dousing. Two senior officials then present the king with the wealth of the kingdom in what is perhaps a reduced version of the longer presentation at the original king-making rite. The event ends with a feast.

Butsayaphisek appears in the Borommakot list of ceremonies with a short description matching that above. Between late Ayutthaya and early Bangkok, the ceremony disappeared. King Chulalongkorn included *Butsayaphisek* in his cycle, but merely repeated the Borommakot-era account and noted that the ceremony had lapsed.

The Palace Law also contains a description of a much more elaborate bathing ceremony termed *Intharaphisek* (c.189–90). The Indian original of the ceremony thus named is a re-enactment of the god Indra traveling to this world to confer on a ruler the five insignia of kingship.[50] The version in the Palace Law, however, shows no trace of this origin. The Ayutthaya chronicles record that this ceremony was performed in the Chakkaphat reign (1548–69) to mark completion of repairs to the palace following a great fire. It may also have been performed in 1496/97.[51] Possibly the account in the law comes from one of these events. The very elaborate ceremony is perhaps a reaffirmation of divine royal power in the wake of the inauspicious destruction of a palace building.

The ceremony extends over twenty-one days. The two main elements of the king-making ceremony—bathing and the presentation of the wealth of the kingdom—appear in an elaborate form. Large amounts of sacralized water are produced, some for presentation to the king and some for bathing various pieces of military equipment and several images of Hindu deities. The officials' presentation

---

[48] Wales, *Siamese State Ceremonies*, 74–75.

[49] Inscription K.806, v. 66, see Sanderson, "The Śaiva Religion among the Khmers," 382.

[50] Maniphin, "Chak nak duek damban."

[51] Cushman, *Royal Chronicles*, 18, 30–31.

of the wealth of the realm to the king extends over several days. In the final stages of the ceremony, there are feasts, distribution of alms, and entertainments that continue for a further month. The most distinctive part of the ceremony, however, comes at the beginning. The palace parade ground is converted into a representation of Mount Meru, where palace staff enact the scene of churning the sea of milk, a mythical account of the creation of the world in both Hindu and Buddhist legend. Perhaps this dramatization symbolizes the revival or recreation of royal power in the wake of an inauspicious event.

This extraordinary ceremony appears to combine the reaffirmation of royal-divine power of the *phisek* bathing ceremony with a propitiation of the Hindu gods, and royal bestowal of alms and entertainments for the populace.

Spirits

The ceremony of *Bophok* (c.187–88) does not appear in the listing of the twelve-month ceremonies, but is introduced with a dating ("On the evening of the 11th waning day ..."), which suggests it was an annual event and possibly part of the cycle. Its meaning is now totally lost. Indeed, a measure of its obscurity is that the Thai title of the ceremony scored only two hits on Google in 2014.[52] At the climax of the ceremony, the king sleeps with a spirit in a scene that recalls Zhou Daguan's account of the Khmer king sleeping with a *naga* princess, a spirit of the earth, to safeguard the realm: "If for a single night this spirit does not appear, the time has come for this foreign king to die. If for a single night he stays away, he is bound to suffer a disaster."[53]

The name *Bophok* probably comes from the Pali-Sanskrit word *pāvaka*, meaning fire, and, by extension, purification. The focus of the rite is *mae yua phra phi*. The three elements of this name are: the type of queen translated elsewhere in the law as head mother; sacred; and the form of address for an elder. The name is rather generic, but hints that it might refer to the spirit of a former queen. Phra Phi may have been an image or a purely imaginary presence. Choti Kalyanamit says there were *jawet* votive tablets of Phra Phi in the nineteenth century, and shows an example from the National Museum (which is no longer on display).[54]

At the start of the rite, shrines for Phra Phi are created in the various residences of the royal wives, children, and grandchildren inside the palace compound. For three days, all courtiers—from ministers down to middle-ranked officials—make worship to Phra Phi. On the following day, Phra Phi leaves her *prasat*, presumably a shrine somewhere in the palace, and travels in a grand royal conveyance, as does the king. The remainder of the procession is almost totally female, including the royal women, female palace staff, wives of senior officials, and wives of the court Brahmans, accompanied by royal children, the court Brahmans, and perhaps a few elderly royal relatives. The Brahmans' wives carry candles and conches, which are standard ceremonial accessories. They also carry several items associated with

---

[52] One of these Google hits was an article on this ceremony by Sujit Wongthes ("Naga sangwat"), and the other was about a television producer who, when making a program on the Palace Law in 2004, appealed "urgently" for information on the word *bophok* and got no responses.

[53] Zhou, *Record of Cambodia*, 49.

[54] Choti, *Photjananukrom sathapattayakam*, 392. The image of a standing woman has a *chada* headpiece, but otherwise the iconography is ordinary.

water, including a golden turtle, golden fish, and *traphang*, usually meaning a pond or lake but perhaps here it means some kind of water container. One carries a knife used for casumunar, a herbal root used extensively in traditional medicine. One of the Brahman wives scatters rice, often a device to chase away evil spirits.

When the procession reaches a point that appears to be close to the river on the north side of the palace, the women leave, and the king goes to sleep with Phra Phi. After emerging, bathing, dressing, and eating, the king makes nine circuits of a royal building and then visits "Uthokkaratsot," a Pali-derived term meaning "ruler of the waters," usually referring to a fierce, female water spirit, sometimes depicted as a servant of Yama, the god of death. The king scatters "rings, gold, and silver." Close by are Brahmans standing by bonfires and also distributing silver.

The king and his four senior queens then enter a "hall of fire" (*rong kun*). Earlier, this hall was occupied by the Brahmans, perhaps in a purification rite. The hall has a fire at the center and then successive rings of balustrades, deities, umbrellas, another fence, votive tablets, another fence, and then ranks of guards and elephants. The concentric pattern may be a mandala. Besides these concentric circles of protection, something extra has been done to block inauspicious forces coming from the direction of the water spirit's shrine. The staging seems designed to protect the king from malicious forces. The Brahmans and the royal wives present the king with sacralized water. The event ends with feasting and entertainments.

The rite is complex, and totally unlike other Ayutthaya royal ceremonies recorded in this source and others. Most likely it is a rite of purification (as the name states) and protection. Females play a prominent role, which perhaps reflects the prominence of females as officiants in other Thai spirit ceremonies. Water is a major theme in the symbolism—including the fish, turtle, conch, *trapang*, and water spirit. Purification by fire is a fundamental part of Brahman ceremonies. The opposition of fire and water is almost universal. Other elements suggest tantric influences, including the protective mandala arrangement of the fire hall, and the sexual element. This may be an inheritance from the tantric influence in late Angkor. Piriya suggests that some images which were deposited in the crypt of Wat Ratchaburana, probably in the 1420s, are tantric in inspiration.[55]

At a guess, this rite propitiates the spirit of a prominent female royal ancestor who died by drowning, hence the role of the water spirit.[56] Sujit Wongthes argues that the rite must have derived from the practice of the Angkor king sleeping with the *naga* princess.[57] This may be true, but any Khmer-derived element in the rite has clearly been greatly transformed and amalgamated with many other elements.

The birth of a royal child, and the preceding pregnancy, occasion several spirit ceremonies, most of which are now totally mysterious (c.192–95).

Discussion

Hierarchy, security, women, war, and ceremony: along with basic housekeeping, these are the primary subjects of the Ayutthaya Palace Law.

---

[55] Piriya, *Roots of Thai Art*, 241, 302–4; and his discussion of texts, 236–39.

[56] On ṃrtoddharah, a tantric rite for the benefit of someone who suffered an impure death, see Sanderson, "Vajrayāna: Origin and Function," 32.

[57] Sujit, "Naga sangwat."

The opening passage and the major theme of the law are about hierarchy and precedence. In part, this is about constructing order and discipline within the royal lineage. In the early to mid-fifteenth century, the Suphanburi and Sukhothai dynasties were becoming closely intertwined,[58] and the law might be an attempt to address the resulting complexity within the royal lineage. But the emphasis on precedence, and especially its public dramatization, is perhaps a more general attempt to establish the principle of hierarchy at a time when society as a whole had increased in complexity.

Several facets of the law reflect the martial character of society in early Ayutthaya. Guarding the city and protecting the body of the king are the second-most prominent themes of the law both in terms of the position in the text and the volume of clauses (i.e., number of pages). The great annual military parade appears early in the list of ceremonies, immediately after the royal bathing, and seems to have been an elaborate event, extending over two days. The elephants—so important in warfare of the early era—are given significant space in the law. The conduct of warfare has a place in the Palace Law because this was the era when a major role of the king was to lead armies. The section on military rewards and punishments suggest an era of hand-to-hand fighting, with a prominent role for duels on elephant back.

The section on the inner palace emphasizes the king's exclusive control over the palace women. While this can be interpreted in several ways, including maintaining the purity of royal blood, the symbolic dramatization of royal power seems to be uppermost. The extreme extent of the king's exclusive control over the palace women is stressed by the immaculate nature of the primary queen, so untouchable by others she cannot be saved from drowning. While the degree of protection diminishes down the social hierarchy, it is striking that men are denied access to *all* women in the palace, including servant girls. All women within the walls are to some extent his royal women.

Ceremony occupies a quarter of the whole text. The major Buddhist ceremonies are missing, and the accounts of many Brahman ceremonies are fragmentary and incomplete. The ceremonies most elaborately described are ones that had disappeared from the ritual calendar by late Ayutthaya.

The bathing rite, which is a conferral of divine power, is central to the ceremony of installing a king. But in early Ayutthaya, this creation of a king does not seem to have been a one-off event. The text mentions no fewer than nineteen ceremonies that included bathing. Some of these are annual, some mark stages in the life of the king, and some are unknown. *Butsayaphisek* appears to have been an elaborate annual re-enactment of the divine conferral of kingly power, with Angkorian precedents. The even more elaborate *Intharaphisek* may have been performed to shore up kingly power after a supremely inauspicious event, such as the destruction of a major palace building by fire. In early Ayutthaya, the divine conferral of royal power was not permanent but had to be constantly repeated.

Other rules and ceremonies for protecting the sacred aura of the palace and the city involve mostly spirits rather than deities. The rite to overcome inauspicious events in the palace uses chickens, which are known in old Tai rites but not in other royal rituals. Most remarkable of all is the lost *Bophok* ceremony: the rite is steeped in imagery of fire and water, masses of women play supporting roles in a way not

[58] See especially Phiset, *Phra maha thammaracha*.

found in other ceremonies, and the king sleeps with a spirit. The rite seems to be about purity and protection secured through propitiating various spirits and making uses of elemental forces.

If these three ceremonies were important in early Ayutthaya, they offer an insight into the cultural context of this era not found in any other document. Their disappearance from the later ritual calendar emphasizes the great change between this earlier era and the late Ayutthaya context, which is better documented and understood.

NOTE ON THE TRANSLATION

The translation is based on the Royal Institute's two-volume edition of the Three Seals Code (2007), which has facsimiles of the 1805 manuscript pages, and on กฎมณเฑียรบาล ฉบับเฉลิมพระเกียรติ, *Kot monthianban chabap chaloemprakiat,* Palace Law, Royal Anniversary Version, two volumes, 2005, edited and annotated by Winai Pongsripian under a project supported by the Thailand Research Fund and initiated by the Thai History Committee of the prime minister's office to produce a revised edition of the law, based on the text edited by R. Lingat in 1938–39 and known as the Thammasat University edition.[59] This translation follows Winai's division into numbered paragraphs but also adds subheadings on the "chapters" of the law.

In his introduction, Winai notes that "the Three Seals Code is full of old words that are difficult to understand ... but no document in the Three Seals Code is as difficult to read and understand as the Palace Law." He provides eight hundred annotations on the text, and acknowledges the contributions to these notes by Prasert na Nagara, Julathat Phayakharanon, and MR Suphawat Kasemsri. Without these notes, explaining a host of words not found in any Thai dictionary, this translation would not have been possible. Many of the annotations here are based on those by Winai and his colleagues. The meaning of many passages remains unclear because of obscure words, lapsed usages, archaic constructions, copying errors, corruptions of the text, and so forth.

As in other early Thai texts, the language is extremely terse, often near-telegraphese. The translation attempts to retain this character by minimizing the addition of words needed to make the English readable. Material [in square brackets] does not appear in the original text but is inserted to make the meaning clearer. Some of these insertions are fragments that seem to have been omitted by copyists. Others are intended to clarify the meaning of the original.

As Thai often neglects to distinguish between singular and plural, it is often difficult to determine whether a passage is referring to one person or several. As English cannot preserve the ambiguity without being very clumsy, here each instance has been guessed according to context. So when a clause mentions a "horse officer," it may mean one or several. There is a similar difficulty with gender.

Thai extracts in the footnotes show the spelling as in the 1805 text. Modern spelling is given only when it is not obvious.

The text mentions many individuals and groups by their official name. Often there is either no obvious English-language equivalent, or the function and position is not clear. For such terms that occur repeatedly, an English version has been

---

59 The information and quotes here come from the "Bannathikan thalaeng" (editor's preface) in the first volume. The preface has no page numbering.

invented and used consistently throughout the translation. These terms are explained in an appendix following the translation.

The division into clauses here follows Winai's edition, which differs from the Khurusapha edition. This table serves as a guide:

Khurusapha	Winai	Khurusapha	Winai	Khurusapha	Winai
10	11	70	75	130	140
20	21	80	85	140	150
30	30	90	97	150	162
40	40	100	109	160	176
50	46	110	121	170	188
60	60	120	130	180	205

THE PALACE LAW OF AYUTTHAYA

1 May there be goodness and beauty![1] In 720 of the [Lesser] Era, on Saturday the 6th waxing of the 5th month in a year of the rat of the era,[2] His Majesty King Ramathibodi Boromma Trailokanat,[3] great crowned divine-human,[4] of pure solar lineage, a future Buddha, a great monarch upholding the Ten Royal Virtues, ruling the realm according to ancient royal tradition, great holy king of kings, the royal foot that maintains the territories and frontiers, great protector of the populace, the great monarch proceeds to sit on the lion throne at the lion window; and[5] His Majesty the Royal Scion[6] of the solar lineage, and His Majesty Phra Phannamesuan[7] sit in

---

[1] ศุภมัสดุ, *suphamatsadu*, a conventional word at head and tail of an announcement.

[2] This date is problematic. It appears to be a date in the Lesser (*chula sakkarat*, CS) Era (CE = CS - 638; see glossary) and would correspond to 1358 CE, just seven years after the founding of Ayutthaya in the chronicles. Several scholars have proposed methods to adjust the date to the reign of King Trailokanat (1448–88), who may be the ruler mentioned later in this sentence. Prince Damrong proposed adding one hundred years to make the year CS 820 or 1458 CE, but this was not a year of the rat. Prasert na Nagara proposed CS 830, as that is the only year in the Trailokanat reign for which the other specifications of the date work, corresponding to March 18, 1468 CE. At this date, Trailokanat was ruling in Phitsanulok. David Wyatt ("Palatine Law," 86) proposed a more complex adjustment with a similar result. Prince Damrong revised his estimate to match. However, Michael Vickery ("Prolegomena," 46) argues that the Lesser Era was not in use in the Trailokanat reign and that this date must have been concocted later "to give that important text a patent of antiquity," possibly during the compilation of the Three Seals Code in 1805.

[3] Boromma Trailokanat, meaning "the great being, refuge of the Three Worlds," an epithet of the Buddha, is generally assumed to refer to the king reigning during 1448–88 according to the chronicles, often referenced in English as King Trailokanat. He received this name when undergoing a tonsure ceremony during his father's reign in 1982 BE [Buddhist Era; 1439 CE] (Winai, "Phraratcha phongsawadan," 111–12). Vickery ("Prolegomena") argues that this king appears under a different name in contemporary inscriptions, suggests the name Trailokanat may have been applied posthumously, and concludes this is further proof that this law was revised during the 1805 compilation of the Three Seals Code (see above note). However, other kings also appear under different names in inscriptions and chronicles, respectively, so Vickery's assumption is unproven. Vickery concedes that Trailokanat seems to have been a legal innovator who may have originated such a law, but suggests that other early kings might equally have been responsible and that thus the date and authorship should remain open.

[4] เทพมนุษย์, *thep manut*, a reference to the theory that eight or eleven gods combine to create a king. The theory appears at the opening of the *Yuan Phai* martial epic, and in the chronicles at the coronation of King Ekathotsarot in 1605 (Baker and Pasuk, *Yuan Phai*, stanzas 1–2; Cushman, *Royal Chronicles*, 199).

[5] Michael Vickery suggests that the list immediately following records "the royalty who were in the king's presence at the moment of proclamation of the law." In other words, these are the titles and relationships in the royal family at a certain time, not a prescriptive arrangement (Vickery, "Constitution of Ayutthaya," 156).

[6] หน่อพุทธางกูร, *no phutthangkun*, literally "shoot of a future Buddha," sometimes หน่อพระพุทธเจ้า, *no phraphuttha jao*, "shoot of the Buddha," a term for a bodhisatta. In the reign of King Ramathibodi II (1491–1529), a royal son of this title was appointed as Great Prince (*upparat*)

audience, and Ekkasattarat,[8] the Great Prince,[9] and primary ministers, the four pillars,[10] major officials, chiefs of the troops, and the inner guard and outer guard of Mahatthai,[11] courtiers,[12] military and civilian, left and right, attend on the royal foot there; thus the King issues royal orders and laws for military and civilian, men and women, monks, Brahmans and teachers, merchants, and all groups of subjects.

Dependencies

2 The Kings who present gold and silver flowers are from twenty cities: the royal city,[13] Si Sattanakhanahut,[14] Chiang Mai, Tongu,[15] Chiang Krai,[16] Chiang Kran, Chiang Saen, Chiang Rung, Chiang Rai, Saen Wi [Hsenwi], Khemmarat,[17] Phrae, Nan, Taithong,[18] Khotrabong,[19] Reo Kaeo,[20] these sixteen cities to the north; to the

---

and sent to rule Phitsanulok, and he later succeeded his father as King Boromracha IV (Cushman, *Royal Chronicles*, 19–20, from the Luang Prasoet chronicle).

[7] พระพรรณเมศวร, probably the king's son, and possibly a copyist error for Phra Ramesuan, a common name for a royal son. Vickery suggests this is "*paramesvara*, a royal title well attested among Malay and Javanese royalty as well as at Angkor" but "not used elsewhere for Thai royalty" ("Constitution of Ayutthaya," 157). The same spelling appears in clause 174.

[8] เอกสัตราช, perhaps a garbled version of Ekathotsarot, a royal epithet meaning a union of eleven gods (เอกาทศรุทร, see note 5); presumably a son who holds the position of the Great Prince (see next note).

[9] พระมหาอุปราช, *phra maha upparat*, "great deputy king." According to clause 3, this is the term for a son of the king by a Head Mother. The Civil List in the Three Seals Code states that a son or younger brother of the king may hold this post with *sakdina* of 100,000 (*KTSD* 1: 219). In Myanmar, the term was used for the deputy king, often the major royal son. In Siam, the term was later used for a minister (not necessarily a royal) who deputized in the king's absence.

[10] The four ministers of the palace, city, lands, and treasury.

[11] Sometime in early Ayutthaya, the four-pillar ministries (see note above) were supplemented by two ministries, Mahatthai and Kalahom, which mainly looked after regions beyond the capital and its immediate domain. The areas under these two ministries shifted from time to time, but Mahatthai usually looked after regions to the north of the capital. Much later, Mahatthai and Kalahom evolved into interior and defense, respectively.

[12] ลูกขุน, *luk khun*, a term with a narrow meaning of "judicial official," but a more general meaning of all senior officials in the court.

[13] นครหลวง, *nakhon luang*, Angkor.

[14] Lanchang, Luang Prabang.

[15] The only record of Tongu (Toungoo) presenting tribute to Ayutthaya appears in the reign of King Ekathotsarot (1605–10), mentioned in the chronicles (Cushman, *Royal Chronicles*, 201–3) and in Dutch records for 1609. Alternatively, this is Tang Au, an old town on the Mekong River above Chiang Saen (Wyatt, "Palatine Law," 88).

[16] In 1538, Tabinshweti attacked Chiang Kran and King Chairacha responded by marching to Chiang Krai and Chiang Kran (Cushman, *Royal Chronicles*, 20). The two places were in the Mon region of southern Burma. Prince Damrong (*Our Wars*, 12, 360 n. 4) first identified Chiang Kran with Kreng, which Phra Phraison Salarak identified with Gyaing, now a river on the road between Mae Sot and Mawlamyine (Moulmein), and later changed to a place near the Three Pagodas Pass, called Ataran by the British.

[17] Chiang Tung, Kengtung in the Shan States.

[18] ไต้ทอง, two possibilities: a town in the Mon country that sent tribute to Ayutthaya after Siamese forces had intervened in a dispute in the Mon country in 1441 (Winai, "Phraratcha phongsawadan," 66–67); or a town in the north of Cambodia (Vickery, "The 2/K.125 fragment," 5, 66). The sequence favors the latter.

south, Uyongtana,[21] Malaka [Melaka, Malacca], Malayu,[22] Worawari,[23] four cities, making a total of twenty cities offering gold and silver flowers.

The lords of great cities who drink the water of allegiance are from eight cities: Phitsanulok, Satchanalai, Sukhothai, Kamphaeng Phet, Nakhon Si Thammarat, Nakhon Ratchasima, Tanaosi [Tenasserim], Tawai [Tavoy].

Regalia and Insignia

3 A royal decree determines that the royal sons and royal grandsons are: a royal son born of the Primary Queen, that is, the Royal Scion; one born of a Head Mother,[24] being the Great Prince;[25] those born from royal children eating provincial cities[26] of first class; those born from royal grandchildren eating cities of second class; those born of royal consorts, being royal youth.[27]

4 His Majesty the Royal Scion has three-tiered *aphirom* regalia;[28] the Great Prince has two-tiered *aphirom* regalia; the royal sons ruling cities have [*aphirom* regalia with] white lotus petals; the royal children and royal youth have *aphirom* regalia with golden petals and *kanching* umbrellas[29] covered with red cloth; the royal youth have

---

19 Phrathat Si Khotrabong is now in the Khammouan Province of Laos, opposite Nakhon Phanom.

20 เรวแกว; the position in the list suggests an old town near Champasak, sometimes called Rakaeo, but there is no record of this as a tributary of Ayutthaya. Possibly it means the Ryukyu Islands, claimed as a tributary because of trading relations; perhaps the composer of the clause was unaware of their location. On his last campaign beyond Chiang Mai, Naresuan defeated a town called Riao (เรียว) according to *Khamhaikan khun luang ha wat*, 15.

21 Tip of the Malay Peninsula, modern Johore.

22 Possibly Sumatra, or "the district on and about the Malāyū river, immediately adjoining Johore on the West" (Gerini, "Historical Retrospect," 11).

23 Maybe Worah Warih, an ancient state in central Java, but more likely a region of the Malay Peninsula. Gerini ("Historical Retrospect," 11) suggested Muar, now on the southwest coast of Malaysia.

24 แม่หยัวเมือง, Prasert na Nagara suggests this is shortened from *mae yu hua mueang*, mother-head-city. In the chronicles, this title is held by Si Sudacan, mother of the infant king Yotfa in 1547–48 (Cushman, *Royal Chronicles*, 21). The term also appears in *Yuan Phai*. The meaning is not clear, and probably changed over time. Here it seems to mean a major queen other than the Primary Queen. In clause 158, it seems to mean the two most junior of the four queens. Elsewhere in the law, it seems to refer to queens ranking below the primary four, possibly consorts who have given birth to a royal child, especially those who bear the king a son. In some usages, it seems to mean queens that come from the (four) principal provincial cities.

25 พระมหาอุปราช, *phra maha upparat*.

26 กิน(เมือง), *kin mueang*, "eating the city," later used to mean ruling a city or province, but may earlier have meant enjoying the revenues, like an appanage.

27 พระเยาวราช, *phra yaowarat*. It is not clear whether this is a collective term or an individual title similar to the Great Prince and Royal Scion.

28 อภิรม, *aphirom*, a term sometimes used for a long-handled, multi-tiered umbrella, and sometimes as a collective term for all "tall regalia," including umbrellas and other items, carried in processions and planted above thrones. Within the ministry of the palace there was a department of *aphirom ratchayan*, tall regalia and royal vehicles, headed by Khun Ratchaphiman, *sakdina* 1,000 (*KTSD* 1: 239).

29 กันชิง, another ceremonial long-handled umbrella in the shape of a *klot*, the umbrella carried by monks.

one elephant, one horse, twenty men, no more; they take betel from a glass-inlaid casket.[30]

His Majesty the Royal Scion travels in a golden carriage. The Great Prince travels in a *nak*[31] carriage. Royal sons eating cities travel in lotus-petal gold carriages.

5 The Primary Queen bathes with a silver thousand-streams;[32] has a royal carriage; has departments of men and women; has a sacred hall;[33] has a hall for audience; has [a hall for] feasting[34] to feed courtiers who pay homage at the New Year[35] and the Sat festival;[36] issues royal decrees;[37] has palace-rear officers; has elephant officers; has horse officers; has shield boats[38] and procession boats.

6 The Royal Scion has a *thoet* throne.[39] The Great Prince sits in the audience hall on a golden bench-throne[40] two cubits[41] tall with a *jiam*[42] cushion. Royal sons eating cities sit on thrones one cubit high with *jiam* with trimming.[43] The royal sons sit on a throne with a *kuatrat*[44] mat with trimming. Royal progeny born from royal sons sit in the palace in order from front to back.

7 When traveling on royal conveyances, the children of the Primary Queen, children of the Secondary Queen, children of the Head Mothers, and [other] royal children sit on conveyances with royal grandchildren and children of royal consorts in order from front to back.

8 Royal sons who eat cities pay homage to His Majesty the Royal Scion. Royal youth pay homage to the royal sons who eat cities.

---

30 เจียด, *jiat*, a lidded container, often octagonal, presented as insignia of rank.

31 นาก, an alloy of gold, silver, and copper with an appearance similar to silver, known among European traders as tutenague.

32 Meaning a shower nozzle, used on ceremonial occasions.

33 หอพระ, *ho phra*, usually a room or small building in which to place images for worship. Within a palace, *ho phra* were granted by the king to royal kin as a form of regalia. Throughout this law, the term refers to a place (other than a throne hall) where the king or other royalty receive people. Often (e.g., clause 160), the *ho phra* is used for gatherings of royal family members rather than courtiers, and might mean the royal *wat*, Wat Phra Si Sanphet.

34 สมโพธ, *somphot*, which might be สมโพธน์, announce, and thus be part of the previous phrase, but more likely สมโภชน์, meaning a communal meal.

35 ตรุด, *trut*, on the 15th waxing day of the 4th lunar month, usually in March–April.

36 สาท, *sat*, a festival falling on the 15th waning of the 10th month, usually in September.

37 ใช้พระราชกฤษฎีกา, *chai phraratcha krisadika*, term for a command by the Primary Queen; see clause 112.

38 To flank her boat during a water procession.

39 เทริด, on a raised plinth with a peaked canopy.

40 เตียง, a flat seat with no arms or back, like a low table.

41 ศอก, *sok*, the length from elbow to finger-tips, 50–60 centimeters.

42 เจียม, a fabric, originally from northern China, made with matted animal hair, usually of a deer.

43 ขลิบ, *khlip*, which may be a mat or, more likely, a trimming on the cushion.

44 กวดรัด, unknown, both syllables may mean "tighten;" possibly a mat made with gold, silver, or other metals.

9 The cities eaten by royal sons are: Phitsanulok, Sawankhalok, Kamphaeng Phet, Lopburi, Singkhaburi. The cities eaten by royal grandsons are: Inthaburi, Phromburi.

10 Those of official rank[45] with 10,000 *sakdina* in the [capital] city travel on conveyances[46] with a *kanching* umbrella of white cloth. Those of official rank of 10,000 *sakdina* from the provincial cities travel on a palanquin with a seat and *kanching* umbrella of white cloth. Those of official rank with 5,000 *na* from the provincial cities travel in conveyances with coated-paper[47] umbrellas. Those of official rank with 3,000 *sakdina* travel in conveyances.

11 Officials of 10,000 *sakdina* who eat the four cities[48] have two peaked umbrellas;[49] a pair of glazed sunshades; a single *kanching* umbrella of red cloth; a cabin-boat with a three-level crab-home[50] roof, eaves,[51] and two slapping posts,[52] fore and aft; palanquin; golden chair;[53] golden *siraphet* hair-bun ornament;[54] three pairs of trumpet, flute, and drum.

Arrival at Audience

12 On arrival at a main customs post,[55] lower all insignia, leaving only the *kanching* umbrella of the palanquin. Lords of cities [come with] a golden *siraphet* hair-bun ornament, *kanching* umbrella of white cloth, betel container, water container, footed *talum* tray,[56] houseboat with a triple roof and eaves, golden palanquin, and golden chair. City governors of 10,000 *na* [come with] a golden *luam* helmet;[57] travel in a conveyance with a *kanching* umbrella of white cloth; have a houseboat with a triple roof and eaves; travel in conveyances[58] patterned completely

---

45 บันดาศักดิ์, *bandasak*, rank and title (Chaophraya, Phraya, Phra, Luang, Khun, Muen, Phan, Thanai) bestowed by the king.

46 Meaning a palanquin or carriage.

47 ทงยู, *thongyu*, paper oiled to be rain-resistant.

48 The four cardinal cities (N, S, W, E): by the late-sixteenth century, these were Phitsanulok, Nakhon Si Thammarat, Tanaosi, Nakhon Ratchasima.

49 ร่มปลิก, *rom plik*, with a raised peak, often made of gold.

50 แมงดาคฤ, *maengda kharu*, presumably shaped like the shell of a *maengda*, a name for several crab species, including the horseshoe crab.

51 บดลาด, *botlat*, "shade-slope," probably part of the roof.

52 สาวตดุก, *sao takhuk*, used to beat a rhythm for the rowers.

53 An article of insignia, introduced from China and hence with a Chinese-derived name, เก้าอี้, *kao-i*.

54 ศิรเพศมวยทอง, *siraphet muai thong*, hair wound in a bun with a gold ornament. Court fashion of the era was to wear the hair long, coiled on the top of head (Chin, "Khrueang pradap sian," 59–60).

55 There was a customs post on the four main water-borne approaches to Ayutthaya, each a few kilometers distant from the city; see Baker, "Final Part of the *Description of Ayutthaya*," 189.

56 ตลุ่ม, *talum*, a tray with an inward-sloping rim, and often a conical lid. In this case the tray is รอง, *rong*, with a pedestal.

57 หมวกล่วม, *muak luam*; *luam* is a soft bag for containing betel, medicine, etc.; perhaps a soft helmet.

58 Given in the original as ลาน, *lan*, unknown, assumed to be ยาน, *yan*, conveyance.

in gold; take betel from a silver casket with black cloisonné on a footed *talum* tray. [Governors of cities of 5,000 *na*[59]] have an ordinary houseboat with triple roof and no eaves, and a square golden *ka-ae* sunshade.[60] Governors of cities of 1,600 *na* [come with] a casket ornamented with glass pieces on a *talum* lidded[61] pedestal-tray, and a vermilion-painted *ka-ae* sunshade.

13 By royal command and decree. When military and civilian officers traveling by boat to audience arrive at the sala,[62] guard staff call on the boats coming down from the *ayaeng* fish traps[63] and *jaklan* fish traps,[64] boats with awnings,[65] and traders' boats not to approach that place. When those coming from the south arrive at the Lime Sala,[66] guard staff call on the boats coming down from the *ayaeng* fish traps and *jaklan* fish traps, boats with awnings, and traders' boats not to approach that place. This command prohibits boatmen on the left and right.

14 Those on land arriving at the twin-roof sala[67] and the Grass Landing Gate[68] alight from elephants or horses, and proceed with their conveyances, palanquins, coated-paper umbrellas, *kanching* umbrellas, and *ka-ae* sunshades from the front of the *wat* to the quarters of the king's-guard archers, up to the rooms of the troops. All those of royal lineage do not walk on the courtiers' way, but walk behind the *wat*, carrying salvers of cloth, betel caskets, salvers supporting caskets, or mother-of-pearl caskets according to their position in the royal lineage as royal sons or royal grandsons.

Guard Zones

15 Authority: from Ten Cowries Landing[69] to the White Elephant Gate,[70] from Ten Cowries Landing to the residence of the King's-guard archers, authority of Phitak Thiwa and Raksa Ratri;[71]

---

59 The flow of the clause suggests this has been omitted.

60 กแอ, *ka-ae*, a Chinese item.

61 กั้ง = กั้น, *kan*, "protect," perhaps meaning a lid.

62 Possibly the *sala trawen*, a guard post opposite the palace on the north bank by the entrance to Lotus Pond Canal.

63 แอย่ง, an Isan word for a type of fish trap.

64 จากลาน, a fish trap woven from bamboo.

65 ป(ระ)ทุน, *prathun*.

66 At the northwest corner of the city, on the north bank.

67 The main building for conducting official business, located in the "outer" section of the palace at the northeast corner.

68 ป(ระ)ตูท่าหญ้า, *pratu tha ya*, probably toward the western end of the north side of the palace. Wat Choeng Tha on the bank opposite was once called Wat Thin Tha, where *thin* means grass, because grass was cut in this area for feeding horses and elephants.

69 On the north of the city, to the east of the palace. A colloquial name coined because the fare each way was five cowries.

70 On the north wall of the palace toward its eastern end, used for taking the royal elephants to bathe in the river.

71 Both of these are *ratchaman* in the ministry of the palace, 200 *sakdina* (*KTSD* 1: 241). *Ratchaman* comes from Sanskrit, meaning a wrestler. Here they are guards keeping the peace but later their duty was enforcing punishments handed down by the courts.

from the White Elephant Gate to the jetty,[72] authority of the major guard;[73]

from the Water Olive Jetty,[74] authority of Muen Thepthawan;[75]

from the conduit[76] past the Gate of Dispelling Misfortune[77] to Chikhan Peak Market,[78] authority of Ja Pram;

from the Phra Wikanesuan[79] Gate to the *wat*, authority of the King's-guard archers;

from the head of the parade ground[80] to the Gate Showing Ram,[81] authority of Bamrue Phakdi;[82]

from the head of the parade ground to the polo[83] ground, authority of the horse officer of the left;[84]

from the polo ground to the casting foundry,[85] authority of the horse officer of the right.

16 Those of 10,000 *na*, 5,000 *na*, and 3,000 to 800 *na* are forbidden to go in procession or ride horses in the parade ground. The horse officer has the authority to prohibit this. If the horse officer does not prohibit it, he is liable to punishment of three types: first, issue only a written notice of the penalty;[86] second, send to Mahatthai to jail; third, send to the King's guard to jail. Any courtier who ignores, opposes, or disputes a horse officer's prohibition is liable to punishment of three

---

72 ขนาน(น้ำ), *khanan (nam)*, a river landing paved with planks.

73 A unit in Kalahom with left and right divisions under Phra Inthep and Luang Phirenthep, both *sakdina* 2,000 (*KTSD* 1: 286–88).

74 ม(ะ)กอกน้ำ, *makok nam*, *Elaeocarpus hygrophilus*. This seems to describe an area on the bank of the river near the northwest corner of the palace.

75 This title does not appear in *KTSD*, but the name indicates a guard of the palace gate. This line should have a "to" phrase that seems to have gone missing.

76 Possibly the inlet of the Pak Tho canal, outside the northwest corner of the palace.

77 ประตูเสดาะเคราะห์, *pratu sado khro*, unidentified.

78 ชีขันตลาดยอด, Peak Market was at the northwest corner of the island. Chikhan might mean "the laughing monk." According to Tri Amatayakul (*Official Guide to Ayutthaya*, 29), Chikhan was the old name for the swamp in the middle of the island, now known as Bueng Phra Ram.

79 ประตูพระวิฆเณศวร, *pratu phrawikanesuan*, a Thai version of the Hindu god Ganesh; unidentified. As this sequence appears to circulate the palace counterclockwise, this may be on the western side.

80 สนาม, *sanam*, here assumed to mean the large open space originally to the immediate east of the Grand Palace, enclosed within the palace during the Prasat Thong reign (1629–56).

81 ประตูแสดงราม, *pratu sadaeng ram*, unidentified. Possibly a palace gate leading out to Wat Phra Ram.

82 Luang Bamrue Phakdi, *sakdina* 1,000, in the ministry of the palace (*KTSD* 1: 237).

83 คลี, *khli*. Polo had spread from Persia to India, Tang China, and elsewhere in Asia, and was often associated with kings. Nothing is known about its arrival in Siam, or the details of the game.

84 Two officers of the major guard reporting to Phra Inthep (*KTSD* 1: 286).

85 โรงช้างหล้อ, *rong chang lo*, which might be ช้างล่อ, decoy elephants, but more likely ช่างหล่อ, casting craftsmen; see clause 22.

86 ภากธรรม (ภาคทัณฑ์), *phakthan*, the punishment is issued in writing, but not executed. Nowadays the term means probation.

grades: first, send to Mahatthai [to jail]; second, send to the King's guard [to jail]; third, tattoo and demote to cutting grass for elephants.[87]

17 From the Gate Showing Ram to Crystal Pond[88] is under the authority of Muen Thowarik.[89] If men or women talk together, sit in the quiet, cast a fishing net, lower a fishhook, set fish traps or nets,[90] sing, play a pipe or flute, bang a drum, recite, dance, yodel, or sing loudly, and if Muen Thowarik can make an arrest, punishment of three grades: first, send to Mahatthai [to jail]; second, send to the King's guard [to jail]; third, tattoo and demote to cutting grass for elephants.

From the right water conduit to the central residence, authority of the right;

from the left water conduit to the central residence, authority of the left.

Authority: from the drum tower[91] to Jao Sai[92] and Peak Market, district of Khun Thoraniban;[93]

from the drum tower to Victory Gate[94] and Jao Sai, district of Khun Tharaban;

from the drum tower to Coconut Quarter[95] [and] Chi Landing[96] to the end of Bang Ian,[97] district of Khun Lokaban;

from the drum tower to Bang Ian on to the palace residence, district of Khun Noraban.

18 Authority to prohibit: from the Palace-Rear Fort[98] to Cloister Gate at the Royal Landing,[99] responsibility of officers of the inner guard of the left and right, half each;

from Cloister Gate at the Royal Landing to Flagstaff Gate,[100] responsibility of the inner soldiers of the left and right, half each;

---

87 An elephant eats 150–170 kilograms (330–375 pounds) of vegetation per day. Several hundred elephants were stabled in Ayutthaya. Cutting grass for elephants was the lowest form of labor, performed by jail prisoners.

88 A pond in the area between Wat Phra Si Sanphet and the throne halls. Until the Prasat Thong reign, this area was not enclosed within the palace walls.

89 Equivalent to *thawarik*, gate-keeper.

90 Three types named: สุ่ม, *sum*, a bullet-shaped trap woven from bamboo; ช้อน, *chon*, a large round or triangular net with a handle; ชนาง, *chanang*, a large hand-held scoop made from woven bamboo, for catching shrimp.

91 A watch tower for spotting fires or enemies approaching, located on the northwest of the Four Ways (*talaengkeng*) crossroads, just south of the palace.

92 เจ้าไสร, unidentified, possibly a spirit shrine.

93 The four officers here are in the patrol department of the ministry of the city, *sakdina* 500 (*KTSD* 1: 231).

94 On the south side of the island, directly below the palace.

95 ป่าม(ะ)พร้าว, *pa maphrao*, in the northeast of the island.

96 ท่าชี, *tha chi*, probably meaning a landing for monks, of which there were several. This is likely in the northeast of the island, along with the other two places in this sentence.

97 บางเอียน, usually Ban Nang Ian, a settlement outside the wall on the eastern side, opposite the current site of the railway station.

98 At the northwest corner of the palace.

99 The Wasukri (Vasuki) royal boat landing on the north side of the Grand Palace, from where a screened cloister ran southward across the palace.

100 On the north side of the palace between the Wasukri landing and the northeast corner.

from Flagstaff Gate to Boundary Landing Fort,[101] from Boundary Landing Fort to the Registration Hall,[102] from the Registration Hall Fort to Fort Sala Phra Sumongkhon Bophit,[103] from Fort Phra Sumongkhon Bophit to the Fort at Wat Ramawat Corner,[104] from the Fort at Wat Ramawat Corner to Grape Garden Fort,[105] responsibility of palace wall guards[106] of the left and right, half each;

from the Grape Garden Fort to the Palace-Rear Fort, responsibility of palace-rear[107] staff of the left and right, half each.

19 Authority over military[108] courtiers. If *phrai* troops are arrogant, aggressive, and break the law, officers of Kalahom [are in charge] with:

for artillery, officer Intharat;[109]
for people, officer Phrommarat;
for boats, officer Thepharat;
for wood, officer Thipparat.

20 Authority over civilian courtiers. *Phrai* troops who commit offenses [concerning] elephants, horses, tusks, rope, boats within the scope of law, grass, and warfare, all these [fall to] the staff of Mahatthai:

sick elephants, elephant tusks, officer Phan Phanurat;[110]
horses, officer Phan Phao;
people, officer Phan Phut;
boats for leading the way, officer Phan Jan.

21 On the water conduit in Crystal Pond: anyone who travels by houseboat, awning boat, cabin boat, or a boat with weapons; or who lies down wearing a hat to cover the head; or men and women who sit together; or who argue, curse, hit one another, sing boat songs; play pipe, flute, fiddle, *jakae,*[111] or lute; or bang a drum, yodel, or sing loudly, [seems incomplete, missing specification of punishment]

---

101 The northeast corner of the palace.

102 ศาลาสารบาญชี, *sala sarabanchi,* near the southeast corner of the palace.

103 The image now in Wihan Phra Mongkhon Bophit was earlier sited slightly to the east of its current site. This fort is probably in the middle of the south wall of Wat Phra Si Sanphet.

104 The southwest corner of Wat Phra Si Sanphet. Either there was a wat of this name there, or Ramawat was the original name of the *wat* built by King Trailokanat and later called Wat Phra Si Sanphet (Royal Institute, *Phra thammanun,* 193).

105 In the middle of the western side of the palace.

106 ชาวกำแพงล้อมวัง, *chao kamphaeng lom wang.*

107 (ท้าย) สนม, *(thai) sanom,* was an area of the palace used for taking care of corpses, detaining royal offenders, and other unpleasant business. In late Ayutthaya, it was in the northwest corner.

108 This clause and the next use the twin terms *thahan* and *phonlaruen,* which later came to mean military and civilian. At this time they appear simply to have meant the officers under Kalahom and Mahatthai, respectively (see note above).

109 All four mentioned here are duty officers in Kalahom, Phan rank, 400 *sakdina* (*KTSD* 1: 279).

110 All four mentioned here are in Mahatthai, 400 *sakdina* (*KTSD* 1: 225).

111 จะเข้, a three-string zither-like instrument shaped like a crocodile, played flat on the ground.

22 If groups of Khaek, Khmer, Lao, Burmese, Meng-Mon,[112] Masumsaeng,[113] Chinese, Cham, Java, [people of] all the various countries, come to walk in the palace-rear, the palace-rear officers have the authority to prohibit them. If they do not prohibit them, or arrest and detain them, bring them to the sala, and hand them over to those supervising the landing, and if they allow those people of various countries to come and go in the palace-rear, punish the officers with death. Foreigners may come and go only to the casting foundry.[114] If they enter the parade ground, the sword officer has the authority to bring them to explain themselves. If the sword officer fails to do so, punish by sending to Mahatthai [to jail].

Royal Travel

23 When the King travels by boat, accompanied in the procession by sword officers, boat officers, gate boats,[115] flanking boats, and shield boats, whether [the King's boat is] stationary or in motion, if the boat of a villain such as a rebel, robber, drunkard, or madman presents the King with an article or a petition, approaching past the gate [boat] of Mahatthai, the gate [boat] of the sword officers, or the gate [boat] of the guard, up to the shield boats and flanking boats, wave cloth; if [the villain] pays no attention, hurl bricks, wood, and swords; if [the villain still] pays no attention, swim over and pull the boat away; if the King sees and summons [the villain] to approach, send a utility boat to receive [what is being presented]; if anyone approaches and is not barred, punish the sword officers, boat officers, and inner guard by chopping their necks and seizing their houses.

In the event of a great storm wind which the royal barge cannot withstand, take flanking boats[116] to assist; if the flanking boats cannot assist, take shield boats;[117] if the shield boats cannot assist, take gate boats to assist the royal barge.

24 If His Majesty the Royal Scion or a royal son approaches inside the gate boats for any purpose, have the [crew of the] gate boats wave cloth; if no attention is paid, have them hurl bricks, wood, and staves;[118] if no attention is paid, have them hurl pikes;[119] if the King sees and summons him to approach, send a gate boat to receive him, not allowing him to come in his own boat; on arrival, he must remain at the gunwales of the boat with a guard officer seated in between; if not done thus, condemned to death.

---

[112] Meng is another term for Mon.

[113] Perhaps an unidentified town on the peninsula, mentioned as มะแสง, *masaeng*, in the *Khamhaikan chao krung kao* (189) as a dependency of Nakhon Si Thammarat.

[114] โรงช้างฬอ, *rong chang lo*, which means the workshop for elephants and mules, but with minor changes of spelling becomes the workshop of the casting craftsmen. Judging from clause 15, this may be in the northeast area of the palace, which contained several workshops. This clause appears to date prior to the Prasat Thong reign when the eastern side of the palace was enclosed by walls.

[115] ป(ร)ะตู, *p(r)atu*, a type of guard boat in royal water processions.

[116] เรือกัน เรือแนม, *ruea kan ruea naem*, two types of boat placed on the flanks of a royal water procession.

[117] เรือดั้ง, *ruea dang*, another procession boat, usually placed at the head and rear.

[118] ไท้หัวด้าย, *mai hua tai*, either a bamboo pole used to anchor a boat, or a length of wood intended as a weapon.

[119] หอก, *hok*, a stabbing weapon with a straight metal blade like a twin-edged knife on a long, usually wooden handle.

25 If the [Primary Queen's][120] royal barge is halted before reaching its destination, all the *hua muen* and *hua phan* of the retainers,[121] heads of the selected men,[122] and palace staff on board are condemned to death. When the royal barge reaches its destination and is already secured, [all the above] go down into the water and swim to land. Anyone who remains in the boat is condemned to chopping the neck.

If the [Primary Queen's] royal barge sinks, the boat staff swims away; anyone who stays with the boat is condemned to death. If the royal barge sinks or capsizes, and [the Queen] is swimming and near death, the retainers and boat staff extend battering rams[123] and throw coconuts for her to cling to, if possible; but if not possible, do not take hold of her; if they take hold and bring her up to survive, they are condemned to death; if they throw coconuts that enable her to survive, reward of ten tamlueng of silver and one golden bowl; if the royal barge sinks and other people see, throw coconuts, and bring her up to survive, they are condemned to severe punishment of death for their whole clan.

If the royal barge sinks, anyone who throws coconuts and approaches at the edge of the bank is condemned to chopping the neck and seizing the house.

For cutting across the front of the royal barge, condemned to death. For crossing close to the royal barge, condemned to death.

26 When the [Primary Queen] travels by boat, should the boats of any courtiers go by a circuitous route and not arrive in time with the royal barge, they are condemned to chopping the neck and seizing the house.

Should any lords, major officials, courtiers, *hua muen,* or *hua phan* pass the royal barge or cut across the front of the royal barge, they are condemned to chopping the neck and seizing the house.

Should any persons approach while cursing or hitting one another and cut in front of *nang thephi,*[124] they are condemned to the same penalty as for passing a royal barge.

Should any person cut across behind the officers of Mahatthai at the outside, in front of the sword officers in the center, or in front of the boat officers on the inside, he is condemned according to the severity of the offense to chopping the neck, seizing the house, tattooing as a grass-cutter,[125] or a suspended sentence.[126]

27 If the King proceeds to the jetty in front of the palace, the inner guard goes down there. If the King proceeds to the Crystal Pond, Haruethai[127] and

[120] In this era, the *ruea prathiap* mentioned in this clause was the boat of the Primary Queen (later the word was expanded to cover boats of other senior female royalty).

[121] ภูดาษ, *phudat*, given in Pallegoix's dictionary as a secretary, especially in the courts. In the context of this clause, this meaning seems unlikely, so "retainer" has been used.

[122] ชาวเลือก, *chao lueak*, a unit of skilled boxers and swordsmen whose members acted as bodyguards for the king and other royalty, especially when in procession.

[123] เสร้า, *sao*, a pole for ramming enemy craft.

[124] นางเทพี, divine lady, probably referring to the Primary Queen.

[125] ลงหญ้าศัก, *long ya sak*, demoted to *phrai* status and put to work cutting grass for elephants.

[126] ถ้าดาบ, *tha dap*, "awaiting the sword."

[127] Luang Haruethai, department head of *phonphun*, right division, in Kalahom, *sakdina* 1,000 (*KTSD* 1: 293).

Ratchaphakdi[128] go down there. If the King proceeds to the area of the water olive[129] and beyond, palace-rear officers, Kanyubat,[130] Ratchasawek,[131] pages, and Indian eunuchs[132] go down there.

If the King travels by barge and [ladies from] the inner palace embark also, only Indian eunuchs, Chinese eunuchs,[133] and boat officers[134] embark.

28 If the King goes to a feasting in the Victory Ground,[135] Moon Ground,[136] or Palace of the Night,[137] rear-palace officers, Haruethai, Ratchaphakdi, Kanyubat, and Ratchasawek attend on him.

If those of 10,000 or 5,000 *sakdina* and courtiers are allowed to pay homage in the Victory Ground, Moon Ground, or Palace of the Night, Haruethai, Ratchaphakdi, Kanyubat, and Ratchasawek announce the name, rank, and position[138] of those paying homage.

If the King travels by royal barge and has any courtiers pay homage, the presiding officer and saber master of the palace-rear announce the name, rank, and position.

29 If the palace staff, rear-palace staff, and inner guard who announce the name, rank, and position do not do so, they are condemned to splitting the mouth; if the event is a royal ceremony or reception of an official guest, death for the whole clan.

If those who announce the name, rank, and position, that is the palace staff, rear-palace staff, and inner guard, do not observe the time and place, and announce all together, they are condemned to cutting the mouth.

30 Order for the inner guard. If the King ascends a hill and enters a cave, goes up to a *prang,*[139] or enters a holy preaching hall, have sword officers enter and search first, then inner guards enter and search, then saber masters search, then Kanyubat searches; and after four searches, invite the King to proceed. When the King proceeds, inner guards stand on both sides, saber masters follow, and the guard officers and sword officers stay at the rear. When the King passes inside, the inner guards stay at the door on the inside, the saber masters stay at the door on the

---

128 Phra Ratchaphakdi was head of the royal warehouse (*KTSD* 1: 267), but much more likely this is a guard, probably the officer of the left division equivalent to Luang Haruethai, who is called Luang Aphaisurin in the Civil List (*KTSD* 1: 293).

129 See note on clause 15.

130 Department head in the king's guard (*raksa phra-ong*), right division, in Kalahom, Luang rank, *sakdina* 600 (*KTSD* 1: 294).

131 Department head in the king's guard (*raksa phra-ong*), left division, in Kalahom, Luang rank, *sakdina* 600 (*KTSD* 1: 295).

132 นักเทษ, *nakthet*, eunuchs from the west, from Arabia, Persia, or India.

133 ขันที, *khanthi*.

134 Here and only here the word translated as officer is ทนาย, *thanai*.

135 Probably meaning the parade ground on the eastern side of the palace.

136 สนามจัน(ทร์), *sanam jan*, an area of garden to the southwest of the audience halls.

137 พิมานรัทยา, *phimanrathaya*, unidentified. Name of a building in the Bangkok Grand Palace built by King Rama I in 1789.

138 ขานขันหมาก, *khan khan mak*, literally, to "call out the betel tray," where betel trays were insignia of rank bestowed by the king.

139 ปราง(ค์), a corncob-shaped tower on a *wat* or palace.

outside, and the sword officers stay at the foot of the stairway. If there is a villain such as a rebel or someone in disguise, or a dog, tiger, bear, cow, buffalo, or poisonous snake, the sword officers, inner guards, and saber masters are condemned to death. If the King travels by royal conveyance accompanied by [ladies from] the inner palace, inner guards do not accompany in great numbers, only the palace-rear guard, Haruethai, Ratchaphakdi, and King's guards[140] come behind.

Horses

31 When the King is traveling by horse, if an elephant officer or elephant staff rides an elephant behind, put the elephant officer's neck in a cangue;[141] for a first offense, an elephant officer may prostrate to beg for royal grace stating that the elephant was out of his control. If the King does not listen[142] and orders an elephant to come behind, ride very slowly so as not to pass the royal mount. If this command is not followed and the royal mount is in danger, have those riding the elephants executed, the whole clan.

When the King travels by horse, elephant officers and elephant staff riding elephants behind the royal mount should stay not too close and not too far away.

32 Order concerning horses. When the King travels by horse, horse officers ride on both sides at the middle, guard officers on both sides at the bit, saber officers on both sides at the tail. When the King travels by horse at night, horse officers and horse masters lead [the horse] by the reins with candles and torches; feed the horse with limes cut open;[143] tighten the halter, holster,[144] and rein; keep the polo mallet in reserve while the King is riding; and have two post horses on hand to fetch replacements quickly in case of damage [to the equipment].

33 When the King is riding a polo horse and summons a *khun muen, hua phan,* or horse master to lead the royal mount by the reins and toss the polo ball, toss lower than the horse's belly, passing behind the tail, not in front of the horse. The horses of the horse officers stay from the head rein to the rear of the royal mount. Anyone who does not follow this order but transgresses is condemned to a suspended sentence, demotion to cutting grass, or execution.

34 All *khun* and *muen* courtiers from 3,000 to 1,600 *sakdina* when riding horses, if their horse tack contravenes regulations, namely saddles and other tack with golden flowers, tooling, and silk, authority of the horse officers [to impose punishment].

---

140 รักษาองค, *raksa(phra)ong,* a unit of the guard in Kalahom, including Luang Kanyubat (*KTSD* 1: 294–95).

141 "Moreover, they put on a cangue sometimes consisting of two long pieces of wood arranged around the neck by means of two crossbars. The cangue is more or less heavy according to the seriousness of the crime. Besides the problem of its weight, it also hinders all movement and especially prevents resting" (Pallegoix, *Description,* 192–93).

142 "Does not listen" means "does not follow this rule."

143 To keep the horse awake, a practice described in *Tamra chang,* elephant manuals.

144 แส้กันชีพ, *sae kan chip,* a holder for a pike or other weapon on the horse's flank.

35 The horse division of the right[145] has authority from the head of the parade ground to the flagstaff, and the horse division of the left[146] from the flagstaff to the end of the parade ground. If lords, major officials, provincial governors, or courtiers of provincial cities ride elephants and horses provocatively close to the front of the horse stables without dismounting, the horse staff are to stop them, and if the riders pay no attention, fine at quadruple rate or double rate.[147]

36 For wives of the four pillars down to wives of those of 1,000 *sakdina*, opening *kanching* umbrellas in front of the horse stables is an offense.

Elephants

37 If the King travels on a royal elephant, horse officers and horse masters[148] who lead or ride horses following the royal mount must not be too distant or too close, but just as should be.

Law on elephants. Elephant officers and elephant masters,[149] rope-head masters,[150] great elephants, medium elephants, howdahs, and mahouts are matters for the department of the special eight elephants.[151] War elephants [have the duty to] attack, and protect camps. The King captures elephants, registered[152] and unregistered.

38 When the King graces to travel by male elephant, war elephant, or medium elephant, follow the regulations by having a goad, fork-trident,[153] stirrups, circling harness, rear harness, and noose.[154] If the King graces to travel by elephant, and an elephant in musth is harnessed as the royal mount, the elephant officers and elephant staff must prostrate to beg for their lives, and not invite the King to mount.

---

145 Headed by Luang Songphon, *sakdina* 2,400 (*KTSD* 1: 256).

146 Headed by Luang Prapphon, *sakdina* 2,400 (*KTSD* 1: 256).

147 In the code called Phrommasak, fines and compensation are graduated according to the *sakdina* of the offender; individual laws then prescribe penalties as multiples of these amounts.

148 ชาวม้าขุนม้าหมื่นม้านายม้า, *chao ma khun ma muen ma nai ma*, i.e., officers of various ranks in charge of horses.

149 หลวงช้าง หมื่นช้าง ปลัดช้าง นายช้าง ท้ายช้าง, *luang chang, muen chang, palat chang, nai chang, thai chang*, i.e., officers of various ranks in charge of elephants.

150 นายต้นเชือก, *nai ton chueak*, "master at the front of the rope," an officer who rides the elephant at the head of a procession.

151 อัษฐคช, *attakhot*, a Pali-derived term for "eight elephants," meaning eight classes of elephant deemed special because of size, color, tusk shape, and other features. Manuals of elephantology described the various lineages of elephants both in the celestial and terrestrial realms. Vishnu (Narai) arranged that a lotus flower be born from a womb with eight petals and 133 pistils, and presented it to Siva (Issuan), who shared it out among Vishnu (Wisanu), Siva, Brahma (Phrom), and Agni (Akhani; the god of fire). The gods then arranged that the petals and pistils be born as elephants in the terrestrial world. From these origins arose the four main lineages of elephants associated with these four deities. Each of these lineages is then subdivided into several sub-lineages, usually eight, for the eight directions, each with distinctive characteristics. See *Tamra chang*, 49–63.

152 Trained royal elephants were registered and given a title and rank.

153 A two-tined weapon.

154 ตระคน, *trakhon*, a strap circling the animal's girth; ซองหาง, *songhang*, a strap that goes around the animal's rear; บาศเชือก, *bat chueak*, a noose for lassoing.

If the King graces to have an elephant lock tusks with the royal mount, and that elephant gains the advantage, putting the royal mount at a disadvantage, [the rider of the opposing elephant] must beg for his life. If the King engages in an elephant duel, the rider of the opposing elephant must restrain his mount and bring him to halt; if he fails, he must [prostrate to] petition [for his life] three times.

If the royal mount encounters a wild elephant, and the wild elephant gains the advantage, putting the royal mount at a disadvantage, the mahout must halt and not use the goad.

If the wild elephant has the advantage, and the King asks for the noose to lasso it, do not give it.

39 Punishment for mahouts in four grades as follows. First, bring the elephant officers and elephant staff to explain to the guard officer, who will take them to prostrate and beg forgiveness. If the King does not grace to listen, send a warrant to inform the overseer and elephant staff to petition the King for their lives. If the King leaves without listening, have them lie down between the tusks for an elephant to impale them, as approved by law. If the elephant officers and elephant staff do not follow the law as stated and the royal mount is in danger, execute the elephant staff, the whole clan.

40 When the King travels to lasso elephants, the middle rider who presents the noose must pay attention to the circumstances. If the wild elephant is below eye-level and the King calls for the noose, give it. If the royal mount is above eye-level and the King calls for the noose, do not give it. If the King slashes [the noose-giver] down on the neck of the elephant [in anger], beg to receive a royal penalty. If not done according to the law, penalty of death.

41 When the royal mount approaches a wild herd in open space and confronts a large wild elephant, if the support elephants and camp elephants equipped with lance and pike on both sides do not approach to help in time, [their riders are] condemned to death.

If the King traveling on a royal mount approaches a herd in open space and the flank elephants, shield elephants, and camp elephants draw close according to procedure, and the King's guards bring the pike elephants and lance elephants who guard the King to intercept and shield according to procedure, yet a wild elephant approaches almost to the royal mount and constitutes a threat, the riders of all those elephants are condemned to death, and the King's guards, *hua muen, hua phan, hua rong*, retainers, and *hua pak*[155] are condemned to be placed in chains for three years; and if the royal mount is thrown into confusion, execute their whole clan.

42 When the King travels to the elephant palace,[156] construct barriers and a disguised camp,[157] place elephants inside the enclosure, and issue an order banning flute, pipe, drum, gong, argument and disagreement, cursing and fighting among the servants and men, singing and shouting, [with punishment] for both officers and

---

155 หัวปาก, where *pak* is an old word for hundred from Chinese, so an officer of lower grade than *hua phan*.

156 Meaning the elephant enclosure that was earlier in the northeast of the island (Hua Ro), and later moved to the current site off the island up the Lopburi River.

157 ค่ายพราง, *khai phrang*, perhaps like a blind for watching the elephants unseen.

men of puncturing the mouth, strapping a pike handle to the legs and parading around the camp. If the camp has been made secure yet an elephant gets out, have the guards impaled; if it is an important elephant, execute the whole clan.

When the King goes to hunt elephants at the elephant enclosure, if Mahatthai and palace staff are missing, they are condemned to the same penalty as deserters from battle.

43 A spirit[158] or forest-walking hunter, who finds an important elephant and gives information to a herd officer, reported to the King, receives a royal gift of a gold bowl weighing ten tamlueng.[159] If he finds a place where the animal wallows, reported to the King, he receives a royal gift of a gold bowl weighing one tamlueng, two baht, a ring with one circle of jewels, and a shirt or cloth.

Send a royal servant. If the royal servant returns to report to the King confirming [the find], [he receives] a royal gift of a silver bowl and a shirt or cloth. When the animal is brought in, the spirit receives a reward of good silver or gold; and the herd officer who knew also and conveyed the information to the King receives a royal gift of good gold, good silver, and a royally-gifted wife.

If the reward is given but the animal cannot be found, the hunter and herd officer are condemned to wear a *klang*[160] and walk searching in the forest for three years. If [the animal is] found, bring to perform a ceremony for seven days, and make a noose from thread for the king to lasso.

When [the elephant is] captured, set up eight screens,[161] eight dance halls, and eight feasting halls for seven days; have entertainments for fifteen days; then embark [the elephant] on a raft and play screens and dances all the way to the capital; on arrival at the capital, have entertainments and feasting for fifteen days.

Warfare

44 Law on royal warfare. When the army goes to war or an enemy approaches the city, lords, provincial governors, major officials, military commanders, chiefs of armies, and regiments assemble elephants, horses, troops, *dang* shields, swords, bucklers, *lo* shields, throwing lances, trigger guns,[162] bows, pikes, and lances, and proceed to the [battle]field. Unit commanders who fight and triumph over the enemy, attested in reports by the army inspectors,[163] receive rewards of a gold casket, *sanop* shirt,[164] promotion, and a stipend for their children and grandchildren.

Anyone who evilly retreats by only one step is condemned to cutting off the head and feet, being paraded around the army, and receiving no support for their children and grandchildren in the future.

---

[158] โขมด, *khamot,* a Khmer-derived word for a spirit like a will-o-the-wisp, perhaps used here metaphorically for a stealthy hunter.

[159] A ตำลึง is sixty grams (about two ounces), equivalent to four baht.

[160] กลัง, a shaming device, made from lengths of bamboo strung around the neck.

[161] Probably for a shadow play or shadow puppets.

[162] ปืนไฟน่า, *buen fai na,* meaning a handheld matchlock rather than a field gun; first mentioned in the chronicles in 1568–69 (Cushman, *Royal Chronicles*, 66).

[163] ยุกระบัด, usually ยกกระบัตร, *yokkrabat*, here an inspector, later the name for a quartermaster and for a royal envoy sent to provincial centers.

[164] สนอบ, royally presented cloth worn only to ceremonies attended by the king or when welcoming state guests.

45 Anyone who succeeds in an elephant duel is rewarded with a golden helmet, *sanop* shirt with gold cuffs, and promotion up to 10,000 *sakdina*; if already 10,000 *sakdina*, a golden umbrella, and golden palanquin.

Anyone who succeeds in an elephant duel in which the enemy loses his head [while] on the elephant is rewarded with a golden tray, golden helmet, golden umbrella, golden palanquin, and a royally-presented wife. If an [enemy] lord is captured, the reward is equal.

Pike troops, sword troops, shield troops, and foot troops who help an elephant and duelist to win victory are rewarded with promotion to Khun rank, good silver and gold, and support for their children and grandchildren in the future. The staff of the elephant duelist receive the same reward.

46 Anyone who rides a horse to battle and takes a head[165] is rewarded with a golden bowl, cloth, and promotion.

A foot soldier who takes a head is rewarded with a golden bowl and clothing.

A foot soldier who takes a horse is rewarded with a silver bowl and clothing.

A *phrai* soldier or King's guard up to 400 *sakdina* who takes a lord is rewarded with good gold, good silver, appointment to eat a city, and a royally-presented wife. If he takes an elephant, he is rewarded with one *chang*[166] of silver, a golden caselet,[167] and clothing.

If a *phrai* soldier, selected man, or secondary man[168] sneaks up to attack an army, slashing and thrusting, and the enemy breaks and flees from the army, he is given one *chang* of silver, a golden caselet, clothing, and promotion to Khun rank.

Anyone who slashes back at the enemy and triumphs is given five tamlueng of silver, a golden caselet, and clothing.

Anyone who fights with two persons and survives to return is rewarded with a golden bowl and clothing.

Anyone who fights with two persons, survives to return, and brings back the enemy's weapons as well, is rewarded with a golden bowl, clothing, and promotion to Khun rank.

47 If the enemy is able to reach the royal pavilion,[169] the sword officers, boat officers, elephant officers, and guard officers surrounding the pavilion have the head and feet cut off, are impaled, and paraded.

If the enemy is able to approach and burn the royal pavilion, impalement.

48 If the army has drawn up in battle formation and engaged to fight an enemy, [anyone who] evilly withdraws by three elephant lengths is executed.

Anyone in an elephant duel who uses the goad to make the elephant retreat, slash him down on the elephant's back, cut off his head, have him paraded, and give no support for his children and grandchildren in the future.

---

165 ได้หัว, *dai hua*.

166 ชั่ง, usually 1,200 grams (under three pounds).

167 ตะหลับ, usually ตลับ, *talap*, a small container, either square or round.

168 ชาวเลือกชาวรอง, *chao lueak chao rong*, probably meaning senior and junior officers; see note on clause 25.

169 พระพลา, *phraphla*, usually พลับพลา, *phlap-phla*, a temporary structure for royalty, here used for viewing the battle.

Anyone fighting on a boat who evilly retreats by one boat length is condemned to be placed in chains; if two boat lengths, [property] confiscated and demoted to cutting grass for elephants; if three boat lengths, execution.

49 Those wielding authority should be attentive to making the royal territory of His Majesty the King prosper so his repute spreads everywhere in every direction. They should conduct themselves by thinking and listening to things of utility in ancient royal legislation, without fail.

Discipline at Royal Audience

50 When His Majesty the King proceeds to an audience hall or any royal building but has not yet arrived, others of royal lineage, *luang mueang, khun, muen, hua phan,* saber masters, and various officials attending on the royal foot may not exit beforehand. When the King has entered, then all may exit following [the King].

51 When attending in the sacred hall, wear upper and lower cloths of white, not black, red, or green.

52 If His Majesty the King has entered an audience hall or any royal building and has not yet departed, and all the lords and high officials have gathered, they must not converse together and make noise in the royal building. If there is anything that should be addressed to the King for discussion, pay homage and beg for his grace. Matters other than these must not be discussed.

53 If anyone of official rank with 10,000, 5,000, or 3,000 *sakdina* speaks aloud in a royal building, on the first occasion, let that person know of the penalty; on the second occasion, issue a written notice of the penalty;[170] on the third occasion, ban that person from attending on the King's royal foot.

54 If anyone of official rank with 2,400, 2,000, 1,600, or 1,200 *sakdina* speaks [in a royal building], on the first occasion, let that person know of the penalty; on the second occasion, have him dragged by hand out of the audience hall and banned from attending on the King's royal foot; on the third occasion, have him dragged by hand out of the audience hall and fined single-rate according to official rank.

55 If anyone of official rank with 1,000, 800, 600, or 400 *sakdina* speaks [in a royal building], on the first occasion, let that person know of the penalty; on the second occasion, have him dragged by hand out of the audience hall, given thirty strokes, fined double-rate according to official rank, and banned from attending on the King's royal foot.

56 If anyone of official rank with 300 or 200 *sakdina* speaks [in a royal building], on the first occasion, give ten strokes; on the second occasion, give ten strokes of the leather lash; on the third occasion, give twenty strokes of the leather lash.

If anyone of official rank with 200 *sakdina* down to *phrai* speaks [in a royal building], on the first occasion, give fifteen strokes of the leather lash; on the second occasion, give twenty strokes of the leather lash; on the third occasion, give twenty-

[170] See clause 16.

five strokes of the leather lash, pierce the mouth, and issue a written notice of the penalty to whoever is the overseer.

57 Any persons who talk or whisper together when attending on the royal foot are condemned to death.

Theft, Disorder, and Misdemeanors

58 Anyone who has the audacity to steal goods prepared by someone to present to the King, or cause them to be damaged or lost in an argument or brawl, and who ignores orders to desist, is condemned to punishment of three grades: first, cut half the fingers of the hand; second, twenty-five strokes of the leather lash; third, fine at double rate.

59 If property of the King goes missing or is damaged in some fashion, those on regular duty in the royal palace must reimburse the cost of the royal property according to its value, large or small; the head of the duty roster pays three parts, his deputy next down pays two parts, and the duty officer one part.

60 When His Majesty the King travels to distribute goods and articles according to the royal pleasure, should anyone steal those things for himself, do not allow this, drag him out by the wrist. If it is one flower or one other item, fine at double rate; if two flowers or two items or more, fine at quadruple rate. The persons distributing those royal gifts must distribute in order [of rank], or else be punished according to the scale of the offense.

61 Among those distributing auspicious gifts of flowers, betel, and water, if anyone picks up a flower and offers to a royal son, punish by cutting off the hand. Anyone distributing water who offers the water before the leather rope[171] is condemned to cutting off the hand.

62 Anyone arguing in the palace violates royal authority and is condemned to fifty strokes of the rattan cane. If any persons curse one another, give a hundred strokes of the rattan cane, then question on the subject of the argument, and fine according to the regulations of the royal city.

63 If any persons of 10,000 to 800 *sakdina* quarrel and come to blows in the royal palace or official sala, give punishment of four grades: one, fine at triple rate; two, fine at double rate; three, fine at single rate; four, issue written notice of penalty.

64 If anyone from *hua phan* up to *hua muen* or *thanai* with official rank and 600 down to 200 *sakdina* comes to blows and creates disorder or damage in the royal palace or official sala, give punishment of eight grades: one, twenty strokes of the leather lash; two, imprisonment for one month; three, expulsion from royal service; four, fine at quadruple rate; five, fine at triple rate; six, fine at double rate; seven, fine at single rate; eight, issue written notice of penalty.

---

171 Possibly this means the recipient must grasp the end of a short piece of rope to ensure both his hands are occupied.

65 Anyone who argues and quarrels in the royal palace, imprison in the cangue for three days. If anyone curses in the royal palace, give fifty strokes of the rattan cane. If anyone comes to blows, peel the fingernails on five fingers of the hand delivering the blow. If anyone grasps a knife, machete, or weapon to cause injury by slashing or stabbing, peel all ten fingernails, then make him state the subject of the dispute, and fine according to the practice of the royal city.

66 Anyone who argues in front of the official sala, place in a cangue in front of the official sala for one day. If anyone curses a courtier, give punishment equivalent to opposing a royal command. If anyone curses and comes to blows within the pillars,[172] and ignores calls to desist, give the same punishment as cursing and coming to blows in that building.

67 If anyone beats or curses a principal elephant or principal horse, cut the hand or mouth.

68 If anyone hits the keeper of an outer gate, give twenty strokes of the leather lash. If anyone hits the keeper of an inner gate, seize and distribute all property, and demote to cutting grass for elephants.

If anyone kicks a palace gate, cut off the foot. If anyone uses a hand to push the palace gate to gain entry, give twenty strokes of the rattan cane. If anyone climbs the palace outer wall, cut off the feet. If anyone climbs the palace inner wall, execution. If anyone carries weapons into the royal palace, the gatekeeper must question to see whether [the purpose] is good or bad; and if [the weapon] is not brought for work, cut off the hand of the person bringing it. If the gatekeeper allows entry without questioning, same penalty for the gatekeeper.

69 If a rebel comes from another city in disguise, or an enemy, dog, horse, cow, or buffalo enters the royal palace, either up to the front of the throne hall or into an audience hall, the palace staff are condemned to death; as for the gatekeeper, put out his eyes.

70 If persons gather to drink liquor in the royal palace, heat liquor until hot and pour into their mouths, then imprison them.

71 Anyone who flies a kite over the royal palace, or throws sticks, clods of earth, bricks, or stones across the palace, is condemned to cutting off the hand; anyone throwing [as above] at an audience hall is condemned to death.

72 Anyone without official rank who sleeps in the royal palace or comes in to sleep, beat the sleeper or anyone who asks to sleep, ten strokes each.

73 If anyone offends against the law, and all those that have the authority under that law do not upbraid him according to the legitimate law, impose punishment on the offender at whatever level, and impose penalty on those with authority who did not upbraid him.

---

172 ประโคน, *prakhon*, large pillars defining a (sacred) space; here probably meaning those around an audience hall.

74 Anyone who makes a key, or reads a mantra or loosening spell to magically open[173] a palace gate, or opens a *khlon* gate[174] to enter into the palace precincts, in order to abduct a female servant or palace maid, or to steal royal property, is condemned to severe punishment and then execution. If the King graciously waives execution, impose punishment of five grades according to royal instruction.

75 Anyone who steals silver, gold, cloth, silk, persons, or royal property and takes these out through a gate, execute both the thief and the gatekeeper.

76 Anyone who has the audacity to dig up and steal the torch posts[175] in the capital, for each ten posts take three posts and fine at 110,000 [? cowries] per post; if in a provincial city, for each ten posts take three posts and fine at 55,000 each.

Anyone who has the audacity to dig up a building for a royal ceremony, or to dig and destroy the city dyke, the city posts,[176] drum tower, or city walls, damaging the aura and security of the city[177] with very malicious intent, the King orders that the villain is either executed, has his hands cut off, or is given 160 strokes of the leather lash, according to the severity of the offense.

Dress

77 A sword officer, boat officer, *hua muen* of the king's guard, *hua muen* of boats, *hua phan*, or saber master who comes through a royal gate or sits in the official sala carrying a royal sword [or casket], yet has not been presented with a sword and casket, the gatekeeper or sala master must take the casket and beat it, and take the sword to present to the King to make another sword. Give the casket to the gatekeeper as reward, and demote the offender to be *phrai* because he should not have carried a royal sword.

If a gatekeeper fails to act according to the law, punish by demoting to cutting grass for elephants.

78 Anyone who tucks a flower behind the ear, wears a red lowercloth, *pairam*[178] pink lowercloth, *karakam*[179] with no border, outer upper cloth covering one shoulder, lower cloth made tight in front and carrying the tail or floating the tail, and enters into the cloister, cloister *taphan*[180] gate, cloister inside the chicken fence,[181] in the

---

173 เสดาะ, *sado*, meaning to loosen or release, name of several spells and techniques in *sayasat* supernaturalism for removing obstructions.

174 โขลนทวาร, *khlon thawan*, a rustic gate constructed for several ceremonies, including welcoming a white elephant and sending troops off to war; here probably meaning using some kind of magic to gain entry.

175 Posts for placing torches for lighting.

176 เสาค่าย, *sao khai*, "camp posts," posts planted around a village or city as part of its protective magic.

177 "Aura and security" refers to the protective magic.

178 ไพร่ำ, from a Tamil word for a jewel, here perhaps used to qualify the pink color.

179 การะกำ, unknown. The word also appears in the *Ramakian* to describe the dress of troops, and may mean dark red.

180 ตะพาน, bridge or jetty, perhaps here meaning the gate to the royal Wasukri landing.

181 รั้วไก่, a fence made of checkered panels to enclose an area for royal ceremonies.

kalabat,[182] in front of an audience hall, the navy gate,[183] or a royal lodge, rip the cloth, smother the flower in dust, and tie [cloth] around the head [of the offender], according to the severity of the offense.[184]

Improper Assignations

79 Any persons from 10,000 down to 1,600 *sakdina* who seek one another out at their houses or at any quiet place, or furtively talk together, or talk in whispers together one-on-one while sitting in the official sala, punish by chopping the neck and seizing the house.[185]

80 Any courtiers who gather together to drink liquor, gamble, or have a cockfight and are seen by others, impose a suspended sentence.

81 If a rear-palace officer goes to meet a courtier or soldier, he is condemned to death.

82 A city governor who goes to meet another city governor in a city is condemned to death.

83 A courtier from 10,000 to 800 *sakdina* who goes to meet a royal son or royal grandson is condemned to death.

The King does not wish for any *khun, muen,* or *hua phan* to favor[186] a royal son, royal grandson, or royal daughter by choosing a good elephant or good horse for them. If there is a royal order for the royal son or grandson to address and inform the King, then royal punishment will be avoided.

84 Anyone who goes to meet and converse with an envoy or royal ambassador is condemned to death.

Oath of Allegiance and Proper Conduct of Officials

85 Anyone from 10,000 down to 600 *sakdina* who sees something wrong, such as people meeting against regulations, misappropriating or stealing royal property, or associating with a woman, anything that errs against the oath of loyalty, or who knows about the matter in some way [because] someone gives information, but has

---

[182] กะลาบาต, *kalabat,* a division of the guard that stands watch by the lamps, with a duty to stand posted along the routes of royal processions. Perhaps here meaning a guardpost.

[183] ประตูทับเรือ, *pratu thap ruea,* unidentified.

[184] While the dress restrictions in other clauses are related to status, these seem targeted against young men hoping to seduce palace women. In late Ayutthaya, the phrase "Din Gate lovers" referred to men who loitered around the gate leading out from the palace to a daily market (see Baker and Pasuk, *Khun Chang Khun Phaen,* 417–18). See also clauses 88 and 142.

[185] In the Thirty-six Laws, there is a law dated 1733 that has similar content expressed in different language. It forbids any unrelated persons, from Chaophraya down to Khun Muen, from meeting in any house or building, and urges a servant accompanying such persons to inform Mahatthai (clause 32, *KTSD* 4: 252). See also notes on clause 105. These laws may date to the era of intense conflict within the royal clan in the early eighteenth century. See Saichol, *Phutthasasana,* 35.

[186] ให้เผื่อใจ, *hai phuea jai,* "give heart to."

not yet informed anyone of royal lineage, or addressed the matter to the King, by law he must inform an inner guard, or else a palace guard, or else a royal page to convey the matter to the royal grace. If the matter has not been conveyed in any way, make a petition to present [the matter] to the King by oneself. Anyone who fails to act thus according to law is held to be in revolt and is condemned to punishment according to the severity of the offense: if severe, execute; if light, place in chains. Impose the same punishment on anyone who fails to bring a matter to address to the King.

86 Any courtier who fails to drink the water of allegiance is condemned to death. If the courtier feigns sickness [as an excuse], drinks the water of allegiance without wearing a *nak* ring or gold ring, or eats rice, fish, *namya* sauce, or sweet rice-water[187] beforehand, or drinks one cup of the water of allegiance and offers [the rest] for others to drink, or who, after drinking, fails to pour the remains on his hair for washing, is condemned to punishment equivalent to that for revolt.

87 Anyone who accepts the receptacle but does not drink it; who does not place an auspicious flower on his head, [but] takes and places it on a betel tray or casket, or drops it in the middle of the audience hall or on the ground; who meets the King's eye; who talks in whispers with others, or walks out and gathers others to talk around the door, is condemned to punishment equivalent to revolt.

88 Any courtier who enters the royal palace daubed with *khrat*[188] or *krajae*[189] oil, sucking *miang*,[190] or wearing a flower behind the ear is in contravention of regulations.

If anyone wears a lower cloth embroidered or patterned with a border on the loose end, have the gatekeeper or hall master rip it apart.[191]

89 If anyone fails to attend in the sacred hall, or fails to attend in front of the royal window, fine in sugarcane according to official rank and give the fine to the elephant staff; if anyone is absent when the King appears, impose the same punishment.

90 When the King travels away from the capital, if anyone on caretaking duty is absent, first time, fine at double rate; second time, fine at triple rate; third, fourth, and above times, fine at quadruple rate.

Anyone on duty after the gates are closed who climbs the wall to go out, punish by cutting off the hand or foot.

91 If a royal palanquin has a collision, or the curtain string breaks, or the curtain cannot be drawn, or the curtain slips or gets tangled, those drawing the curtain on that same string are condemned to chopping the neck and seizing the house.

---

187 เข้ายาคู, *khao yakhu*.

188 คราด, a flower in the Compositae genus.

189 กระแจ, a floral mixture used as a cosmetic.

190 A type of tea that can be used like chewing tobacco.

191 See note on clause 78.

92 Any *hua muen* of boats holding the flag at the prow who causes the pole to break or be blown down into the water, or who holds the flag upside down, punish by chopping the neck and seizing the house and servants; if [the occasion is] a royal ceremony for official guests to pay homage, execute the whole clan.

93 Any *hua muen* of the palace-rear, presiding official,[192] or saber master holding *aphirom* regalia who causes the pole to break and fall, punish by chopping the neck and seizing the house; if [the occasion is] a royal ceremony for official guests to pay homage, execute the whole clan.

94 If an official guest is paying homage, anyone who fails to attend in audience is fined according to official rank.

95 When an official guest arrives and enters to pay homage, if any of the various military or civilian officers do not wear the lowercloth and uppercloth that are *sanop* cloth presented by the King, but wear other lowercloth and uppercloth, it is inappropriate and unattractive.

96 If the *sanop* cloths presented by the King have been worn elsewhere for improper reasons so they look dreary, anyone wearing such bad-looking old cloth at a time when an official guest comes and enters to pay homage is first expelled from the audience hall, called to account for himself, and punished as follows: first time, issue punishment in writing; second time, give three strokes and place in the cangue.

97 The *sanop* cloths presented by the King should be worn for appropriate reasons, namely for royal ceremonies of the new year and Sat festival,[193] entertainments, and when the King travels. If the cloth is old, send it to the overseer to be presented in the royal quarters[194] and a petition made to the royal grace for the King to present a [new] *sanop* cloth. If such a petition has not been made in time, other *sanop* uppercloth and lowercloth should be found to wear in order to avoid looking bad.

98 Anyone who is informed by his overseer or finds out for himself that it has been fixed for an official guest to pay homage to the King, but does not come by the appropriate time, punish by expelling from royal service and fining at double rate according to official rank.

99 Courtiers, major officials, lords, *phra*, *luang*, and city governors who no longer hold their rank and position must surrender their *phrai som*[195] [to the King] and not feed them.

---

[192] สมุหประทาน, *samuha prathan*, later used to mean one of the four-pillar ministers.

[193] สาด (สารท), a festival falling on the fifteenth waning of the tenth lunar month, usually in September. *Sat* is derived from a Pali word for season. A special sweet, *krayasat*, made from new rice, sugar, peanut, and sesame, is presented to the monks. Some believe the dead return to the human world on this day—thus, merit made for them on this day is especially effective.

[194] ราชรโหฐาน, *ratcharahothan*, "royal private place."

[195] From the seventeenth century, *phrai* were allocated to senior officials to assist in their work, especially in provincial cities. Nobles were often able to convert these men into

Official Duty

100 Royal kin, *hua muen*, and *hua phan* in all departments undertake whatever royal service the King gives them.

Anyone sent to attend judicial court proceedings, the King requires him to remain until the matter is completed and then come to attend on the King's royal foot. If [the matter] is not over, the King requires that he not come. If there is anything to report to the King, come and report. If the matter is completed and there is a royal order to attend, come. If that person comes himself [with no order given], he is in violation of the King's royal authority.

101 Henceforth, the King does not wish to have many judicial court officials. Only one *phudat* clerk and two *samian* clerks are approved by royal order, and those people will have recompense[196] for royal service. Those persons who failed in their duty and did not show respect to the royal directive cannot claim recompense for royal service.

102 If a principal elephant or principal horse is sick, but the matter is not informed to the King, and the principal elephant or principal horse dies, demote [the offenders] to cutting grass for elephants.

If a principal elephant or principal horse is sick and is not cared for, imprison as for a serious offense, or fine at double rate.

103 If there is news of an enemy approaching, lords, major officials, and courtiers are to come and sit in the sala. If any person does not come, punish as for revolt, fine according to the offense.

104 If the King sends anyone on royal service, and that person has paid homage and taken leave, yet remains at his own house or any other place, and after three days has not gone, send another person instead, place the offender in chains until the person gone on royal service returns, then release him.

105 If lords of wild[197] states and tributary states, or *phra, luang, khun,* and *muen* sent by the King to govern cities or to make war, do not send reports of progress[198] but come themselves, and bring wealth to use as bribes, or take away *phrai* from the King's domain,[199] the King sees that these petty rulers wish to be major rulers, and orders their necks chopped and their houses seized. If the King graciously waives execution, seize all that part of their property due to the king, issue a suspended sentence, [or] demote them to be *phrai* cutting grass for elephants.[200]

---

personal retainers, and kings passed laws to get them back. See, for instance, Old Royal Decrees 23 (dated 1727), *KTSD* 5: 37–43.

196 บำเหนด, *bamnet*, a payment made in reward for some service.

197 สามล, *samon*, "wild country" in the Pallegoix dictionary.

198 หนังสือบอกศุขทุก, *nangsue bok sukthuk*, "letter telling of happiness and sorrow."

199 ราชธานี, *ratchathani*, the capital and its immediate surroundings.

200 This law is similar in content to Old Royal Decrees clause 23, dated 1727: "if any governor, acting governor, or someone sent to war does not send a report, and is not sent for, yet comes himself, he is in the wrong, penalty of death" (*KTSD* 5: 37–43).

106 If a report of progress has arrived, and a letter has not been sent to fetch [someone] but the person arrives, have him trussed up in front of the official sala for three days, then fined at single, double, or triple rate, dismissed from royal service, and placed in chains for one month. If the King graciously allows him to remain [in royal service], place him in chains for fifteen days. If the letter is found in transit, the King orders a demotion: if 10,000 *sakdina,* reduce to 5,000; if 5,000 *sakdina,* reduce to 3,000; and so on, by degrees, to 400; and fine according to rank at single, double, or triple rate; and imprison for fifteen days, so this should not be a model [for others].

107 Anyone in royal service with official rank must be on duty daily without fail. Anyone who is lazy and misses royal service should recognize his own fault, and if unable to make the effort required, should resign from royal service so as not to look bad.

108 Anyone who wishes to make the effort [to serve] but is incapacitated by sickness should report the incapacitating sickness to his overseer, request for a physician in royal service to make an examination as proof, then pay homage to the King and ask for the King's grace to remain in royal service but undertake duties only as befitting his capacity to perform.

109 If anyone condemned to punishment does not find out about his punishment in time, but then finds out and requests for the punishment to be served, the punishment should be waived.

Anyone who should be on service without fail but is lazy and misses royal service, if that person recognizes his fault and requests to be punished, administer the appropriate punishment. If the person does not recognize his fault in missing royal service a great deal, does not pay attention, and does not resign from royal service, the overseer of that person should examine the matter, pay homage, and propose a befitting punishment to the King's grace.

110 If any *chaophya, phya, phra, luang,* city governor, major official, courtier, royal kin, *muen,* or *hua phan,* all those having recompense, makes the effort to serve the King without fail, and the King presents something to that person, it is unbefitting for a lazy person to be dissatisfied. If anyone who by nature is lazy shows dissatisfaction, dismiss that person from royal service and relieve him of his property.

111 For anyone from 10,000 down to 800 *sakdina* who disobeys a royal order, punishment of four types:

for disobeying an oral royal order, punish by splitting the mouth;
for failing to implement a royal order, punish by execution;
for failing to follow a royal order, cut the mouth;
for disobeying a written royal order, fine at quadruple rate.

112 For disobeying a royal decree of Her Majesty the Primary Queen [? fine at quadruple rate]; for disobeying a royal command of the Secondary Queens or His Majesty the Royal Scion, [? fine at triple rate]; [for disobeying a royal command] of royal sons eating cities, fine at double rate.

113 For implementation of a royal decree [of the Primary Queen], seal to Khun Janthrathit.[201]

For implementation of a royal command by the secondary queens or Royal Scion, seal to Khun Inthrathit.

If a royal order, an Indian eunuch carries it; [if] secondary queens or the Royal Scion, a [? Chinese eunuch] carries it.

114 Anyone who fakes royal articles,[202] punish by cutting off the hand from the wrist down.

Anyone who fakes a royal order, a royal decree, or royal command is condemned to death.

115 When anyone addresses His Majesty the King on any matter, let that person continue speaking until finished, then if the courtiers in attendance on the King see that words are incorrect, let them address a correct version to the King.

If the matter is about the self, the King does not allow a person to speak himself.

If anyone requests to petition about property of any kind, the King does not allow the matter to be addressed to the King in the presence of the petitioner.

116 If a saber master or Mahatthai master speaks to a royal descendant, overseer, or official anywhere to quickly take up and implement an official matter on royal command of the King, [but] the official matter of the saber master or Mahatthai master is vexing and cannot be taken up and implemented, the matter should forthwith be addressed to the King. Anyone who ignores such a matter and does not address it to the King is condemned to punishment on the scale of the offense.

117 Anyone in charge of work in a department who does not know his job and mixes up right and wrong is considered by the King to have done his duty imperfectly.

118 If the King speaks on any government matter connected with law or custom, it is considered a ruling to be followed. Anyone who objects may petition in opposition one, two, or three times. If the King does not listen [to the petitions], the matter is closed; do not try to speak to the King in private.

If the King does not listen [to the petitions] and hence the ruling is to be followed, anyone who does not act on this command is considered by the King to have violated royal authority.

119 A commander of the guard must be loyal to His Majesty the King; not annoy the King; be minded to uphold what is right and true; take care to command courtiers, overseers, and *hua muen* to surround the King for protection; prevent people going out at the wrong time of day or night; and be attentive to the sign of

---

[201] This means that the order carrying a seal is sent to Khun Janthrathit, who, along with Inthrathit in the next sentence, are heads, respectively, of the left and right divisions of *phra sanom* (royal consorts) in the ministry of the palace with Okphra rank and 3,000 *sakdina* (*KTSD* 1: 246–7).

[202] เครื่องต้น, *khrueang ton*, probably clothes or food.

anything abnormal on the part of royal kin, *hua muen*, *hua phan*, and people good or bad who secretly talk together on covert matters. If he knows of any such matter, he must not ignore it, and if he can find ways to put a complete end to the matter, he must do so. If the matter should be informed to the King, he should do so; and if he ignores the matter, he is condemned to the same punishment as the wrongdoer.

120 Anyone appointed by the King to a senior post[203] must be steadfast and loyal in thinking what is of benefit to the King.

Any animate being or inanimate thing[204] which can nourish the capital, bring it to present to the King to enhance the wealth of the realm. Be mindful of the authority of royal commands. If anyone does not act according to the royal wish, but embezzles or steals [these items] to sell or exchange, forgetful of his duty, the King holds that person to be in violation and condemns to punishment of three grades.

121 If the King presents a primary wife to a lord, and if that woman does anything wrong, only scold and beat her to subdue her and make her fearful, do not cause that lady to fall dead or lose her female form; failure to comply is liable to punishment of three grades.

If the King presents a royal daughter, royal granddaughter, or royal consort of high rank to a royal son, royal kin, lord, *phra*, *luang mueang*, *khun*, *muen*, or *hua phan* who receives a recompense and enjoys royal favor, if there is anything wrong, even punishable by death, have the case informed to the [minister of the] palace[205] to be presented to the King for punishment at whatever level according to the severity of the offense.

122 The head of any department may not carry a royal sword.[206] If the King sends a royal sword to a head of department, do not receive it, on pain of heavy punishment, but have a page receive it, or otherwise be condemned to death. Anyone carrying a royal sword in the retinue of the King must not unsheathe it. When presenting a royal sword to the King, hold the sharp edge towards oneself and the blunt edge towards the King; if it is presented wrongly, condemned to death.

123 If the King is angry at anyone and calls for the royal sword, officials must not present him with the sword; anyone who does so is condemned to death.[207]

124 In the event of a fire, enemy attack, or a tiger, cow, buffalo, or elephant on the rampage, or bandits brawling, if the King is sleeping, wake him to manage the matter.

---

203 อธิบดีศรีสมุหนายกรักษาองค, *athibodi si samuha nayok raksa ong*, this may mean a post of ministerial rank.

204 สวิญาณกทรัพ อวิญาณกทรัพ, *sawinyanaka-sap awinyanaka-sap*, property with or without a soul.

205 มณเฑียรบาล, *monthianban*, Phraya Thammathibodi, 10,000 *sakdina*, one of the "four pillars" (*KTSD* 1: 237).

206 พระแสง, *phra saeng*, a short twin-edged regalia sword.

207 Seni Pramoj (*Pathakatha*, 78–79) argued this clause demonstrated that "The Palace Law is a law that the absolutist king promulgated to apply to himself, to limit his own power." In contrast to the Western idea that the king can do no wrong, "the king in the Palace Law accepts that he can do wrong and has this law written because he does not wish to do so."

125 If there is a fire in the palace or near the palace by day or night, bring executioners[208] to station in the parade ground; command that the good horses and good elephants near the fire be removed without creating confusion; and check to bring hooked machetes and fire-beaters.[209] Staff must assemble at every place to go wherever the King instructs. If the fire is near the stables for elephants or horses or near the buildings for troops or [royal] articles, heads of the guard take men to help extinguish the fire. Do not ignore [these orders] and rescue your own possessions; anyone who rescues their own possessions is caned severely.

126 The King forbids *chaophya, phra, luang, khun, muen, phan,* those holding official rank, from mischievously letting their siblings or servants appropriate the tax from fields, gardens, or market dues. Failure to comply is considered a violation of royal authority.

127 In the case of forest trees, rocks, or pillars that mark the boundary of any territory or any city, the king forbids cutting the branches of these trees, or digging up rocks and breaking them into pieces, on pain of punishment of three grades.

The Inner Palace

128 Servants of the King's foot must know about royal service in the palace during the first watch, which the King forbids to be written down. If royal sons, royal daughters, and royal grandchildren move about during the first, second, third, or fourth watches,[210] it is against the King's regulation. Their retainers are to forbid them to move about, and if they fail to forbid them as stated here, are condemned by the King to be caned and then executed.

129 The King issues a royal command to organize the *chamae* court ladies[211] to nurse and raise royal sons, royal daughters, and royal grandchildren, and to ensure the royal children are well-versed about correct behavior and the King's affairs. If a court lady sees a royal son, royal daughter, royal grandchild, court lady, or royal consort do wrong within the palace, she must pay homage and inform the King; if she fails to do so, the King considers she has wronged against royal authority, and condemns her to be caned and then executed.

130 Anyone who is lover with a court lady or royal consort is executed to die over three days, and the woman is executed also.

If anyone speaks with a servant girl of the inner palace, holds her hand, or touches her shoulder, and she cries out at the top of her voice to let people know, and pinches and scratches, demote the man to cutting grass for elephants. If the

---

[208] ทลวงฟัน, *thaluang fan*, "stab and slash" officers, four *hua muen* in Mahatthai, 400 *sakdina* (*KTSD* 1: 225).

[209] พร้าขอ, *phra kho*, a large knife with a hooked blade on a long handle, and กระตร้อน้ำ, *kratronam*, a pole ending in a triangular frame to hold cloth steeped in water, for beating roof fires.

[210] The first watch is 1800–2100 and the fourth is 0300–0600.

[211] ชะแม่, from เจ้าแม่, occasionally ชาวแม่, a term that appears many times in this part of the law (translated as "court lady"). It appears to cover all women in the inner palace except for the queens, consorts, and royal kin.

woman was complicit, give her twenty strokes of the leather lash, then submit her to public shaming and do not allow her to enter the palace.

131 Anyone who cuts a hole, breaks a screen, or parts a curtain[212] or fence is punished the same as for an offense with a consort; slash his neck and seize his house.

Anyone who takes a royal consort out of the palace, slash his neck, seize his house, and demote his wife and children to cutting grass for elephants. If a royal consort escapes from the palace, whether by land or by water, anyone who tells her the way to go is to be arrested, submitted to interrogation, and have the neck slashed and house seized; as for the consort, execution.

132 If a male and female palace servant are lovers, give the male fifty strokes, seize his property, and demote him to cutting grass for elephants; give the female fifty strokes of the leather lash, then cut her[213] and submit her to public shaming, and either make her an embroiderer, or give her to a royal child or grandchild.

133 A consort or palace maid who associates with a woman like a man with a wife is condemned to fifty strokes of the leather lash, then tattooed on the neck, taken for public shaming around the royal palace, and either made an embroiderer, or given to a royal child or grandchild.

134 A royal consort or palace maid who cuts a hole, breaks a screen, or parts a curtain or fence is condemned to death. A woman who carries regalia, a servant of the inner palace, or senior governess[214] [who commits the same offense is condemned to] twenty strokes of the leather lash.

135 Any woman who brings liquor into the palace, give twenty strokes of the leather lash.

136 A court lady, royal consort, or palace maid who has anything to say to an overseer shall address that matter to the King. If any persons argue and curse one another in the palace, and the matter irritates the royal ear, the King considers it an offense with punishment of fifty strokes of the rattan. If any person grasps a knife or cleaver to slash and kill, peel off the fingernails, then allow that person to explain himself. If the slashing causes injuries, cut off the hand on the side that was carrying the knife or cleaver, then impose a fine appropriate to the injury.

137 If a servant woman in the palace goes to meet and associate with a monk-teacher, give her twenty strokes of the leather lash, and have the monk expelled from the *wat*.

138 Anyone who seizes or grabs any unmarried or widowed woman serving in the palace is considered by the King to have committed a punishable offense. If the woman was complicit, give her twenty-five strokes of the rattan. Give the man fifty

---

[212] บ้าน, *ban*, house, in the original but ม่าน, *man*, curtain, in the similar passage in clause 134.

[213] สับ, *sap*, meaning to slice or cut in some way.

[214] ท้าวนาง, *thao nang*, "chief lady," a general term for any of the senior officials in charge of the administration of the inner palace.

strokes of the leather lash, then impose a fine according to rank, and deposit the fine proceeds in the royal treasury. If inside the palace, give the man the same punishment as for abducting someone from the palace.

139 If a man and woman talk together inside the palace and connive to be lovers, give twenty strokes of the rattan. If the man is in palace service, give fifty strokes of the leather lash. If the woman is in palace service, execution.

140 If anyone approaches and speaks with a royal servant inside the palace, make enquiries to establish the truth, give thirty strokes to the woman, and give fifty to the man as a suspended sentence.

141 If anyone takes an unmarried woman working in the palace to bed as wife without informing the King, and the King comes to know somehow, punish both with thirty strokes of the leather lash, and fine the man according to rank.

If anyone takes an unmarried woman working in the palace to bed as wife, and someone knows but does not inform the King, give twenty-five strokes of the leather lash, and fine according to rank.

142 Any courtier who brings books of poetry into the palace to seduce palace maids and inner palace servants is condemned to death.

An inner female servant who associates with a male outsider bringing books of poetry is condemned to death.

143 It is an offense for royal sons, royal daughters, Indian eunuchs, Chinese eunuchs, and heads of the houses of hunchbacks and dwarfs to go beyond the customs posts or guard posts.

144 If a court lady, consort, or palace maid, who has never trespassed on a forbidden place, does trespass, senior governesses are to forbid her and, if she does not listen, punish her.

A court lady, royal consort, or palace maid in attendance in the palace must not trespass on the throne. If she trespasses on the throne, senior governesses are to forbid her and, if she does not listen, punish her.

145 The King appoints the sentinelles[215] to summon the court ladies and royal consorts evening and morning to take care of lighting torches and fires. Heads of the sentinelles are to check on every one of the court ladies and royal consorts without fail. Any incident must be reported to the King. If there is any matter of concern [such as the] sickness or death of a father, mother, relative, or sibling, give a report to the King. If anyone willfully fails to report something to the King, the King considers it an offense subject to punishment of three grades: one, slash the neck and seize the house; two, dismiss as servant; three, fifty strokes of the leather lash.

146 If the King summons a minister, court lady, or royal consort for a royal matter in secret, and if anyone makes enquiries, do not tell anything; if anything is told, punishment of six grades.

---

[215] โขลนจ่า, *khlon ja*, female guards in the inner palace.

147 If a villain has the audacity to steal royal property from inside the palace and takes it to sell in the palace, cut his foot or hand from the ankle/wrist down. If he takes the stolen goods out of the palace, execute the thief and the gatekeeper. If the King graciously waives execution, fine the thief quadruple rate. If the thief has stolen essential[216] articles from the palace to sell, mortgage, or exchange in some way, give fifty strokes of the leather lash, cut off his hand, then fine at double rate for the articles, and punish any accessories to the sale with fifty strokes of the leather lash and half the fine imposed on the thief.

148 If servants in the palace go out by themselves, or are sent out [for some purpose], and if anyone abducts them to sell or make love to, give the abductor fifty strokes of the lash, tattoo his face, place a *chaleo*[217] on his forehead [and take him] around the city with a man banging a gong. Hasten to bring money to release and redeem the victim. If that person is aged thirteen or above, give fifteen strokes of the leather lash; if sixteen or above, give twenty-five strokes and send him back to his master; if he is not afraid and abducts a second time, cut off the hand or foot.

149 If people quarrel, fight, slash and stab, causing bloodletting in the palace, or if a servant woman, whether slave or free,[218] gives birth to or aborts a child in the palace, the King orders an offerings ceremony at his palace: erect a ritual hall at the four gates, with four five-level *baisi* for offerings, and a pair of chickens for each gate; string a circle of thread made from cotton or *lalang* grass around the palace; invite monks to chant Buddhist verses for three days; fetch Brahmans who know about offering ceremonies to make the offerings according to custom; lay on dancing, *phinphat*[219] ensembles, gongs, and music at all four gates; when the ceremony is finished, release the chickens outside the city to take the inauspiciousness, evil, danger, and misfortune out beyond the King's capital.

Brahmans

150 If a Brahman teacher, yogi, *phokhi*,[220] *adan*,[221] Saivite, or *phayari*[222] is guilty of a sex offense,[223] liquor offense, concealment offense,[224] theft offense, robbery offense, revolt offense, drinking liquor, taking life, adultery, stealing the King's property, or sedition, all of these according to the degree of severity: fine at double rate; fine at

---

216 เครื่องสรรพเหตุ, *khrueang saphahet*, "things for all purposes."

217 เฉลว, a stigma device made from plaited bamboo, used as a mark of shaming.

218 ทาศไท, *that thai*.

219 พินพาท, an ensemble including wind, string, and percussion instruments.

220 The Indian word *bhogi* comes from *bhuj*, enjoy, and implies worldliness or sensuousness, here in counterpoint to the asceticism of the yogi.

221 อาดาร, from Sanskrit *aadhyana*, meaning first or foremost, now a division of Brahmans from Kerala in southwest India, more usually known as Namboodri Brahmans. Chiraphat Phrapanwitthaya thinks the word derives from Andal, the only female among the twelve Alvar, Vaisnavite saints of south India (Royal Institute, *Phra thammanun*, 104, n. 156).

222 พญารี, Payyari, a division of Brahmans, originally from Karnataka, who migrated to Kerala in southwest India; also a term for Brahmans that engage in trade.

223 The first six items in this list have a suffix ฉินท์, *chin*, "cut," meaning that they destroy the offender's status as a Brahman.

224 พินทุฉินท์, *phinthuchin*, concealing one's status as a Brahman.

quadruple rate with copper; if condemned to death, cut his *sangwan* breast ornament, cut his sacred thread, and expel him to another city. [This seems to mean that a Brahman who commits a capital offence is expelled rather than executed, as execution might be inauspicious.]

151 The chief judges,[225] deputy judges,[226] chief scribe,[227] chief astrologer,[228] chief physician of the front,[229] and chief physician of the rear[230] have the authority and duty to prescribe royal traditions according to ancient procedure; and to prescribe ceremonies as laid down in the Veda texts, including the ceremonies of the twelve months, the sixteen major royal ceremonies,[231] and *Pathomaphisek,*[232] *Ratchaphisek, Intharaphisek,*[233] *Sangkhramaphisek,*[234] *Ajariyaphisek,*[235] and all the bathing ceremonies according to the manuals of knowledge; and to arrange officiants who have correct knowledge to direct the procedure. The presiding officers, military and civilian, [who oversee] the staff will receive money for these matters equal to that of the officiant.

152 For giving a royal name to the reign,[236] to Her Majesty the Primary Queen, or to royal children and grandchildren of first and second rank, [the Brahman will] receive cloth and a silver hat, big or small, depending on whether first or second rank. The special name[237] given to all with royal appointments must be appropriate to the rank and the post. If [the Brahman] gives a name that is inauspicious, or arranges officiants without appropriate knowledge, or carries out supernatural anointing with liquid or smoke,[238] or reads a manual incorrectly, punish the chief scribe by tying up suspended;[239] punish a chief judge, deputy judge, chief astrologer, or chief physician of the front and rear by hanging large beads[240] around the neck.

153 Since the past, the posts of astrologers of the front and of the rear are separate, under the following hierarchy:

astrologer of the front, Phra Horathibodi, deputy Phokhun Chotisastrajari;

---

225 The two Phra Maharatchakhru, 10,000 *sakdina* (*KTSD* 1: 265).

226 Phrakhru Phichet and Phrakhru Phiram, 5,000 *sakdina* (*KTSD* 1: 265).

227 Okphra Si Phuriyapricha, usually known as Phra Alak, 5,000 *sakdina* (*KTSD* 1: 272).

228 Phra Horathibodi, 3,000 *sakdina* (*KTSD* 1: 275).

229 Phra Si Mahasot, 1,600 *sakdina* (*KTSD* 1: 262).

230 Phra Sisak, 1,600 *sakdina* (*KTSD* 1: 262).

231 โสฬศกรรม, *solotkam.*

232 ปัถมาพิเศก (อภิเษก), "primary bathing ceremony," a ceremony of appointment involving bathing or water pouring.

233 See clause 189.

234 สังครามาภิเศก, "warfare bathing ceremony."

235 อาจาริยาภิเศก, "teacher bathing ceremony."

236 การแผ่นดิน, *kan phaendin,* presumably meaning a king.

237 นามวิเสศ, *nam wiset,* meaning the ราชทินนาม, *ratchathinanam,* a name given by the king for the holder of a specific post.

238 ชุบโหมเวทมนทร, *chup hom wetmon. Chup* means to coat (with liquid). *Hom* is the Brahmanical practice of burning ghee as worship. *Wetmon* is a word for supernatural practices (*saiyasat*).

239 Tying the hands to something over the head, usually to facilitate whipping.

240 ประคำ, *prakham,* a form of public shaming.

astrologer of the rear, Phra Lokathip-horathibodi,[241] deputy Phokhun Thephakon.

The front astrologer performs royal service at the front, taking care of the Brahman royal ceremonies, namely the ceremonies of the twelve months, except for the Triyampawai Swinging Ceremony which falls to the astrologer of the rear.

The astrologer of the front looks after the royal ceremonies of military processions, warfare, and royal business of the front, and all the royal business of the military. If he cannot be found, Khun Choti deputizes.

The astrologer of the rear looks after the royal business of the rear, issuing commands to the Indian Brahmans, the royal Swinging Ceremony, and all matters of the Primary Queen, Secondary Queen, Head Mothers, court ladies, royal consorts, and the royal children of first and second rank. If the department head of the front or rear cannot be found, the department deputy issues documents instead.

154 For decorating the image for [the ceremony of] burning rice[242] for any department, officer, official, or officials of any department or city: the astrologer of the front has servants[243] of the Brahmaracha to decorate the image to go to the ceremony of burning rice; the astrologer of the rear has servants of the Siwathit[244] to decorate the image to go to royal ceremonies along with the officials of that day. Phraek has the astrologer of the front, Chainat has the astrologer of the rear.[245]

155 When calculating Songkran and Cutting the Year,[246] a document[247] is issued in each case.

If there is an eclipse, a document is issued in each case similarly, and the King provides money for the ceremonies along with discarded uppercloths and lowercloths[248] for both Songkran and eclipses. At an eclipse of the moon, the King provides silver stamped with an image of the moon, and at an eclipse of the sun, gold stamped with an image of the sun, one baht per person.

---

241 In the Civil List, he has Luang rank, 1,600 *sakdina*. The two deputies have Khun rank, 800 *sakdina* (*KTSD* 1: 275).

242 See note on clause 186.

243 ข้า meaning ข้ากัลปนา, *kha kalpana*, often translated as "temple slaves," people donated to a religious institution for various purposes.

244 ศรีวาทตย; the word appears in the chronicles, early in the reign of King Narai (1656–88), when the king had four images of Siva cast to make merit including "one statue of Siva the Sun standing up, a little over a sok [cubit] and a khup [span] in height," all covered in gold and "reserved for worship in the performance of the holy royal ceremonies" (Cushman, *Royal Chronicles*, 243). The Brahmaracha earlier in the sentence is also probably a specific image of Brahma.

245 Meaning unclear. The original has แพต, *phaet*. Winai Pongsripian and Prasert na Nagara proposed this is an error for "Phraek Siracha," a place close to Sanghkaburi, about eight kilometers from Chainat. Alternatively, this means แพทยา, *phaetya*, and refers to someone in the department of physicians; and เมืองไชนาถ, *mueang chainat*, is a copyist's error for another Brahman officer, perhaps Luang Rachanithan (see *KTSD* 1: 262–63).

246 เพตร์ (เผด็จ) ศก, *phet sok*. These are calculations for fixing the annual calendar.

247 ฎีกา, *dika*, here meaning a written document with a calculation.

248 Meaning unclear, but possibly the cloths worn by the king at the ceremony are subsequently given to the Brahmans.

If the Brahman astrologers calculate planetary positions, [outcome of] warfare, or auspicious times wrongly, punish by having large beads hung around the neck.

156 *Si Suphasawat*[249]

5th month	royal ceremony of Cutting the Year when Caitra[250] takes the field
6th month	*Phaisakha* ceremony;[251] royal plowing
7th month	offering water to wash the royal feet
8th month	entering Buddhist Lent
9th month	*Tulaphan* weighing ceremony[252]
10th month	*Phatharabot*;[253] the *Sat* festival[254]
11th month	*Asayut*, boat racing
12th month	*Jongpriang* ceremony, floating lanterns
1st month	boat chase; swinging ceremony of *Triyampawai*
2nd month	*Butsayaphisek* ceremony;[255] holy cow circulates for feeding[256]
3rd month	*Thanyatho* ceremony[257]
4th month	*Samphatcharachin*[258]

Court procedure and dress

157 Royal activities in sequence

0700, dawn	proceed to the Mangkhala [-phisek, Throne Hall]; open for the palace and consorts to attend
0800	eat *namya* and sweet boiled rice[259]
0900	proceed to the sacred hall; open for the palace, palace-rear, inner guards, Haruethai, Ratchaphakdi, outer guards, and guards of the upcountry cities to attend
1000	call for food to eat; proceed to bedroom

[249] สรีศุภสวัสดิ, "sacred beautiful good." The Thai calendar is a compromise between an old Thai lunar system and the Indian Surya Siddhanta solar calendar. In the version used here, the year begins with the lunar cycle in November–December.

[250] แจตร, *jaet*, Thai-Sanskrit for the fifth lunar month, Caitra, in March–April.

[251] ไพศากขย, today usually called Visakha Puja, on the full moon day of the sixth lunar month, marking the birth, enlightenment, and death of the Buddha.

[252] A ceremony to overcome inauspiciousness by weighing royal property against the king stepping on the other end of scales, and gifting that property to the Brahmans (see clause 178).

[253] See note on clause 179.

[254] See note on clause 97.

[255] See note on clause 183.

[256] See note on clause 185.

[257] See note on clause 186.

[258] A ceremony honoring the various guardian spirits of the city, later part of ceremonies for Songkran new year (*Tamra phraratchaphithi kao*, 13–15).

[259] ยาคู, *yakhu*, made with young rice and sugar.

1100, 1200	open for the inner palace [to attend]
1300	private
1400	open at the throne hall for royal children, royal grandchildren, old consorts, young consorts, court ladies, inner *okjao*, outer *okjao*,[260] and palace maids to attend
1500	open for the outside, lords with *sakdina* from 10,000 down to 800; consider matters of the realm; dismiss court cases
1600	private
1700	proceed to the sacred hall
1800	proceed to the inner audience hall; affairs of the inner palace
1900, evening	open for the outside; consider matters of war
2000	consider matters of the city
2100	consider the essence of ancient events
2200	call for food to eat
2300	open for astrologers and royal scholars to discuss matters of dhamma
2400	open for *sepha*,[261] music
0100	open for tales
0200	[blank]
0300	enter bedroom; fetch attendants of curtains and mosquito net on the first shift

158 Placing of ladies at royal appearances.

After proceeding to the throne hall, royal consorts bring betel, drinking water, fans. Next beside, the two royal wives[262] on *jiam* mats[263] with trimming and seven-pocket velvet cushions.[264] Next beside, the Head Mothers, Phra Ratchathewi and Phra Akkachaya, on three-pocket cushions. Next beside, royal children, first and second class, on *jiam* mats with trimming or mats with trimming; royal

---

[260] ออกเจ้า, probably meaning senior female members of the royal household who no longer have regular duties but are retained for certain expertise, especially in ceremonies.

[261] เสภา, a form of storytelling with stylized recitation; see Baker and Pasuk, *Khun Chang Khun Phaen*, 909–10. Sujit Wongthes (*Matichon Sutsapda*, May 24, 2013) argues that in this context, *sepha dontri* refers to a group of royal musicians.

[262] พระภรรยาเจ้า, *phra phanraya jao*, apparently meaning the two most senior queens, Phra Akharamahesi and Phra Akhararatchatewi, as the other two of the four major queens are mentioned in the next sentence.

[263] เจียม, a floor covering, originally from northern China, made with matted animal hair, usually of a deer.

[264] Cushions with seven stuffed pockets.

grandchildren, first and second class, on mats with trimming; head governess;[265] sixteen court ladies who follow the King into the inner palace hall; sixteen court ladies who look after money; twenty-four court ladies who attend to general matters; seven court ladies on duty in daytime; twenty court ladies who take care of education; twenty court ladies who oversee servants; sixteen court ladies who oversee places [in the palace]; thirty-two palace maids; forty-eight dancers; four chief governesses[266] who accompany inside the palace; and four chief governesses who accompany outside the palace. The first royal aide[267] sits in front of the head governess; royal aides sit in front of the court ladies.

159 [On the inner][268] terrace: Okjao Thamma;[269] wives of 10,000 *na*, 5,000 *na*, and 3,000 *na*; wives from the ordinary provincial cities;[270] supervisor of the residence of royal children; supervisor of the residence of royal grandchildren; sentinelles who go to the throne hall; sentinelles who direct the dancers and heads of dancers.

On the outer terrace: Phra Si Manorat,[271] Phra Si Aphai, Khun Ratchakhan, and Khun Mano, the four deputies; Indian eunuchs and Chinese eunuchs; Muen Si Saowarak and Muen Sanphet;[272] Nai Ja;[273] head of the palace maids; pages; dwarfs; hunchbacks.

160 Four royal wives,[274] royal sons, and royal grandsons pay homage and drink the water in the sacred hall; all others sit in the Mangkhalaphisek [Throne Hall].[275]

161 The King's articles[276] include: the great crown; royal ear-rings; armbands;[277] garland decorations; great breast chain; waist chain; ornaments for the left and right

---

265 แม่เจ้า, *mae jao*, Thao Worajan, head of the inner palace staff, an office usually held by a senior woman of the royal lineage, 1,000 *sakdina* (*KTSD* 1: 221).

266 ออกเจ้า, *okjao*, see note on clause 157.

267 สนองพระโอษฐ, *sanong phra-ot*, "respond to the royal mouth." Currently this means somewhat older members of the royal lineage employed in the palace service, usually translated as "ladies-in-waiting." In later clauses (e.g., 178), the term seems to mean the four assistants of the head governess, Thao Worajan, namely Thao Somsakdi, Thao Sopha, Thao Sisatja, and Thao Insuriya, all *sakdina* 1,000 (*KTSD* 1: 221). Here it is qualified with เอก, *ek*, first, so perhaps means just one of these, with the other three in the second clause of the sentence.

268 Assumed, to match the outer terrace in the next paragraph.

269 See note on clause 158. Thamma here may be a name, or mean those who have religious expertise.

270 เมียหัวเมืองเทียร, *mia hua mueang thian*. This form (which appears only this once) could be the same as *mae yua mueang*, translated as Head Mother.

271 Okphra Si Manorat and Luang Ratchakhan, *sakdina* of 1,000 and 500, respectively, are both Chinese eunuchs in the ministry of the palace, under Okya Phrasadet, the royal chamberlain. Phra Si Aphai does not appear in the Civil List but is probably the same, and Khun Mano may be another who appears in the list as Luang Si Manorat, 1,000 *sakdina* (*KTSD* 1: 242–43).

272 Two of the four heads of the royal pages, 1,000 *sakdina* (*KTSD* 1: 223).

273 A title of several of the royal pages (*KTSD* 1: 222).

274 Phra Akharamahesi, Phra Akhararachathewi, Phra Ratchathewi, Phra Akharachaya.

275 Date of construction unknown; first mentioned in the chronicles in the Naresuan reign; destroyed by lightning and fire in the Prasat Thong reign, and replaced by the Wihan Somdet Throne Hall, completed in 1636.

276 เครื่องราโชปโภค (ราชูปโภค), *khrueang ratchupophok*, royal articles of (everyday) use.

hand, seven bands; three rings for each finger; blouse;[278] trousers;[279] britches;[280] red wool [lowercloth];[281] ankle bracelets; slippers; end of King's articles.

162 Royal articles of the Primary Queen and Secondary Queen:[282] golden crown and shoes, three-level umbrella; royal seat.

Royal articles of Phra Ratchathewi and Phra Akharachaya: crown; helmet for bun with swan tail;[283] velvet and woolen shoes; two-level umbrella; *thewiyan* palanquin with dragon rampant.[284]

163 Royal children of first and second rank: helmet with round bun; shirt showing rank in gold pattern.

Royal grandchildren of first and second rank: jeweled head ornament for hair in bun; *phrae* silk cloth in ordinary star pattern.

164 Head governess, royal aides: hair ornament; patterned silk cloth; colored *phrae* silk cloth.

Court ladies: hair bun with topknot ornament[285] and waving flowers.[286]

Palace maids, dancers, household heads: hair ornaments.

Sentinelles: sparkling lacquered hair ornament.

165 Wives of 10,000 *na* from the four provincial cities at ceremonies: jeweled head bun ornament; *khaorop*[287] silk lowercloth.

Wives of the four pillars: jeweled hair bun ornament; *jomruat*[288] silk lowercloth.

Wives of 5,000 *na* and 3,000 *na*: jeweled head ornament; uppercloth with golden borders on both shoulders.

166 *Khun muen* of palace maids, royal conveyances, and tall regalia: rabbit-ear hairband;[289] white shirt; white lowercloth with colored lower border.

---

277 พาหุรัศ, *phahurat*, perforated gold inlaid with gems, worn on the upper arm. An example was found in the crypt of Wat Ratchaburana (*Jittrakam lae sinlapa watthu*, 73).

278 ขนอง, *khanong*, a dress for public appearance, waist-length with long sleeves and a round or "lotus" collar.

279 กั้งเกญ, *kangken(g)*, tight, down to the knee.

280 สนับเพลา, *sanap phlao*, close-fitting trousers ending below the knee, often with a flared cuff, now part of the costume for traditional dance.

281 รัตนกำพล, *rattana kamphon*, lowercloths of various kinds.

282 "Ratchathewi" in the original, but clearly a mistake, as she appears in the next line.

283 พระมาลามวยหางหงษ, *phra mala muai hang hong*. Chin Youdi ("Khrueang pradap sian," 61, 95) identified one of the headpieces found in the crypt of Wat Ratchaburana with this description. The headpiece is like a pillbox, made from gold filigree, with two short tail flaps hanging on either side of a hair bun on the nape of the neck.

284 เทวิยานมีมกรชู, *thewiyan mi makhon chu*, a conveyance for queens. (Choti, *Photjananukrom sathapattayakam*, 251, has a picture of an example in the museum of Wat Ta Sao or Wat Yai, Phitsanulok.)

285 เกี้ยว, *khieo*, a garland of flowers made from silver, gold, or other metal around the topknot.

286 ดอกไม้ไหว, *dok mai wai*, flowers made from metal waving on wire stems.

287 เคารพย, a type of silk.

288 จมรวจ, a type of silk.

Royal Ceremonies

167 Royal ceremonies with bathing are: *Bophok;*[290] *Phetsok* [cutting the year]; *Lot jaet;*[291] *Samphatsachin; Phatrabot; Chawian phra kho* [circle the holy cow]; *Tulaphan* [weighing ceremony]; *Butsayaphisek;*[292] *Ratchaphisek* [ascent of the throne]; *Intharaphisek;*[293] *Khotchakam* [elephant ceremony]; *Prathomaphisek, Prathomakam, Mathiyomakam, Udomkam;*[294] *Ajariyaphisek;*[295] *Uparakha* [eclipse]; and *Prapdaphisek* [victory celebration]. These seventeen ceremonies involve bathing.

168 For the bathing, there is a golden bath with a pipe that spreads into a thousand streams; scented water in sixteen flasks;[296] and flowered water in sixteen flasks. The officiant Khun Sayamphon goes up to pour water into the golden bath. The presiding official carries a bathing tray and circles in front to wash the royal foot.[297] [Minister of the] Treasury brings soaked cloth; [minister of] lands brings conch water; Brahman priests, Mahethon and Phichet, bring *klot* water.[298]

At the ceremony, the presiding official offers a *baisi* to the King; Yanprakat[299] offers a prayer[300] to the King; Itsararaksa offers a blessing; Inthon beats the Indra drum,[301] Siket hits the victory gongs, and Khun Dontri beats the *mahorathuek* drum.

169 The ceremony of the Primary Queen is the same. The Brahman priest-teachers bring all four deputies [to do the rite instead], and dispense with the thousand streams of gold and silver. There is no bathing for the three [other] queens.

170 On the fifth waxing day of the fifth month in the evening in the great parade ground there is a parade of troops with various weapons—swords, *dang* shields, *khen* bucklers, *lo* shields, pikes, spears, guns, crossbows, bows—wearing shirts and

---

289 หูก(ร)ะต่าย, *hu kratai*, "rabbit ears," the name for several articles with a bow-knot shape, including a scarf, but here probably a hair band.

290 เบาะพก; see note on clause 187.

291 ลดแจด, from the Sanskrit term for the fifth month, Caitra; a ceremony for the *naksat* new year. See clause 191.

292 See clause 183.

293 See notes on clause 189.

294 Believed to be four ceremonies marking the life-stages of the king. According to the chronicles, King Ramathibodi II performed ปฐมกรรม, *pathom kam*, translated by Cushman as "the rite of Primary Karma," in CS 859, 1497 CE (Cushman, *Royal Chronicles*, 18; *Phraratchaphongsawadan krung kao chabap luang prasoet*, 20).

295 Appointment of Brahmans.

296 คนโท, *khontho*, a jug, often with an elaborate spout like an extended goose's neck, an item of regalia, probably of Persian origin.

297 The original has ช้าง, *chang*, elephant, which makes no sense; assumed to be a copyist error for ล้าง, *lang*, wash, as in the same phrase in clause 176.

298 Holy water made by Brahmans, carried in a กลศ *klot*, lidded jug.

299 Phra Yanprakat, *athibodi horadajan*, a post that originally belonged to a head Brahman who led prayers and appeals to the gods in offering rituals, 3,000 *sakdina* (*KTSD* 1: 265).

300 สโลก, *salok*, from Sanskrit *sloka*, a verse form.

301 เภรี, *pheri*, a general word for drums.

helmets without fail. Each division of military, civilian, troops, and *phrai* [appears] in the parade ground according to skill.

Pavilions for elephants are erected around the courtyard. All ten *khun han*[302] ride on elephants standing beside the walls of the courtyard, inside and outside. Sword officers and boat officers follow on left and right, riding fighting elephants; elephant officers and *muen* of elephants, inner and outer; a large group of royal kin; all four provincial city governors riding polo horses; horse officers of the royal kin.

Hua muen of the king's guard and *hua muen* of boats are interspersed in the procession according to line; *muen chai* stands at the front of the drums; *muen ja sapkan sakonkan*[303] stand at the front of the elephants; inner guards of the left and right sluice the elephants and clear away elephant dung; pour water and place sugarcane plants;[304] major guards close the bolts, and ride elephants to chase away the horses; elephant officers ride horses to lure the elephants; Senanon[305] and horse staff [come behind]; all of this under the command of Phan Phanurat.[306] In front of the stairway, [head of] elephants of the left, head of elephants of the right, [Khun Ngam[307]] Mueang wait at the courtyard sitting [facing] the lion's back [window].[308]

171 The chief scribe receives a royal order; a royal aide receives [it from] the scribe; Khun Rat receives [it from] a royal aide; orders to mount an elephant and send the order to Phan Phan[?urat]. If he mounts a horse and sends the order to Phan Phao:[309] wrestling, boxing, polo tossing. [If the order] is sent to Phan Phut,[310] and the *hua phan* sends the order to the stairway, *nai rong* of Mahatthai goes to receive it; if ordered by Khun Rat, Muen Niron[311] of Kalahom has the work.

Inner guard, Mahatthai, Kalahom, master of the rolls, major guard, [minister of the] palace—these six people walk in front of the royal kin. People riding fighting elephants and polo horses come to pay homage at the carriage;[312] *muen ja* of the palace polo tossers and Nakhonban come at the front; Thepnarai, wrestlers, boxers, Ngam Mueang,[313] and elephants all stand on the spot.

172 Then after dawn, 0700, Mahatthai in formation stage a procession in the center of the courtyard on the left and on the right. Troops of all types enter in procession with elephants and stand in formation in the parade ground. In the lion

---

302 หาร, probably ทหาร, *thahan*, soldier.

303 สรรพการสกลการ, unknown; both terms may mean something like "all kinds of things/matters."

304 รดน้ำทอดอ้อย, *rot nam thot oi*; in the ceremony of *thot chueak* from King Chulalongkorn's time, elephants are anointed with sacred water.

305 Khun Senanon, head of the right division of royal horse (*asa wiset*), 800 *sakdina* (*KTSD* 1: 275).

306 An official of Mahatthai, 400 *sakdina* (*KTSD* 1: 225).

307 Perhaps the officer mentioned at the end of clause 171.

308 The lion window where the king appears.

309 Phan Phaonurat, same as Phanurat, above.

310 Phan Phutanurat, same as Phanurat, above.

311 Deputy for accounts in Kalahom, 800 *sakdina* (*KTSD* 1: 278).

312 ระแทะ, *rathae*, a little wagon.

313 Khun Ngam Mueang ("protect city"), officer in the ministry of the city, 800 *sakdina* (*KTSD* 1: 229).

window, there are tall umbrellas, nine-level, seven-level, six-level, five-level, three-level, two-level, and one-level, and raised lotuses of silver, gold, and *nak*; the throne of His Majesty the Royal Scion is on the terrace to the left; the throne of His Majesty the Great Prince in front of the swordstore[314] is two cubits high[315] with a roof in *chaphop*[316] pattern and four curtains spread at the back;[317] the royal sons who eat cities [have a bench-throne] one cubit and one span high with a pavilion[-style] sloping[318] roof; royal sons in youth have a bench-throne[319] one span high; all the royal grandchildren [? sit on something] fore and rear; the Chief Scribe stands on a bench-throne ten cubits high, ringed by red cloth; the royal aides sit next to the scribe; Khun Rat sits in front in an empty space between; the four *hua phan* sit between the heads of the connected swordstores; *nai rong* sits also; the Indra drummers and *mahorathuek* drummers stand in front, with dancers to left and right.

There are three rounds of *mongkhrum*:[320] when the King first arrives; *mongkhrum* by the court ladies during feasting; *mongkhrum* by the pages in the evening; and various sports.[321]

173 When the King first arrives: luring elephants; bullock carriage fight; water buffalo fight; sheep fight; elephant fight; bald-headed people fight; chicken-flapping; polo tossing; wrestling; hitting shields; slashing; sword fight; tricks; horse polo.

174 After dawn, 0700: elephants enter and stand in formation in the parade ground.

0800, elephants are in place; at the marquee[322] courtiers beat the *mahorathuek* drum one time; elephants are taken out to stand with decorations at a place open for courtiers.

0900: the *mahorathuek* drum is beaten twice; the King proceeds to the sacred hall; open for royal children and royal grandchildren to call on the King.

1000: the *mahorathuek* drum is beaten three times; the King proceeds to the throne hall; the Chief Scribe goes up; royal aides, Khun Rat, and *hua phan* enter and sit; the parade ground is closed to prevent people entering; the King is invited to proceed to the throne hall; [the drum is] beaten five times; the King comes out and is open for royal kin to pay homage; [the drum is] beaten seven times; horses are

---

314 In late Ayutthaya, there were three "twin" buildings in the northeast corner of the palace, in front of the audience halls, used by officials to conduct business.

315 Meaning, raised from the ground.

316 ชภบ, unknown.

317 พนัก, *phanak*, usually meaning a backrest, but here probably meaning at the rear.

318 บดลาด, *bot lat*, guessed.

319 เตียง, see note on clause 6.

320 A ritualistic drum performance, probably originating from India, played as part of royal ceremonies in the Ayutthaya period, and revived in early Bangkok. Players wearing *lomphok* (conical hats) and long *khrui* (robes) act as deities attending a festival at Mount Kailash. The leader calls out names such as "Lotus bud blooming," "Dragon lashing tail," and "Wind blowing," and the team performs the appropriate drum sequence and dance (*Saranukrom watthanatham thai*, central region, vol. 11, 5297; Flood and Flood, *Dynastic Chronicles*, 1: 237).

321 The original has คิลา, *khila*, which could mean medicine, but is more likely a mistake for กีลา, *kila*, sports.

322 บราม, *bram*, probably ปะรำ, *param*, a temporary structure with a thatched or cloth roof.

called to lure elephants; *rabeng* dance,[323] left and right; sword dance, left and right; *rabam* dance in the style of *mongkhrum*; Phan Phan leads *mongkhrum* in front of the drum; stick fight; throwing pikes; playing *phaen*[324] and shooting arrows with wooden tips; ducking under the noose or leather rope; the *mahorathuek* drum is beaten nine times; the elephants are removed; feasting, *mongkhrum* by court ladies, then polo tossing. If there are official guests in attendance, and if the King plays polo on a post-horse, His Majesty the Royal Scion, Somdet Phra Phannamesuan-jao,[325] royal children of 10,000 *na* and 5,000 *na*, first and second rank, royal kin governing provincial cities, the four horse officers, and Khun Rat toss the polo ball. If the King plays polo, a *chaophya* tosses the polo ball. End of the great parade.

175 Sixth month, plowing [ceremony].[326] Chaophya Janthakuman pays homage at the sacred hall; the King graciously presents a royal short sword;[327] Phra Phonlathep[328] pays homage, has the power to command; the King graciously reduces his royal authority, and does not present his face at the window, does not decide court cases, does not have audience with courtiers, and does not venture out. Chaophya Janthakuman has an elephant-mounting platform in front of the *wat*[329] and goes in procession riding an elephant. Thenceforth there are ceremonies for three days. Courtiers, *hua muen, phan* of 100 *na* [to] 100,000 *na*,[330] local officials in the ministry of lands, and *khun muen* of the courts, all of them attend in the procession.

176 Seventh month. Courtiers offer water to wash the royal feet[331] at the jeweled lion nine-level *benja*[332] throne with gold umbrella, *nak* umbrella, silver umbrella, and five-color[333] umbrella. The King proceeds up to the *benja* throne of nine levels and seven levels. On the left is Khun Ratchaphaet;[334] on the right is the presiding official of 10,000 *na*. The four provincial city governors go up first. The four pillars of

---

323 A dance performed by males, originating from south India.

324 แพน is a large screen, often made of woven wood or bamboo, similar to a Roman *scutum*, carried in front by advancing soldiers to block various missiles, here used as a target for arrows.

325 See clause 1.

326 จรดพระอังคัล, *jarot phra angkhan*.

327 พระขรรค, *phra khan*. Thus symbolically transferring his kingly authority.

328 The minister of lands (*KTSD* 1: 231).

329 The original is พุทธาวาศ, *phutthawat*, the public area of a *wat*, excluding the monks' residences. The *wat* is not named but is probably Wat Phra Si Sanphet.

330 An odd phrase, as no official had *sakdina* as low as 100 or as high as 100,000; probably it should be 1,000 to 10,000.

331 Little is known or understood about this ceremony, which had disappeared by the Bangkok era. King Chulalongkorn speculated that it was a chance for senior officials, who had no part in the ceremony of installing a king, to offer water to the king (Chulalongkorn, *Phraratchaphithi*, 402–4). Woraphon (*Sathaban kasat*, 97–98) suggests it is a display of subordination and loyalty, symbolized by the noble receiving betelnut from the king on his head, redolent of the form of words *rap duai klao* for receiving a royal order "on one's head."

332 A type of throne with a high plinth, canopy, and curtains.

333 เบญจรง, *benjarong*.

334 Phra Si Mahosot Ratchaphet, head of the department of physicians of the front (กรมแพทยาหน้า, *krom phaethya na*), 1,600 *sakdina* (*KTSD* 1: 262).

10,000 *na* down to [officials of] 1,600 *na* and 5,000 *na* come behind. The presiding official receives: from [those of] 10,000 *na*, a gold water-carrier;[335] from 5,000 *na* and 3,000 *na*, a *nak* water-carrier; from 1,600 *na*, a silver water-carrier. Outside the balustrades[336] and outside the umbrellas, *hua muen* of the King's guard go in procession in file, leading with a rope Phra Prab and Phra Chayanuphap,[337] to stand at the golden bath for placing the royal foot. After the offering of water to wash the royal feet is complete, the King proceeds out to a feasting. A water-carrier of water is placed on the head [? of each noble, above, offering water] and a cloth wrapped around the head and the water-carrier. The King offers three betel nuts, received on the head.[338]

177 8th month, nothing.

178 9th month, Tulaphan royal weighing ceremony.[339] Erect a weigh scale in the middle of the Mangkhalaphisek Throne Hall; place wealth of various kinds on the left side; the King and Primary Queen step on the right side. Below, palace staff sit outside a curtain. Inside the curtain are the four chief judges,[340] the presiding official Phra Si Akharat holding the royal short sword, Phonlathep holding a lute,[341] [minister of the] palace holding a betel flower,[342] and Phra Yommarat[343] holding a *phaenchai* pipe.[344] Khun Si Sangkon[345] blowing a conch, Phra Intharo beating the Indra drum, Phra Nonthiket beating victory gongs, and Khun Dontri beating a *mahorathuek* drum go with the King. The four royal aides,[346] wives of 10,000 *na* from the four provincial cities, and the Primary Queen in a *thewiyan* palanquin go in procession in front of the King. The people in procession in front there, the wives of the four chief astrologer-judges, and wives of the four pillars make nine circuits. The King steps [on the scale], then the Primary Queen steps [on the scale], then the King proceeds out to the feasting, [distributing?] on the left silver, on the right gold and *phrae* silk cloth.

---

335 กลออม (กระออม), *kra-om*, a container for water, made of woven bamboo lined with dammar (Choti, *Photjananukrom*, 39).

336 ราชวัต, *ratchawat*, a railing or balustrade placed to mark the boundary of an area used for a ritual, or a temporary barrier made with a lattice of bamboos bound with bamboo lath.

337 Chayanuphap and Prap Traijak are the names of the two elephants of King Naresuan during the famous elephant duel in 1593. Possibly these were the titles of the king's two principal mounts.

338 Golden betelnuts found in the crypt of Wat Ratchaburana are believed to have been used in this or a similar ceremony (*Jittrakam lae sinlapa watthu*, 73).

339 According to Quaritch Wales (*Siamese State Ceremonies*, 199), this ceremony has antecedents in India, and in Siam "fell into disuse in the middle of the eighteenth century."

340 The two chief and two deputy judges described above.

341 พิน, usually พิณ, a string instrument.

342 A betel flower made from gold, used in several ceremonies for auspiciousness.

343 Minister of the city.

344 แพนไชย, *phaen chai*, a blown musical instrument made of gold.

345 An *athibodi horadajan* in the Brahman department, 3,000 *sakdina* (*KTSD* 1: 265).

346 See clause 158.

179 10th month, Phatharabot festival.[347] Throw rope, brace rope. Pay homage. Feast the courtiers. Drink water of allegiance.[348]

180 11th month, Atsayut boat racing ceremony.[349] There is *mongkhrum* of left and right, dancing, [*ma*]*horathuek* drums, Indra drums, music. Morning, the King wears the royal crown and royal adornments.[350] Midday, the King wears a golden *mala* helmet with flower garlands. Evening, the King wears a bright *mala* helmet and pink breastcloth. The Primary Queen [and?] the royal wife[351] wear a golden *mala* helmet, lowercloth of *phrae* silk with a gold pattern, and blouse. Phra Akharachaya wears a plain helmet, lowercloth in star pattern, and blouse. The royal children and grandchildren have hair in a bun and wear a blouse. Royal consorts have hair with a winged ornament[352] and a breastcloth on both shoulders. Glorious Victory[353] is the King's barge. Lion Visage[354] is the barge of the Primary Queen. Glorious Victory and Lion Visage are placed at the rear. If Glorious Victory loses, there will be overflowing joy and happiness; if Glorious Victory wins, there will be an era [of hardship].

181 12th month, Trong Priang festival.[355] Lower a set of lanterns down to float on water. Erect four firework towers at a Meru with two sitting halls. The King boards a boat with a five-level *benja* and a four-level throne for the Primary Queen, three-level for the Head Mothers,[356] two-level for royal children, and one-level for royal grandchildren. Royal consorts wear bright[357] pink uppercloths. Lanterns are all five-level. The courtier's fish boats are in attendance in front of the *benja* boat; crocodile boats[358] guard on both sides with *dontri* music on the left and *mahori* on the right.

---

347 Phatharabot is the constellation where the moon resides in the tenth month. This is a Brahman ceremony of self-purification in preparation for the Sat festival (Chulalongkorn, *Phraratchaphithi*, 416–17).

348 These fragments were perhaps notes by a scribe. They refer to ceremonies that are not covered in this account, including *Thot choek*, an elephant ceremony, and the ceremony of drinking the water of allegiance, both usually in the fifth month.

349 อาสยุช, usually อาสวยุช, *atsawayut*. There is an elaborate account of this ceremony during the Ekathotsarot reign (Cushman, *Royal Chronicles*, 204).

350 See clause 161.

351 พระภรรยา, *phra phanraya*, which might here be a qualifier for the Primary Queen, or mean all the other major queens, but more likely refers to the Secondary Queen, Akhararatchatewi, since another of the queens is mentioned by name in the next sentence.

352 สนอง, *sanong*, a winged hair ornament.

353 สมรรถไช, *samanthachai*, a royal barge with raised gunwales.

354 (ไกร)สรมุข, *(krai)soramuk*, a barge for the queen.

355 ตรองเปรียง, later Jong Priang, a Brahman lantern ceremony to honor Siva, Brahma, and Visnu on the full moon of the 12th month. In the version, based on an Indian original, recorded in later manuals and practiced in the Bangkok era, the lanterns are hoisted on posts for fifteen days, and on the first day, the king anoints the three main posts with cow fat (*Tamra phraratchaphithi kao*, 9; Wales, *Siamese State Ceremonies*, 288). Possibly in this account, the description of this festival has gone missing, and the title is now attached to an account of an early version of Loi Krathong.

356 แม่หยัวเจ้าเมือง, *mae yua jao mueang*.

357 สุกหร่ำ, *sukram*; *suk*, ripe, is used as a qualifier for color; perhaps หร่ำ = หร่าม, splendid, hence "bright."

358 เรือตะเข้, *ruea takhe*.

Flat[359] boats have a lantern in each boat. When the King boards, blow horns and cheer three times. Have screen dancing.[360] Feast the courtiers and inner palace, then cut the anchors, untie the moorings, raise three cheers, and let the flat boats float in procession. Cut the anchor of the royal-throne boat to float along down river. On reaching [Wat] Phutthaisawan,[361] light fireworks, and play screens. The King boards the Glorious Victory barge with the four major wives. Royal children, royal grandchildren, and royal consorts travel in royal barges up to the side of [? Wat] Ko Kaeo.[362]

182 Royal ceremony of boat chasing.[363] The King wears a bright[364] *mala* helmet. Her Majesty the Primary Queen wears a bright [something] on the throne. Royal children and royal grandchildren have hair in the form of a bun.[365] Royal consorts with hair in winged ornaments sit two in front, two behind, wearing a gold-bordered breastcloth on both shoulders, with a curtain tied to posts as a back-rest, only chest-high. Phya Mahasena[366] beats a gong. On reaching the end of Ban Run,[367] the King disembarks and stands to fan. Then on reaching the Victory Gate, the King beats time.[368]

183 Feast of the auspicious circles of flowers.[369] Her Majesty the Primary Queen arranges *krajae* and floral powder. Wives of the King[370] prepare betel. Royal sons,

---

[359] เรือเอน, *ruea en*, guessed. The word usually means leaning or bent.

[360] หนังระบำ, *nang rabam*.

[361] A large *wat*, dating to early Ayutthaya or before, sited on the off-island bank in the middle of the south side of the city.

[362] On the off-island bank near the southeast corner of the city.

[363] ไล่เรือ, *lai ruea*, more usually *lai nam*, chasing the water, a ceremony to make the water level fall after the rains in time for the harvest. Writing around 1600, Diogo da Couto described the event: "When they want this river to switch to draining away ... the king goes out of the city with all of his great lords, in [a procession of] many vessels grandly gilded and adorned, with many festivities and playing of musical instruments of all sorts. It is said that the king goes to expel the water out of the kingdom. Among all of his festive occasions, this is the main one." The highlight of the event was a boat race "with voluminous shouting, frequent screams, and much clamour." Breazeale, "Portuguese Impressions of Ayutthaya," 54.

[364] See note on clause 181.

[365] เศียรเพศมวย, *sian phet muai*.

[366] Minister of Kalahom.

[367] Down the river toward Bangkok around five kilometers, almost to Wat Prot Sat.

[368] ส้าว, usually beating with a stick to keep time for oarsmen. In other descriptions of this ceremony, the king beats the water with a regalia sword and orders the water to fall. Perhaps that is what is intended here.

[369] ดอกไม้วงมงคล, *dokmai wong mongkhon*, usually called Butsayaphisek, held in the second month when the sun is in conjunction with *butsya*, the eighth *naksat* constellation, Prasesepe in Cancer, which has five stars seen as a garland, hence this name. Wales (*Siamese State Ceremonies*, 120) claimed, "The object of the ceremony is said to have been the maintenance of the welfare of the kingdom, presumably by means of reinforcement of the king's divine powers." This ceremony (*puṣyābhiṣekaḥ*) is found in a mid-tenth century Angkor inscription (K.806, v. 66), which describes how the king was "reconsecrated to his office annually by the royal chaplain and the royal astrologer" through "a stream of nectar poured from one hundred golden vases." The "nectar" was melted butter and the king sheltered under a blanket (Sanderson, "Śaiva Religion among the Khmers," 382). The ceremony lapsed after the fall of Ayutthaya in 1767 (Chulalongkorn, *Phraratchaphithi*, 69).

royal grandchildren, and Head Mothers prepare betel. Courtiers and royal aides prepare food trays. Royal sons and palace cooks prepare food trays [for officials of] 10,000 *na* [down to] 5,000. Thao Inthakalaya[371] arranges food trays for courtiers. Thao Yotmonthian[372] arranges rice pancakes. Phonlasena arranges brewed liquor. Surin[373] arranges distilled liquor.

Then, after dawn, 0800, the King proceeds to bathing and perfuming. At 0900, the King dresses and proceeds to the sacred hall. Royal sons and grandchildren, outside and inside, pay homage in the sacred hall. Royal sons and daughters and the four royal wives address the royal foot. At 1000, the King proceeds to the Mangkhalaphisek [Throne Hall]. Indian eunuchs beat claves, then when the sound stops, an overture is played in the sacred hall. Lords, major officials, and courtiers prepare themselves, set their faces to beware, and wait to hear the claves. The King proceeds to the throne hall. After a silence of six minutes, claves, horn, and conch play, and the curtain is drawn to reveal [the King]. Phrayan Prakat[374] offers a verse. Phra Issuan Raksa[375] offers a blessing. Phra Ratchapurohit and Phra Khruphiram[376] offer conch water. Phra Mahethon and Phra Phichet offer *klot* water.[377] Mahasitthi[378] offers [something]. Lords, major officials, and courtiers pay homage. [Minister of the] Palace offers a flower circle of auspiciousness, *krajae* powder, and betel. Kalahom offers the *phayu* military; [Okya] Decho[379] offers the *thahan* military. [Phraya] Jakri[380] offers the *phonlaruen* civilians. Palace offers musical instruments.[381] Musicians wait to hear a royal command. Then the King orders to bring food trays. A *khlui* pipe leads a song.[382] *Nai rong* carry and place the royal food trays and first-rank food trays. Muen Jong prostrates, gets up to stand, and then places the betel. The royal aides offer flowers to the royal sons, and place betel. Maha Bamrue distributes auspicious flowers and betel to the lords, provincial governors, major officials, and courtiers. The royal sons indicate who should take [the betel]. If anyone else takes, penalty of cutting off the hand. After the distribution of betel, Muen Tharakamnan offers gold and silver flowers and a betel bowl [? to the King]. Muen Thin accepts [? on the King's behalf].

---

370 พระภรรยาเจ้า, *phra phanraya jao*, which sometimes seems to refer to the Secondary Queen alone, and sometimes to all the queens other than the Primary Queen.

371 In the outer division of royal cooks, 400 *sakdina* (*KTSD* 1: 222).

372 In the outer division of royal cooks, 400 *sakdina* (*KTSD* 1: 222).

373 Perhaps Khun Surin Sombat, officer of the great treasury under the Treasury of the Great Wealth (*KTSD* 1: 267).

374 The chief astrologer, *sakdina* 3,000 (*KTSD* 1: 265).

375 This name does not appear in the Civil List, but there is Issuan Thibodi, a department head in the Brahman section, *sakdina* 1,000 (*KTSD* 1: 266).

376 The second pair of chief judge and deputy judge (see above and *KTSD* 1: 265).

377 The first pair of chief judge and deputy judge.

378 Khun Mahasithi Wohan, a deputy in the department of scribes, 1,000 *sakdina* (*KTSD* 1: 272).

379 One of two military heads in Kalahom with 10,000 *sakdina*, equivalent to a minister (*KTSD* 1: 280).

380 Minister of Mahatthai (*KTSD* 1: 224).

381 In the original เครื่องเลี้ยง, *khrueang liang*, feeding things, but probably a mistake for เครื่องเสียง, *khrueang siang*, musical instruments.

382 ขลุ่ย, a woodwind instrument rather like a recorder.

184 Triyamphawai bathing ceremony.[383] Phra Si Akkharat offers cloth. Phra Phonlathep offers water. Phra Ratchapurohit and Phrakhru Aphiram offer conch water. Phra Mahethon and Phra Phichet offer *klot* water. Phrayan Phrakat offers a verse. Phra Issuanraksa offers a blessing. Khun Wisutthaphot[384] offers rice, flowers, roasted rice, young rice, and crisped rice. [Minister of the] Palace receives royal young rice.

185 Chawian royal ceremony.[385] Phra Kosupharat[386] stands facing to the north. In front is a pile of charcoal for fire, two cubits tall. Two horns are plated with gold and decorated with nine gems. Four hooves are [plated with] gold and decorated with nine gems. *Tap*[387] plates on the ears, gold wire around the shoulders, and a silk rope decorated with *thamo*[388] under the belly. The division of gold and jewels[389] [brings] silver, gold, bright *phrae* silk, a golden salver to carry grass, and a golden flask filled with water. Royal sons feed the grass [to the cow]. A *baisi* and a footed bowl are placed in front. The four chief Brahmans are at the four corners. Phrayan Phrakat and Issuan Raksa perform a rite of worshipping fire from evening until dawn. Then at 0900, the King proceeds. [Minister of the] Treasury carries the royal short sword of victory. [Minister of the] Palace carries bathing articles. [Minister of the] City carries a water basin. Wives of 10,000 *na* and 5,000 *na* go in procession with the Primary Queen clockwise around nine circuits. The King carries a golden lotus. The Primary Queen carries a silver lotus. Phra Phonlathep carries a salver with popped rice to feed the royal cow. The King proceeds up to bathing, then to a ceremonial feasting. Courtiers pay homage, in order of procession. Elephants stand where umbrellas and balustrades are placed as in the Tulaphan ceremony.

186 No [ceremony of] burning rice.[390]

---

383 The swinging festival. Unfortunately, the details seem to have been lost.

384 An officer in the ministry of land, 400 *sakdina* (*KTSD* 1: 231).

385 This ceremony does not appear in the account of royal ceremonies from the Borommakot reign (*Khamhaikan khun luang ha wat*, 106). King Chulalongkorn (*Phraratchaphithi*, 61) believed it had long disappeared.

386 The "holy, beautiful, jeweled cow."

387 ตาบ, usually a breast ornament, lozenge-shaped.

388 ถมอ, usually meaning stone.

389 กองสุวรรณรัตน, *kong suwannarat*.

390 This refers to *Thanyatho*, meaning "burning rice," mentioned above in clause 156, a ceremony held after the harvest and threshing, possibly originally designed to kill pests or disease in the gleaning, but converted into a royal ceremony to predict the prospects of the following season's crop. In one manuscript version, a representative of the king and other officials go in procession, each holding a candle and a bundle of straw. When they set light to the straw, a group of fifty to seventy men riding buffaloes charge in to seize the rice and scatter the officials away (*Tamra phraratchphithi kao*, 9–10). In another version, from King Borommakot's reign, three straw umbrellas are set alight, four teams compete to seize them, and the result foretells the coming season (*Khamhaikan khun luang ha wat*, 106). The ceremony was performed in the early Bangkok era in a more sedate form along with various entertainments, but had disappeared by the fifth reign (Chulalongkorn, *Phraratchaphithi*, 106). Wales (*Siamese State Ceremonies*, 228) thinks this was a thanksgiving ceremony, deriving from an old Indian ceremony of the fire god, Agni, but his account is speculative.

187 The royal ceremony of *bophok*.[391] Erect a ceremonial hall with a fire at the center. The four chief Brahmans, four deputies, astrologers, and physicians sit in a group as presiding officials. Outside them is a balustrade. Place offerings for the deities of the nine planets. [Among] the eight directions,[392] the inauspicious direction is at the northwest, [the site of] Uthokkarat.[393] Erect a silver umbrella, gold umbrella, *nak* umbrella, five-color umbrella, and balustrade outside this first level with a chicken fence,[394] votive tablets[395] of silver, gold, *nak*, and five-color. Outside this one level, have a solid fence, and outside the solid fence have elephants, sword officers, boat officers, and guard officers stand in formation.[396]

At the royal residence,[397] have a throne hall and a sacred hall for Queen Phra Phi,[398] another at the residence of the Primary Queen and the royal wife,[399] another at the residences of the two Head Mothers,[400] another at the house of the royal children, and the houses of the royal grandchildren and royal consorts.

---

[391] เบาะพก, *bophok*, probably distorted from ปาวก, *pāvaka*, a Pali-Sanskrit word meaning fire and, by extension, purification or purifier, especially in an invocation of fire in an old Brahmanical ordeal of carrying a heated ball: *pāpaṃ punāsi vai yasmāt tasmāt pāvaka*, "You are called 'purifier' (pāvaka) because you purify (*punāsi*) sin (*pāpam*)" (Yelle, *Semiotics of Religion*, 44, 77). The purpose and significance of this ceremony is unknown. MR Suphawat Kasemsri suggested it might be the inauguration of a new residence for a queen. More likely, the ceremony is somehow related to the Angkor rite, described by Zhou Daguan in 1296 (Zhou, *Record of Cambodia*, 49): "Inside the palace there is a gold tower, at the summit of which the king sleeps at night. The local people all say that in the tower lives a nine-headed snake spirit which is lord of the earth for the entire country. Every night it appears in the form of a woman, and the king first shares his bed with her and has sex with her. Even his wives do not dare go in. At the end of the second watch he comes out, and only then can he sleep with his wives and concubines. If for a single night this spirit does not appear, the time has come for this foreign king to die. If for a single night he stays away, he is bound to suffer a disaster." Sujit Wongthes ("Naga sangwat") suggests *bophok* derives from Khmer words meaning "pierce the belly," but this is unlikely. The Angkor rite may be related to the prominence of tantric beliefs in late Angkor, and there are tantric traces in this ceremony (see notes below), but also many other influences.

[392] Probably this is a (*maha*)*thaksa* diagram (Thep, *Horasat nai wannakhadi*, 521–29).

[393] อุทกราช, ruler of the waters, a type of water spirit, usually female, otherwise called รากษส, *raksot*, and in Pali, *udaka-rākṣasa*, black and very evil, sometimes depicted as servants of Yama, the lord of death.

[394] See note on clause 78.

[395] จรเหวด, more usually เจว็ด, *jawet*.

[396] This appears to be a mandala, and has traces of a tantric initiation ceremony, including the bathing at the end of clause 188 (Sanderson, "Vajrayāna: Origin and Function," 88).

[397] พระตำหนัก (ตำหนัก), *phra tamnak*.

[398] แม่หยัวพระพี่, *mae yua phra phi*. Probably this is an image. Choti (*Photjananukrom*, 394) shows an image of a *jawet* tablet, dating from the nineteenth century and now in the National Museum. In some tantric traditions, devotees have a personal idol, kept in a casket, and brought out for occasional worship (Sanderson, "Vajrayāna: Origin and Function," 20–21). But Phra Phi in the ceremony described here may have been insubstantial, a pure spirit.

[399] Probably the Secondary Queen, see note on clause 180.

[400] Here and in the next clause, this is แม่หยัวเจ้าเมือง, *mae yua jao mueang*. This might mean "wives of provincial governors" but more likely a copyist has inserted *jao* in the usual term for the Head Mothers.

188 On the evening of the 11th waning day of the month,[401] courtiers from 10,000 down to 1,000 *na* pay homage at the ceremony of Queen Phra Phi for three days.

On the 14th waning of the month, take royal conveyances and sixteen Brahmas[402] to receive Queen Phra Phi in the *prasat*. After dawn, 0800, summon the royal conveyances *thewiyan, thippayan,* and *phrayanumat* for the King with white umbrella of nine levels, seven levels, five levels, four levels, three levels, and two levels to shade, and thirty-two Brahmas; and for the Primary Queen, [umbrellas of] five levels, four levels, three levels to shade, and sixteen Brahmas. The wives of first class of 10,000 and 5,000 *na*, royal aides, walk in front of the royal wives with [umbrellas of] three levels, two levels for shade, and eight Brahmas. Wives of 5,000 *na* and courtiers walk in front of the Head Mothers, left and right, with [umbrellas of] two levels and raised lotuses for shade, and eight Brahmas. Wives of 3,000 *na* and old court ladies walk in front of Queen Phra Phi. The wife of Phra Purohit[403] holds golden candles; the wife of Phra Phiram carries a conch; the wife of Phra Mahethon carries a golden fish; the wife of Phra Phichet carries a golden turtle;[404] the wife of Phra Thepharat[405] carries a *traphang*;[406] the wife of Phra Jakrapani[407] carries a salver with popped rice; the wife of Phra Athaya[408] carries a casumunar[409] knife; the wife of the chief astrologer scatters rice.

Arriving at the *mondop* of Queen Phra Phi, the King halts. In front of the King, Phra Si Akkharat holds the royal short sword, then come the royal aides, royal children and royal grandchildren, Phra Madurat,[410] Phra Matucha,[411] and Phra Athikanyomahathibodi.[412] Behind the King come the Primary Queen, then the royal wives, Head Mothers, left and right, and twelve palace maids. The saber masters of the palace-rear escort her out from the foot of the *prasat*.[413] The saber masters of the front escort her out from the Gate of the Water Olive. Horn and conch invite the ladies to leave. Then the King proceeds to sleep with Queen Phra Phi. When he awakens from sleep, the King bathes, eats, is adorned with perfume, cosmetics, and royal decorations, and proceeds to the sacred hall. The King makes nine circuits, then goes to Uthokkaratchasot,[414] and scatters rings, gold, and silver. [Each] deity has a bonfire with a Brahman to perform worship and scatter silver for everyone.

---

401 Unfortunately, *which* month is not specified, but probably the third, same as clause 186.

402 พรหม, *phrom*, possibly a misspelling of Brahman, but the correct spelling appears in the next clause.

403 These are the wives of the two pairs of chief and deputy judges.

404 Vishnu's first two incarnations are as a fish and a turtle, and he carries a conch.

405 Another deputy in the Brahman section, 3,000 *sakdina* (*KTSD* 1: 265).

406 ตระพัง, a Khmer word usually meaning a pond or lake, so perhaps some kind of water carrier.

407 Another deputy in the Brahman section, 3,000 *sakdina* (*KTSD* 1: 266).

408 *Ratchahoradajan*, "royal astrology teacher," deputy to the second chief judge, 3,000 *sakdina* (*KTSD* 1: 265).

409 ไพล, *phlai*, a tuberous root, *Zingiber casumunar/purpureum*, used for treating wounds, nausea, and headaches.

410 มาดุราช, maybe มาตุลา, *matula*, a maternal uncle.

411 A grandparent on the maternal side.

412 Unidentified.

413 This is probably the same as the *mondop* mentioned a few lines above, presumably referring to a shrine where Phra Phi usually resides

414 อุทกราชสศ, see note on clause 187. Presumably an image of a water spirit.

After the circuits are complete, all five royals proceed by royal foot into the hall of fire and all five sit on golden bench-thrones. [The minister of the] Palace stands carrying a salver for bathing. Phonlathep brings water. Purohit and Phiram give conch water. Mehathon and Phichet give *klot* water. The royal wives, Head Mothers, Khun Inthon, and Khun Janthon[415] follow on left and on right carrying salvers for bathing. Phra Thepharat and Phra Jakrapani give conch water. Phra Thammasat[416] and Phra Athaya give *klot* water. When finished, the King proceeds up to the throne hall to feast the courtiers. There is *mongkhrum* left and right, Khula[417] stick fighting, ducking under a leather rope, playing *phaen*,[418] throwing pikes, and shooting bows. Royal sons and the Primary Queen [stand?] on the right; royal daughters on the left; royal children and grandchildren, royal consorts, and the head of the royal maids on the left; Indian eunuchs on the right; Chinese eunuchs on the left.

189 Royal ceremony of Intharaphisek.[419] Erect a Mount Meru one *sen* and five fathoms high[420] in the center of the parade ground with an image of Indra sitting on Mount Meru, Isinthon and Yukhunthon one *sen* high, Karawik[421] fifteen fathoms high, Mount Krailat[422] ten fathoms high, an inner ring of golden umbrellas, middle ring of *nak* umbrellas, outer ring of silver umbrellas, and outside that a balustrade and five-color umbrellas. Under the umbrellas stand images of deities. Outside the umbrellas and balustrade, have a chicken fence,[423] paper umbrellas, images of *yak* ogres[424] and *khonthan* musicians;[425] a *raksot*[426] standing at the foot of Mount Meru;

---

[415] See clause 113.

[416] *Ratchahoradajan* and deputy to the first chief judge, 3,000 *sakdina* (*KTSD* 1: 265).

[417] คุลา, possibly a branch of Tai Yai or Shan.

[418] See note on clause 174. Here the three phrases, "playing *phaen*, throwing pikes, and shooting bows" should probably be read as one activity.

[419] The name comes from an old Indian ceremony based on a legend of Indra flying down in his chariot to present the five insignia of kingship: crown; sword; cane; fan and whisk; slippers. However, the Siamese version is completely different, focusing on a dramatization of the legend of churning the ocean of milk at the creation of the world. According to the chronicles, Intharaphisek was performed in the Chakkaphat reign (1548–69) after repairing damage to the palace by a great fire, but no details are given. It may also have been performed in 1496/97, when the chronicles state the king "ให้เล่นการดึกดำบรรพ," *hai len duek damban*, "had the Dükdamban festivities performed," using the same phrase for the churning as appears later in this clause (Cushman, *Royal Chronicles*, 18, 30–31; *Phraratchaphongsawadan krung kao chabap luang prasoet*, 20). Intharaphisek is also mentioned at Angkor under Jayavarman VII and in Pagan under Kyanzittha (1084–1113); see McGill, "Art and Architecture," 57–68; Maniphin, "Chak nak duek damban."

[420] Fifty meters.

[421] Isinthon/Isadhara, Yukhunthon/Yugandhara, and Krawik/Karavika are three of the seven mountain ranges around Mount Meru in the Three Worlds cosmology.

[422] ไกรลาศ, Mount Kailash.

[423] See note on clause 78.

[424] ยักษ, common term for mythical giants or ogres.

[425] คนธรรภ (คนธรรพ์), Gandharva, musicians in the heavens and the Himavanta Forest.

[426] See note on clause 187.

and images of *khochasi, ratchasi, singto, kilen,*[427] serow,[428] elephant, cow, buffalo, tiger, and bear. Have images of deities sitting on every mountain: on Krailat, an image of Lord Issuan as lord and Nang Uma as lady; on the peak of Mount Meru, an image of Lord Indra; images of Asura at the middle of Mount Meru; an image of Lord Narai sleeping on water at the foot of Mount Meru; and a seven-headed *naga* wrapped around Mount Meru. Outside the area, have *asura* standing outside the wall, halls for dance, firework towers, and fireworks. Mahatthai, Bamrue,[429] royal aides, and child guards dress up as the hundred *asura*. Pages dressed up as the hundred deities, Pali, Sukrip, Mahachomphu,[430] and 103 monkey retainers pull the ancient *naga* to churn the sea of milk[431] with *asura* pulling at the head, deities pulling at the tail, and monkeys at the end of the tail. Mount Meru has one side gold, one side *nak*, one side crystal, and one side silver. Mount Yukhanthon is gold, Isinthon *nak*, Karawik silver, Krailat silver. Around the outside of the arena have elephants, horses, and the four troop divisions.[432] [Those of] 10,000 *na* wear a jeweled hair ornament, shirt, lowercloth of *khaorop phrae* silk; 5,000 *na* wear a golden helmet, shirt, and lowercloth of *jamruat phrae* silk; 3,000 *na* wear a helmet of foreign *phrae* silk, shirt, and lowercloth of *phrae* silk; 2,400 *na* down to 1,200 hold silver and gold flowers according to post. With popped rice and flowers, they pay homage. Brahman teachers, yogi, *phokhi, adan,*[433] *taba,*[434] and Saivite sit inside the balustrade.

190 First day, *athiphat;*[435] 2nd day, flatten and erect; 3rd day, build and erect; 4th day, finish completely; 5th day, pull the ancient *naga;*[436] 6th day, set up three jars of nectar water, three-headed elephant, albino horse, Usupharat,[437] *garuda, nang dara*[438] in front; bring various weapons, elephant gear, rope nooses, victory pikes, shields, goads, spears,[439] lance-goads, and bathe with nectar water a hundred images of the

---

427 All mythical creatures. *Khochasi* is a lion with an elephant's trunk, *ratchasi* and *singto* are lions, all from the Himavanta forest in the Three Worlds cosmology. *Kilen* is an animal from Chinese legend with a deer's body, a dragon's head, and a single horn.

428 A small goat antelope found mainly in steep limestone terrain.

429 See note on clause 15.

430 Two monkey brothers and a monkey king from the Ramakian.

431 ชักนาคดึกดำบรร(พ์), *chak nak duek damban*, literally: pull the *naga* very deep until milk comes; a re-enactment of a Puranic scene in which deities churn the sea of milk by using Meru as a pivot rotated by a *naga* wrapped around the mountain, creating many powerful substances, including the nectar of immortality. Maniphin Phromsutthirak suggests that this ceremony comes from the Khmer, and that the churning scene in the bas-relief of Angkor Wat may depict this ceremony. In the Puranic version of the story, Vishnu is present, but in the Angkor bas-relief, Indra is present, as here (Woraphon, "Phaplak sathaban kasat," 233–34; Maniphin, "Chak nak duek damban").

432 จัตุรง(ค์), *jaturong*, from Sanskrit *caturanga*, literally: four-limbed, meaning the four divisions of an army—elephant troops, chariot-born troops, cavalry, and infantry; a term for troops in general.

433 See clause 150.

434 ตบะ, *taba*, Sanskrit tapa, ascetic practice of self-denial.

435 อธิภาศ, unknown, possibly something like "great place," probably a ceremony. Wales (*Siamese State Ceremonies*, 123) suggests a "discourse."

436 See clause 189.

437 Nandi, the bull mount of Shiva, see clause 185.

438 นางดารา, "star lady," perhaps similar to an *apsara*; also a female character in Ramakian.

439 โตมร, *thomon*, a thrown weapon.

deities and ancients that churn the sea of milk—Lord Issuan, Lord Narai, Lord Indra, and Lord Phitsawakam.[440] Following custom, bring golden sets of articles to offer for blessing. Up to the 7th day, Brahman teachers offer blessing. On the 8th day, lords offer blessing. On the 9th day, offer elephants, horses, and the four divisions of troops. On the 10th day, offer the twelve royal treasuries. On the 11th day, offer *suai* taxes, and the seven taxes and dues.[441] On the 12th day, offer the city. On the 13th day, bring nectar water. On the 14th day, bring the rewards of the deities; on the 15th day, rewards of the lords; on the 16th day, rewards of the courtiers and *muen*; on the 17th day, royal gifts to Brahman teachers; on the 18th day, scatter alms from trees of plenty;[442] on the 19th, 20th, and 21st days, for three days scatter gold and silver. Have entertainments for one month. Erect an image of Kumphan[443] one *sen* tall on the terrace, and have pages acting as monkeys jump out of his ears, eyes, nose, and mouth. When the ceremony is finished, the King proceeds in a royal carriage to give alms around the city. End of the Intharaphisek ceremony.

191 The royal ceremony of Cutting the Year takes place in a side-hall[444] to the left of the throne hall in the center. [Minister of the] Palace, inner guards, Haruethai and Ratchaphakdi,[445] consorts of left and right attend, and Nilawan[446] and others attend for Cutting the Year. After dawn, 0800, the King proceeds to *lot jaet*.[447]

For the ceremony of *lot jaet*, have a lodge for bathing the monks. In the water place a curtain [? to divide into] inner and outer areas, a throne at the center, and a bush with trunk wrapped in red cloth. In the area inward of the bush: the two royal wives, royal children, royal grandchildren, head governess, royal consorts, and courtiers, all of them. In the area outside the bush: royal sons, royal grandsons, [officials of] first class 10,000 *na*, second class 10,000, 5,000 to 1,000 *na*. After feeding the monks, the King sleeps. When the King awakens, he proceeds down to bathe and dress in a complete set of patterned [cloths]. The King proceeds up to the sacred hall, and at midday proceeds down to bathe and put on a complete set of jewels. Feast the courtiers, inner and outer. Have *mongkhrum*, left and right, Kula stick fighting, playing *phaen*, ducking under the leather rope, passing through the noose, throwing pikes, and shooting bows. The losers feast the royal sons on a

---

440 พิศวกรรม์, Visvakarma, artificer of the gods.

441 สัดพัทยกร, *sathapathayakon*; the *pathaya* part means a portion due to the king, and the last syllable is *akon*, a tax.

442 กรรมพฤกษ, *kammaphruek*, after Kalapaphruek, mythical trees of plenty in the Himavanta Forest. This is a form of almsgiving in which money is inserted in limes, which are spiked on artificial trees, and then scattered as alms.

443 กุมภัณฑ์, Pali: Kumbhanda, is a genus of potbellied giants or deities who play various roles in Buddhist cosmogony, including forming the retinue of Wirunhok/Virudhaka, guardian of the south, and sometimes appear as guardians in *wat*. Possibly this scene is related to Kumphakan (กุมภกรรณ, Kumbhakarna in the Ramayana), a brother of Thotsakan (Ravana), or one of the many other *kumphan* characters from Ramakian who fight in many battles with Rama's monkey troops; see, for example, "Kumphakan ok suek" (Kumphakan Goes to Fight, and following chapters). It could be that these battles are the inspiration of this performance. At Prasat Phnom Rung, Buriram, there is a stone carving of a huge Kumphakan with fighting monkeys crawling all over his body.

444 บรัด (ปรัศว์), from a Sanskrit word meaning a royal building beside a main building.

445 See clause 27.

446 A Brahman who also pushes the swing at the swinging festival.

447 See note on clause 167.

three-level *prasat*; the royal grandchildren in a one-part pavilion;[448] [officials of] first class 10,000 *na* in a five-level *mondop*; 10,000 *na*, second class in a three-level *mondop*; 5,000 *na* in a three-part royal-house;[449] 3,000 *na*, 2,600 *na*, in a two-part house; 1,400 *na* and 1,200 *na* in a one-part house with screening; 1,000 *na* in a one-part house; 800 and 600 *na*, under a marquee[450] with edging; 500 *na* and 400 *na*, on paper.[451] Lords, provincial city governors, four pillars, major officials, and courtiers [? are given] three sets of lower and upper cloths. Within evening, the King proceeds to bathe, be adorned, and go down to board a boat. Lords and courtiers put on lowercloths and go down into the water at the same time. When the King bathes at the head of the water at the sand palace, the ceremony of *lot jaet* comes to an end.

192 When the Primary Queen is pregnant, perform the ceremony of the *man* tree.[452] The guardian spirit of the city, *jetawan*,[453] is fastened to a *samrong* tree.[454] Wives of 10,000 *na* walk in front of the royal carriage for all seven days of the rite. Courtiers pay homage and give blessings for auspiciousness, according to official rank. Erect a house for [lying by the] fire with five rooms, and seven halls. The work is the responsibility of Kalahom.

193 At the birth, [minister of the] Palace hits a gong. [Minister of the] Treasury offers wrapping cloth of sixteen seals. [Minister of the] City offers fifty criminals' wives.[455] Phonlathep offers sixteen flasks of water. Khun Si Sangkon blows a conch. Conch troops blow horns and hit twenty victory gongs. Khun In and Khun Jan[456] boil hot water. Mahathep and Mahamontri[457] take care of things. Haruethai and Ratchaphakdi bring a [spirit-]doctor of the great spirit and great specter[458] to discard a spirit's head.[459] Phra Sitthisan[460] goes without morning rice. Kuman-raksa goes without midday rice. Kuman-phet[461] goes without evening rice. The chief astrologer and Phra Thepharat calculate the birth time. When the newborn has been bathed, royal children receive [the infant] and pass to a royal aide who passes to a wet

---

448 คูหา, *khuha*, cave or a cave-like building.

449 ราชคฤห, *ratchakharueha*.

450 ปราม, see note on clause 174.

451 เพลา, *phlao*, a kind of *sa* paper, made from mulberry fibre.

452 หมัน, several trees in the Cordia family, especially *Cordia cochinchinensis*, that grow in mangrove swamps or near water; an auspicious tree, probably because the name is a homophone for "secure."

453 เจดวัน, unknown, but may be a miscopying of เจตคุก เจตคุปต์, *jettakhuk/p*, one of the protective spirits of the city, a Thai representation of Chitragupta, assistant to Yama, the god of death.

454 *Sterculia foetida*, bastard poon, java olive, hazel sterculia, or wild almond tree.

455 The wives would have been locked up as surety after their husbands had fled to evade arrest.

456 See note on clause 113.

457 Two department heads of the inner guard of the left and right, respectively, Luang rank, 2,000 *sakdina* (*KTSD* 1: 283–84).

458 ผีหลวง หลวงโขมด, *phi luang luang khamot*.

459 A rite of decapitating a doll so that the doll absorbs any inauspicious forces.

460 Department head of medicine doctors of the left, Okphra rank, 1,400 *sakdina* (*KTSD* 1: 263).

461 Khun rank, 400 *sakdina*, in the department of medicine doctors. Kuman-raksa is not in the Civil List, but there are three others with a "Kuman-" name (*KTSD* 1: 263).

nurse. 0700, bring a spirit-doctor[462] to release the inauspiciousness of the embroidery frame. 0800, open for courtiers to pay homage. Place the royal child on a nine-jeweled salver. Royal children and grandchildren raise their hands and faces to pay homage.

194 Dawn, morning rite of blessing for success for three days. Golden salver, weight of five *tamlueng*; golden plate, weight of five *tamlueng*; golden sheet, weight of ten *tamlueng*; golden mortar, weight of fifteen *tamlueng*; golden pestle, weight of five *tamlueng*; golden excrement scoop, weight of one *tamlueng*. Wet nurse first class, three; wet nurse second class, seven; wet nurse third class, nine; caring aunts, four; caring grandmothers, two; cradling-standing maids, four; cradling-going maids, four; maids in house, eight; doctors, six; doctors to overcome ill fortune, twenty; embroiderers, twenty; fan and whisk, twenty; lullabyers, thirty; golden basin,[463] weight of fourteen *chang*.

195 For seven days, perform the rite of the splendid peak;[464] receive nine-jewel rings, nine pieces. Perform the rite of spoon-feeding rice; receive ten *chang* of silver and two *chang* of gold. Perform the rite of spoon-feeding banana for the same amount. Blessing for good fortune at every place.

On ascending the cradle, receive gold weight of four *chang*. On performing the rite of *atsaja thai*,[465] the rite of *tharok*,[466] the rite of *jongbat*,[467] the rite of *yot fong man*,[468] receive a golden egg, weight of five *tamlueng*; [the rite of] fifty people [bringing?] hot water, [receive] silver [weight of] one *chang*. On performing the rite of moving to the river,[469] receive ten *chang* of silver, three *chang* of gold, a hundred people, three elephants, and three horses. On performing the rite of shaving the topknot, [receive payment] equal to going down to the landing,[470] performing the rite of mounting the horse, the rite of mounting the elephant, ordination, approaching menstruation.[471]

196 The Primary Queen feasts half; wives of the King feast half;[472] Head Mothers half; royal children half; royal grandchildren half; royal consorts half; by hierarchy of princely rank.

---

462 หมอปัตติเสดาะเคราะห์, *mo patti sado khro*; *sado khro* is a common term for rites to combat inauspiciousness and misfortune. *Patti* is a Khmer-derived word with meaning similar to *sado*. The significance of the embroidery frame (สนัดดึง สดึง, *sadueng*) is unknown.

463 สาคน, *sakhon*, a large semi-spherical basin of copper or bronze, often with a lion's face design on the side, used for making sacred water or washing.

464 ยอดศรี, *yotsi*, unknown.

465 อาสจไทย, unknown.

466 ถารถ, maybe ทารก, *tharok*, infant.

467 จองบาท, *jongbat*, unknown, perhaps "fasterning the foot."

468 ยอดฟองมัณ, unknown.

469 จรดคงคา, *jarot khongkha*, unknown.

470 ลงท่า, *thao long tha*, unknown.

471 จวรอุหลบ, *juan ulop*.

472 Meaning half of the amount of the Primary Queen, and so on, halving at each step of the hierarchy.

Punishment of Royal Family and Palace Staff

197 If a royal consort, *okjao*,[473] palace maid, serving palace maid who carries regalia, or in-house sentinelle incurs punishment, heavy or light, send her to the consort executioners, Muen Fat and Muen Jom.[474] If a consort is condemned to death, have her wear britches before execution. If she is executed without britches, the executioner receives the same punishment as the errant royal consort. If executing a royal consort, place her in a sack, and do not allow the corpse to be seen. If the corpse is seen, it is an offense.

198 If a royal son faces punishment, place him in chains and a frame, that is, put him in chains. If he is a royal child of first class, golden articles; if a royal child of second class, silver articles; if a royal child outside the palace, send to Phithak Thiwaraksaratri;[475] if a royal child in the palace, send to the palace-rear executioners, left or right. The jail in the palace-rear, at the water olive,[476] and the jail outside in Phra Phikanet[477] are for light offenses.

199 If a heavy offense, exile to another city, that is, Phetchabun, Jantabun [Chantaburi], or Nakhon Si Thammarat. Send [as escort] two saber masters of the front, two saber masters of the rear, and an inner guard to carry the order. Command a *phinet*[478] inner boat with boats of sword officers in procession in front and boats of palace staff and *hua muen* of the King's guard following behind. On arrival, the saber masters and inner guards disembark first and take the ruling to the governor and local officials for them to arrange a place with a house appropriate to the severity of the offense, in the center of the city. The house is to have three rooms, walls of wood fastened with metal, and a hole five cubits deep dug under the belly of the house, covered over with planks. Above, have locks and bolts according to the order. Have [the offender] placed either upstairs or down in the hole depending on the severity of the offense. If condemned to death, down in the hole.

200 While en route, if a boat of anyone—saber master, lord, provincial city governor, major official, courtier from 10,000 to 600 *na*, or someone escorting royal children or forwarding goods and presents—approaches in contravention of law, the saber masters have the authority to detain that person as in revolt to be punished according to the severity of the offense.

In the city where [the offender] is being imprisoned, if anyone goes to meet, speak, or give gifts and offerings to him, that person is condemned to death.

---

[473] See note on clause 157.

[474] หมื่นฟาด(เพลิงล่า) หมื่นโจม(สงคราม), Muen Fatphloengla and Muen Jomsongkhram, two of the four *thaluangfan*, ทลวงฟัน, stab-slash officers, in the department of the palace overseeing royal consorts, 600 *sakdina* (*KTSD* 1: 246–47). Presumably these officials applied punishments lighter than execution in the case of "light" offenses.

[475] See clause 15.

[476] See clause 15.

[477] พระพิคเนศ, a Thai term for the Hindu deity Ganesh. This appears to be the name of an area of the city close to the palace (see clause 15).

[478] ในพิเนศ, unknown; perhaps meaning a boat from the area called Phra Phikanet in the previous clause.

201 If [the offender] is condemned to a severe penalty including death, send him to the executioners of the rear and saber masters of the rear to take for execution at [Wat] Khok Phya.[479] The saber officers sit *thaptak*.[480] Senior sword officers sit and watch. The head executioner prostrates three times, hits with a length of sandalwood, then lowers [the body] into a hole. If any saber officer or executioner takes the [victim's] cloth and gold rings, penalty of death. When being hit, [the offender] is supported on a trimmed mat and cushion.

Forms of Address, Vocabulary, Precedence

202 Command concerning the Royal Palace in the throne halls at *somphatsachin* festival, festival of unfolding and storing rope,[481] paying homage and feasting courtiers, paying homage and drinking the water of allegiance. Her Majesty the Primary Queen, Secondary Queen, Head Mothers, His Majesty the Royal Scion, royal sons, and royal grandsons pay homage in the sacred hall. The royal sons and royal grandsons sit in the sala. All of the royal scholars and Brahman teachers sit in the sala together according to custom.

203 Royal grandchildren living outside the palace and lords of cities travel in a canopy boat, take betel from a pedestal salver or *talum* tray; anything more than that is an offense. Royal grandchildren take betel from a mother-of-pearl casket or mother-of-pearl salver; more than that is an offense. Only royal grandchildren living in the palace may use a *kanching* umbrella covered with red cloth; those living outside the palace use a *kanching* umbrella covered with ordinary white cloth.

204 When addressing the king, a royal son who becomes the Royal Scion of the front side calls himself "Somdetphra No Jao." When Somdetphra No Jao enters in audience inside the palace, people accompanying him carry a betel salver, water kettle, and *kaphae*,[482] one person [for each item]. Other than those carrying these, only four other people may enter.

205 The regalia of the King are called: the *mala* helmet, *kasa* cloth,[483] and *phrakhan* short sword; salver for betel; salver for water; [? salver for] powder; [? salver for] costume; elephant mount; horse mount; barge; carriage; *aphirom* umbrella; *kanphirom* umbrella; *bangsun* shade; *phachani* fan; and *jiam* mat. Comestibles are called rice *sawoei*, water *sawoei*, things *sawoei*, *miang* and betel *sawoei*.

206 When responding to the King, use the form [to call oneself] "Phraphutthajao kha." When addressing him, [call oneself] "Phraphutthajao kho krap thun." If conversing, use the form "Jao nang kamom trat sang/chai."[484]

---

479 A *wat* to the north of the island where several royal executions took place.

480 ทับตัก, "covering lap," maybe sitting cross-legged with the feet on the lap.

481 Inspection of elephant harness, in the fourth month.

482 กะแพ, unknown.

483 กาษา, unknown.

484 This appears to be an instruction to those attending audience. The clauses from here to the end seem to be drafts or notes, never finalized.

207 If appointed as *luang, khun, muen,* from *luang, khun, muen* down to *phan, thanai,* do not use the name as *luang, khun, muen, phan,* or *thanai* in the Grand Palace. People in the royal palace who may take betel from a dome-shaped[485] casket [are those] from Luang Kalahom, Luang Ja Saen [upward]; other than them, people may take betel only from a *mong*[486] casket with silver ears.

208 All the royal sons, if they have anything to address to the King, use the form "Phrajao luk thoe" followed by their name. When a royal son attends in audience in the royal palace, he may be accompanied by one person carrying a casket for betel, one carrying a casket for water, and only three others. On reaching the palace, put the betel and water caskets down on a bench or *talum* tray.

209 All the royal articles are to be called: *mala*-helmet *song;*[487] *pha*-cloth *song;* casket betel *sawoei;*[488] casket water *sawoei;* powder *song;* elephant *thinang;*[489] horse *thinang;* boat *thinang; kanching* umbrella; *yanumat* palanquin, *khanphirom* umbrella; comestibles to be called rice *sawoei,* water *sawoei,* things *sawoei, miang* and betel *sawoei.* Fan[490] with handle decorated with mother-of-pearl and leaf[491] painted with vermilion, inscribed with a pattern in gold.

210 If responding to the King, use the form "Phra Phutthajao kha"; if addressing the King, "Kha Phraphutthajao kho thun." If conversing, use the form "Phra-ong jao trat sang trat chai." If appointed as *khun, muen, phan,* or *thanai* in the department of the royal children, do not use the name as *khun, muen, phan, thanai* in the royal palace.

211 As for [people in] the department at the rear, the King orders that they be called according to the custom of the royal children.

---

485 ทรง มัน, *song mon,* in the shape of a *mondop* roof.

486 มอง, unknown.

487 This and other clauses in this final section are more like notes than finished drafts. ธรง, usually ทรง, *song,* is the royal vocabulary for "wear."

488 เสวย, *sawoei,* is the royal vocabulary for "eat."

489 ธี่นั่ง, "place to seat," is the royal vocabulary for a conveyance.

490 ภัด, usually, พัด, *phat.*

491 ใบ, *bai.* This and the fan are articles of regalia.

Appendix

Translation of Royal and Official Names

Several terms for ranks and positions are translated consistently throughout.

Royal Kin

พระมหาอุปราชา	*phra maha upparacha*	Great Prince
หน่อพุทธางกูร	*no phuttharangkun*	Royal Scion
ราชกุมาร	*ratchakuman*	royal son
ราชนัดดา	*ratchanatda*	royal grandson
ลูกเธอ	*luk thoe*	royal children
หลานเธอ	*lan thoe*	royal grandchildren

Queens

The structure and terminology changed over time. Several clauses, particularly at the start of the law, describe a structure of four queens, consisting of two principal queens:

พระอัครมเหษี	*phra akharamahesi*	Primary Queen (of the right)
พระอัครราชเทวี	*phra akhararatchatewi*	Secondary Queen (of the left)

each of whom has a deputy:

พระราชเทวี	Phra Ratchathewi	for the Primary Queen
พระอัครชายา	Phra Akharachaya	for the Secondary Queen

However, some clauses may have been added after this structure changed, leading to some confusion. Also, there is another term:

พระภรรยา(เจ้า) Phra Phanraya (Jao)

This term sometimes seems to refer to the Secondary Queen, and sometimes seems to be a collective term for those queens other than the Primary Queen.

แม่หยัว(เจ้า)เมือง *mae yua (jao) mueang* Head Mother

This term seems to refer to queens ranking below the primary four, possibly consorts who have given birth to a royal son, or perhaps either a royal son or daughter. In some usages, it seems to mean queens who come from the (four) principal provincial cities. Again, the meaning of the term may have changed as palace practice changed.

สนม *sanom* consort

Other Women in the Palace

แม่เจ้า *mae jao* head governess
Thao Worajan, the head of the female palace administration.

ท้าวนาง *thao nang* senior governess
Probably meaning Thao Worajan and her four deputies, the five senior ladies in the palace administration.

ออกเจ้า *okjao* chief governess
Probably the same as *thao nang*.

สนองพระโอษฐ์ *sanong phra-ot* royal aide
Literally meaning "respond to the royal mouth," this term is used for various people in close attendance on the king. In many places, these are probably the *thao nang*.

ชะแม่ *chamae* court lady
It appears to be a collective term covering all women in the inner palace except for the queens, consorts, and royal kin.

กำนัล *kamnan* palace maid
Probably a general term for the female staff in the inner palace, but in some usages may include consorts; the line between staff and consorts may have not been very clear.

Officials

ตำรวจ	*tamruat*	guard
ทหาร	*thahan*	soldier
ท้าวพญา	*thao phya*	lords
บันดาศักดิ์	*bandasak*	official rank
มุกขมนตรี	*mukhamontri*	major officials
ลูกขุน	*luk khun*	courtiers
องครักษ์นารายณ์	*ongkharak narai*	King's guard

Various officers with a *khun* title are translated as follows:

ขุนโขลง	*khun khlong*	herd officer
ขุนช้าง	*khun chang*	elephant officer
ขุนดาบ	*khun dap*	sword officer
ขุนม้า	*khun ma*	horse officer
ขุนเรือ	*khun ruea*	boat officer
ขุนโรง	*khun rong*	support officer
ขุนแวง	*khun waeng*	saber officer
ขุนสนม	*khun sanom*	palace-rear officer

And similarly:

นายช้าง	*nai chang*	elephant master
ชาวช้าง	*chao chang*	elephant staff

Titles transliterated, not translated:

นาย	*nai*
พัน ,หัวพัน	*phan, hua phan*
ขุน	*khun*
หมื่น ,หัวหมื่น	*muen, hua muen*
หลวง	*luang*
พระ	*phra*
พญา	*phya*

Weights and Length

บาท	*baht*	15 grams
ตำลึง	*tamlueng*	60 grams
ชั่ง	*chang*	1,200 grams
เส้น	*sen*	40 meters
วา	*wa*	2 meters, one fathom

Glossary

aphirom อภิรม—A term sometimes used for a long-handled, multi-tiered umbrella, and sometimes as a collective term for all "tall regalia," including umbrellas and other items, carried in processions and planted above thrones.

asura อสูร—A demon; an inhabitant of the netherworld

bodhisatta โพธิสัตว์—A Buddha-to-be; the Buddha in a previous life

casket เจียด *jiat*—A lidded container, often octagonal, presented as insignia of rank

chaophraya เจ้าพระยา—A lord; in late Ayutthaya, the title of the highest rank in the official nobility

dhamma ธรรม *thamma*—The teaching of the Buddha; nature; justice; truth

four pillars จตุสดมภ์ *jatusadom*—The four original departments of royal government: palace, land, city, and treasury

garuda ครุฑ *krut*—A mythical bird, based on an eagle with a human torso; the mount of Vishnu

Issuan อิศวร—Iswara, common Thai name for the god Siva

Himavanta, Himaphan หิมพานต์—In the Three Worlds cosmology, the area beyond human habitation, populated by animals, many of them fantastic, and visited by deities; modeled on the Himalayas

Kalahom กลาโหม—One of the two major ministries, overseeing the south, and later the military

kalpa กัลป—An era

kinnari กินรี—Mythical female creature, half-bird, half-human

Lanchang ล้านช้าง—A Lao polity, once with its capital at Luang Prabang

Lanna ลานนา—A Tai polity, centered on Chiang Mai, controlling the upper valleys of the Chaophraya River system, absorbed into Siam in the late-nineteenth century

Lesser Era จุลศักราช—*Chula Sakkarat*, CS; a calendrical system, CE minus 638

Mahatthai มหาดไทย—One of the two major ministries, overseeing the north, and later the civilian administration

Mon มอญ—A language and ethnic group, related to Khmer, mostly found in southern Myanmar

Mount Meru พระสุเมรุ, *phra sumeru*—In Buddhist cosmology, the center of the universe

naga นาคา—A mythical snake, modeled on a cobra

Narai นารายณ์—Narayana, common Thai name for the god Visnu

nak นาก—Alloy of gold, silver, and copper with an appearance similar to silver, known among European traders as tutenague

official sala ศาลาลูกขุน(ใน) *sala luk khun (nai)*—A building where senior officials held court in the "front" section of the palace

phrai ไพร—A commoner with obligations of labor service to a king or noble

Phrakhlang พระคลัง—Minister of the treasury, from mid-Ayutthaya onward, overseeing trade and foreign relations

Ramakian รามาเกียรติ์—The Thai version of the Ramayana epic from India

rishi ฤๅษี ดาบศ, *ruesi, dabot*—A hermit or ascetic

sakdina, na ศักดินา, นา—A numerical system of ranking status, ranging from ten thousand for a *chaophraya* to five for a slave

sala ศาลา—A pavilion; a building without walls; sometimes shorthand for the official sala (see above); may refer to an audience hall with open sides

sentinelle โขลนจ่า, *khlon ja*—Female guards in the inner palace

Siam สยาม—Former name of Thailand; in mid- and later-Ayutthaya era, equivalent to today's Central Region, with spurs west to Tanaosi (Tenasserim) and east to Khorat

Songkran สงกรานต์—Thai new year, in mid-April

Three Jewels (Triple Gem) พระศรีรัตนตรัย, *phra si rattanatrai*—The Buddha, the Dhamma (teaching), and the Sangha (monkhood)

Three Worlds ไตรภูมิ, *traiphum*—The cosmology of Theravada Buddhism, particularly as represented by the *Traiphum Phra Ruang*, a text believed to originate from the Sukhothai era

wai ไหว้—Gesture of greeting and respect by joining the palms in front of the chest or face

wat วัด—Buddhist temple or monastery

yokkrabat ยกกระบัตร—An official sent from the capital to a provincial city to act as the king's spy, and later as a magistrate

Publication History of the Three Seals Code and Palace Law

Based on Pimpan Paiboonwangcharoen, "Kotmai tra sam duang: Kan sueksa ton chabap tua khian lae chabap tua phim" [Three Seals Code: Study of Manuscript and Printed Versions], in *Kotmai tra sam duang: waen song sangkhom thai* [Three Seals Code: Mirror of Thai Society], Vol. 1, ed. Winai Pongsripian (Bangkok: Thailand Research Fund, 2004). Additional information from Ishii, "Thai Thammasat," 151–54, 202–3.

Note: all entries refer to the complete Three Seals Code, unless otherwise indicated.

1849 Planned edition of Three Seals Code in two volumes by Phraya Krasaponnakit (Mot Amatyakun), proscribed by King Rama III before printing completed. Copy of first volume in the National Library.

1862–63 Dan Beach Bradley, with the permission of King Mongkut, printed a two volume edition, using Mot Amatyakun's manuscript, entitled *Nangsue rueang kotmai mueang thai* [Book on Laws of Siam], including complete Three Seals Code plus a law on robbery from the Third Reign. Ten printings.

1876–78 Three Seals Code printed in sections in issues of the *Royal Gazette*.

1880 Samuel Smith printed *Siamese Domestic Institutions: Old and New Laws on Slavery* (Bangkok: S. J. Smith's Office), including the "Code on Slavery" from the Three Seals Code and related regulations.

1895–97 Luang Damrong Thammasan (Mi) printed two-volume edition, including the Bradley version plus additional laws, as *Kotmai, mai prakat, phraratchabanyat kao mai sueng yang khong chai yu nai patjuban* [Old and New Laws and Decrees Still in Use at Present] (Bangkok: Bamrungnukunkit).

1901 Prince Ratchaburi published a two-volume edition of extracts from the laws as a handbook for judges, known as *Kotmai ratchaburi* [Ratchaburi Laws]. (Bangkok: Lahuthot).

1928 Jean Burnay, "Texte de la loi laksana moradok d'apres le manuscrit Vajirañāṇa *nithisat mo 12* CS. 1167," *Journal of the Siam Society* 22, 2: 117–51. Thai text of the "Code on inheritance," transcribed from the manuscript version of the Three Seals Code.

1930 Nithisat Printers published a facsimile version of the Three Seals Code manuscript as *Prachum kotmai phak 1* [Collected Laws, Part 1].

1930 Luang Pradit Manutham (Pridi Banomyong) published *Prachum kotmai thai* [Collected Thai Laws] (Bangkok: Nithisat). Includes the Thammasat, Tenets of Indra, and codes on debt, marriage, inheritance, miscellaneous laws, and the palace law, and a photographic facsimile of the manuscript version.

1930 Jean Burnay and Robert Lingat published *Lois siamoises, Code de 1805 A.D. xiv: Lois diverses, texte* (Bangkok: Imprimeria de l'Assomption), an edition of the "Code on miscellaneous subjects" transcribed from the manuscript version of the Three Seals Code.

1931 Wachirayan Library published *Kotmai ratchakan thi 1 chabap tra sam duang aiya luang lae aiya rat* [Three Seals Edition of Laws of King Rama I, "Code of Crimes against Government" and "Code of Crimes against People"] (Bangkok: Wachirayan Library). Published as a cremation volume.

1935 Sathian Lailak et al. published the Bradley version without the additional law on robbery in *Prachum kotmai prajam sok lem 1–2*.

1938–39 Thammasat University published a three-volume version, edited by Robert Lingat, as *Pramuan kotmai ratchakan thi 1 C.S. 1166 phim tam chabap luang tra sam duang* [Law Code of King Rama I, 1805, Printed following the Three Seals Edition].

1962–63 Ongkankha Khong Khurusapha (government printers for textbooks, etc.) published a five-volume edition, based on the Thammasat University edition with corrections, entitled *Kotmai tra sam duang* [Three Seals Code]. Third edition 1994.

1978 Thammasat University's Fine Arts Department published a single-volume edition, based on the Thammasat University edition, entitled *Rueang kotmai tra sam duang*.

2005 Two-volume edition of the Palace Law, edited by Winai Pongsripian, published by the Thailand Research Fund as *Kot monthianban chabap chaloemprakiat* [Palace Law, Royal Anniversary Edition] on the occasion of the two-hundredth anniversary of the Three Seals Code and the sixty-year jubilee of the reign of King Bhumibol Adulyadej.

2007 Royal Institute published a two-volume edition with facsimiles of the manuscripts and transcription, entitled *Kotmai tra sam duang: chabap ratchabanditsathan* [Three Seals Code, Royal Institute Edition].

2015 Royal Institute published an annotated edition of the Thammasat and Tenets of Indra, entitled *Kotmai tra sam duang: phra thammasat lae lak inthaphat* [Three Seals Code: Thammasat and Tenets of Indra].

BIBLIOGRAPHY

Aroonrut Wichienkeeo. "Lanna Customary Law." In *Thai Law: Buddhist Law. Essays on the Legal History of Thailand, Laos and Burma,* ed. A. Huxley, 31–42. Bangkok: White Orchid, 1996.

Attachak Satyanurak. "The Intellectual Aspects of Strong Kingship in the Late Nineteenth Century." *Journal of the Siam Society* 88 (2000): 72–95.

Baker, Chris. "Ayutthaya Rising: From Land or Sea?" *Journal of Southeast Asian Studies* 34, 1 (2003): 41–62.

———. "The Grand Palace in the *Description of Ayutthaya*: Translation and Commentary." *Journal of the Siam Society* 101 (2013): 69–112.

———. "Final Part of the *Description of Ayutthaya* with Remarks on Defence, Policing, Infrastructure, and Sacred Sites." *Journal of the Siam Society* 102 (2014): 179–210.

Baker, Chris, and Pasuk Phongpaichit, tr. and ed. *The Tale of Khun Chang Khun Phaen.* Chiang Mai: Silkworm Books, 2010.

———. *Yuan Phai: A Thai Military Epic Poem.* Chiang Mai: Silkworm Books, forthcoming.

Bradley, Dan Beach. *Phraratchaphongsawadan krung si ayutthaya chabap mo bratle* [Royal Chronicles of Ayutthaya, Bradley Edition]. Bangkok: Kosit, 2006 [1864].

Breazeale, Kennon. "Portuguese Impressions of Ayutthaya in the Late Sixteenth Century." In *500 Years of Thai-Portuguese Relations: A Festschrift,* ed. Michael Smithies, 50–58, Bangkok: Siam Society, 2011.

Busakorn Lailert. "The Ban Phlu Luang Dynasty 1688–1767: A Study of the Thai Monarchy during the Closing Years of the Ayuthya Period." PhD dissertation, SOAS, University of London, 1972.

Caron, François, and Joost Schouten. *A True Description of the Mighty Kingdoms of Japan and Siam.* Bangkok: Siam Society, 1986 [1663].

Channarong Bunnun. "Phra Thammasat." In *Nitipratya thai: prakat phraratcha prarop lak inthaphat phra thammasat lae On the Laws of Mu'ung Thai or Siam*, ed. Winai Pongsripian and Wirawan Ngamsantikun. Bangkok: Thailand Research Fund, 2006.

Chatraphon Jindadet. "Kan borihan ratchasamnuek fai nai ratchasamai phrabat somdet phra chulachomklao chaoyuhua" [The Inner Court Administration in the Reign of King Chulalongkorn]. *Warasan ruam botkhwam prawatisat* [Journal of the Historical Society] 25 (2003): 145–200.

Chin Youdi. "Khrueang pradap sian" [Headdresses]. In *Jittrakam lae sinlapa watthu nai kru phraprang wat ratchaburana jangwat phranakhon si ayutthaya* [Murals and Artefacts in the Crypt of Wat Ratchaburana, Ayutthaya Province], 57–62. Bangkok: Fine Arts Department, 2015 [1958].

Choti Kalyanamit. *Phojananukrom sathapattayakam lae silpa kiao nueng* [Dictionary of Architecture and Related Arts]. Bangkok: Muang Boran, 2005.

Chulalongkorn, King. *Chotmaihet phraratchakit raiwan phraratchaniphon nai phrabat somdet phra julajomklao jao yu* hua [Diary of Royal Activities of His Majesty King Chulalongkorn]. 24 volumes. Bangkok: Fine Arts Department, 1934–65.

———. *Phraratchaphithi sipsong duean* [Royal Ceremonies of the Twelve Months]. Bangkok: Khlang Withaya, 1960 [1911], 3rd printing.

Collins, Steven. "The Discourse on What is Primary (Aggañña Sutta), an Annotated Translation." *Journal of Indian Philosophy* 21 (1993): 301–93.

Crosby, Kate. *Theravada Buddhism: Continuity, Diversity, and Identity*. London: Wiley Blackwell, 2014.

Cushman, Richard D. *The Royal Chronicles of Ayutthaya*. A synoptic translation by Richard D. Cushman, ed. David K. Wyatt. Bangkok: Siam Society, 2000.

Damrong Rajanubhab, Prince. "Tamnan kotmai mueang thai" [History of Thailand's Laws]. In *Phraratchaphongsawadan chabap phraratchahatalekha* [Royal Chronicles, Royal Autograph Edition]. Bangkok: Fine Arts Department, 1999.

———. *Our Wars with the Burmese*, trans. Phra Phraison Salarak and ed. Chris Baker. Bangkok: White Lotus, 2001.

Day, Tony. *Fluid Iron: State Formation in Southeast Asia*. Honolulu: University of Hawai'i Press, 2002.

Dhani Nivat, Prince. "The Old Siamese Conception of the Monarchy." *Journal of the Siam Society* 36 (1947): 91–106.

Doniger, Wendy, and Brian K. Smith, tr. *The Laws of Manu*. Calcutta: Penguin, 1991.

Drago, Roland. "Robert Lingat (1892–1972)." *Revue internationale de droit comparé* 24, no. 3 (Juillet–Septembre 1972): 702–4. Viewed at: www.persee.fr/web/revues/home/prescript/article/ridc_0035-3337_1972_num_24_3_15031 (accessed December 1, 2015).

Drekmeier, Charles. *Kingship and Community in Early India*. Stanford: Stanford University Press, 1962.

Flood, Thadeus, and Chadin Flood, tr. and ed. *The Dynastic Chronicles, Bangkok Era, The First Reign, Chaophraya Thiphakorawong Edition*. Tokyo: Center for East Asian Cultural Studies, Vol. I, Text, 1978; Vol II, Annotations and Commentary, 1990.

Forchammer, Emil, tr. *King Wagaru's Manu Dhammasattham: Text, Translation and Notes*, preface by John Jardine. Rangoon: Superintendent of Government Printing, 1892.

Gerini, G. E. "Historical Retrospect of Junkceylon Island, Part 1." *Journal of the Siam Society* 2, no. 2 (1905): 2–148.

Gervaise, Nicolas. *The Natural and Political History of the Kingdom of Siam*, trans. John Villiers. Bangkok: White Lotus, 1998 [1688].

Ghosh, Lipi. *Tai Cultural Heritage in Northeast India: A Study of the Tai-Ahoms*. Bangkok: Institute of Thai Studies, Chulalongkorn University, 2003.

Griswold, A. B., and Prasert na Nagara. "A Law Promulgated by the King of Ayudhyā in 1397 A.D. Epigraphic and Historical Studies, No. 4." *Journal of the Siam Society* 57, no. 1 (1969): 109–48.

———. "King Lödaiya of Sukhodaya and His Contemporaries. Epigraphic and Historical Studies, No. 10." *Journal of the Siam Society* 60, no. 1 (1972): 21–152.

Heeck, Gijsbert. *A Traveller in Siam in the Year 1655: Extracts from the Journal of Gijsbert Heeck*, trans. Barend Jan Terwiel. Chiang Mai: Silkworm Books, 2008.

Huxley, Andrew. "Thai, Mon and Burmese Dhammathats: Who Influenced Whom?" In *Thai Law: Buddhist Law: Essays on the Legal History of Thailand, Laos and Burma*, ed. A. Huxley, 81–132. Bangkok: White Orchid Press, 1996.

———. "When Manu Met Mahasammata." *Journal of Indian Philosophy* 24, no. 6 (1996): 593–621.

———. "The Importance of the Dhammathats in Burmese Law and Culture." *Journal of Burma Studies* 1 (1997): 1–18.

Ishii, Yoneo, Mamoru Shibayama, and Aroonrut Wichienkiew. *Computer Concordance to the Law of the Three Seals*. Bangkok: Amarin, 1991. Index available at: http://adap.crma.ac.th/KotmaiTraSamDuang/index.html (accessed December 1, 2015).

Ishii, Yoneo. "The Thai Thammasat (with a Note on the Lao Thammasat)." In *The Laws of South-East Asia*, ed. M. B. Hooker, Vol. 1, 43–203. Singapore: Butterworths, 1986.

———. *Sangha, State and Society: Thai Buddhism in History*, trans. Peter Hawkes. Monographs of the Center of Southeast Asian Studies, Kyoto University, 16. Honolulu: University of Hawai'i Press, 1986.

Jacq-Hergoualc'h. *Étude historique et critique du livre de Simon de La Loubère 'Du Royaume de Siam', Paris 1691*. Paris: Editions Recherche sur les Civilisations, 1987.

Jakkrit Uttho. "Khwam samphan khong kotmai tra sam duang kap kotmai chabap chaloeisak thi phop nai hua mueang tang tang" [Relationship between the Three Seals Code and Laws Found in Provincial Centers]. In *Kotmai tra sam duang: waen song sangkhom thai* [Three Seals Code: Mirror of Thai Society], ed. Winai Pongsripian, 61–116. Bangkok: Thailand Research Fund, 2004.

Jittrakam lae sinlapa watthu nai kru phraprang wat ratchaburana jangwat phranakhon si ayutthaya [Murals and Artifacts in the Crypt of Wat Ratchaburana, Ayutthaya Province]. Bangkok: Fine Arts Department, 2015 [1958].

Kaempfer, Engelbert. *A Description of the Kingdom of Siam 1690*. Bangkok: Orchid Press, 1998 [1727].

Kern, Fritz. *Kingship and Law in the Middle Ages*, trans. S. B. Chrimes. Oxford: Blackwell, 1939.

Khamchan sansoen phrakiat somdet phra phutthajao luang prasat thong [Poem in Praise of King Prasat Thong]. Bangkok: Fine Arts Department, 2000.

Khamhaikan chao krung kao [Testimony of the Inhabitants of the Old Capital]. Bangkok: Chotmaihet, 2001.

Khamhaikan khun luang ha wat [Testimony of the King Who Entered a Wat]. Bangkok: Sukhothai Thammathirat University, 2004.

Kotmai tra sam duang: phra thammanun [Three Seals Law: Phra Thammanun]. Bangkok: Royal Institute, 2010.

Krisda Boonyasmit. "Khrongsang kotmai tra sam duang: kan phicharana mai" [The Structure of the Three Seals Code: A Reconsideration]. In *Kotmai tra sam duang: waen song sangkhom thai* [Three Seals Code: Mirror of Thai Society], ed. Winai Pongsripain, Vol. 2. Bangkok: Thailand Research Fund, 2004.

———. "Nueaha khong kotmai tra sam duang" [Content of the Three Seals Code]. In Royal Institute, *Kotmai tra sam duang: chabap ratchabanditsathan* [Three Seals Code: Royal Institute Edition]. Bangkok: Royal Institute, 2007.

———. "Nueaha khong phra thammanun" [Content of the Phra Thammanun]. In *Kotmai tra sam duang: phra thammanun* [Three Seals Code: Phra Thammanun]. 3–14. Bangkok: Royal Institute, 2010.

KTSD. *Kotmai tra sam duang* [Three Seals Code]. Five vols. Bangkok: Khurusapha 1994 [1805].

La Loubère, Simon de. *A New Historical Relation of the Kingdom of Siam*, trans. A. P. Gen. London: n.p., 1793.

Lammerts, D. Christian. "The Dhammavilāsa Dhammathat: A Critical Historiography, Analysis, and Translation of the Text." MA dissertation, Cornell University, 2005.

———. "Buddhism and Written Law: Dhammasattha Manuscripts and Texts in Premodern Burma." PhD dissertation, Cornell University, 2010.

———. "Narratives of Buddhist Legislation: Textual Authority and Legal Heterodoxy in Seventeenth through Nineteenth-Century Burma." *Journal of Southeast Asian Studies* 44, no. 1 (2013): 118–44.

———. *Buddhism and Written Law: Dhammasattha Literature and Jurisprudence in Burma, c. 1200–1850*. Forthcoming.

———. "A Narrative of the Origins of Burmese Written Law." Unpublished manuscript.

Lingat, R. "Note sur la revision des lois siamoises en 1805." *Journal of the Siam Society* 23, no. 1 (1929): 19–27.

———. "Review of *Commentaire des lois sur les epoux*, par le Pha:ja Vĩnăisŭnthon." *Journal of the Siam Society* 24, no. 2 (1931): 211–13.

———. "Influence hindoue dans l'ancien droit siamois." *Etudes de sociologie et d'ethnologie juridiques*. Paris, Editions Domat-Montchrestien, 1937.

———. "La conception du droit dans l'Indochine Hînayâniste." *Bulletin de l'École française d'Extrême-Orient* 44, no. 2 (1947–50): 163–87.

———. "Evolution of the Conception of Law in Burma and Siam." *Journal of the Siam Society* 38, no. 1 (1950): 9–31.

———. *The Classical Law of India*. Berkeley: University of California Press, 1973.

———. *Prawatisat kotmai thai*. Two vols. Bangkok: *Foundation* for the Promotion of Social Sciences and Humanities Textbooks, 1983 [1938].

Loos, Tamara. *Subject Siam: Family, Law, and Colonial Modernity in Thailand*. Ithaca: Cornell University Press, 2002.

———. "Sex in the Inner City: The Fidelity between Sex and Politics in Siam." *Journal of Asian Studies* 64, no. 4 (November 2005): 881–909.

Low, James. "On the Law of Mu'ung Thai or Siam." *Journal of the Indian Archipelago and Eastern Asia* 1 (1847): 327–429. Facsimile in *Nitipratya thai: prakat phraratcha prarop lak inthaphat phra thammasat lae On the Laws of Mu'ung Thai or Siam*, ed. Winai Pongsripian and Wirawan Ngamsantikun. Bangkok: Thailand Research Fund, 2006.

Maniphin Phromsuthirak. "Chak nak duek damban lae phraratcha phithi intharaphisek" [Churning of the Sea of Milk and the Intharaphisek Royal Ceremony]. In *Srichamaiyajan*, ed. Winai Pongsripian et al. Bangkok: Chulalongkorn University, 1997.

McDaniel, Justin T. *Gathering Leaves and Lifting Words: Histories of Buddhist Monastic Education in Laos and Thailand*. Chiang Mai: Silkworm Books, 2008.

McGill, Forest. "The Art and Architecture of the Reign of King Prasatthong of Ayutthaya (1629–1656)." PhD dissertation, University of Michigan, 1977.

Nai Pan Hla. *Eleven Mon Dhammasāt Texts*, collected and translated in collaboration with Ryuji Okudaira. Tokyo: The Centre for East Asian Cultural Studies for UNESCO and the Toyo Bunko, 1992.

O'Kane, John. *The Ship of Sulaiman*. New York: Columbia University Press, 1972.

Pallegoix, Jean-Baptiste. *Sapha phajana phasa thai: sive Dictionarium Linguae Thai* [Dictionary of the Thai language], second edition. Paris: Jussu Imperatoris Impressum, Bangkok 1896 [facsimile edition by Thailand Ministry of Education, 1999].

———. *Description of the Thai Kingdom or Siam*, trans. Walter E. J. Tips. Bangkok: White Lotus, 2000.

Panyat chadok [The Fifty Jatakas]. Bangkok: Petchkarat, 2011.

Phiset Jiajanphong. *Phra maha thammaracha kasatirat kan mueang nai prawatisat yuk sukhothai-ayutthaya* [King Phra Maha Thammaracha: Politics in the History of the Sukhothai-Ayutthaya Era]. Bangkok: Matichon, 2010.

Phojanukrom sap wannakhadi thai samai ayutthaya khlong yuan phai [Dictionary of Words in Thai Literature: Defeat of the Yuan]. Bangkok: Royal Institute, 2001.

Phraratchaphongsawadan krung kao chabap luang prasoet [Royal Chronicles of Ayutthaya, Luang Prasoet Edition]. Bangkok: Saengdao, 2001.

Pimpan Paiboonwangcharoen. "Kotmai tra sam duang: kan sueksa ton chabap tua khian lae chabap tua phim" [Three Seals Code: Study of Manuscript and Printed Versions]. In *Kotmai tra sam duang: waen song sangkhom thai* [Three Seals Code: Mirror of Thai Society], ed. Winai Pongsripian, Vol. 1, 33–60. Bangkok: Thailand Research Fund, 2004.

Piriya Krairiksh. "A Revised Dating of Ayudhya Architecture (II)." *Journal of the Siam Society* 80, no. 2 (1992): 11–26.

Piriya Krairiksh. *The Roots of Thai Art*. Bangkok: River Books, 2012.

Pitinai Chaisaengsukkul. *Kotmai haeng anajak sayam: wijai phuen than* [Law of the Siamese Kingdom: Basic Research]. Bangkok: Samcharoenphanit, 1994.

———. "New Source Material of the Siamese Kingdom." In *Thai Law: Buddhist Law. Essays on the Legal History of Thailand, Laos and Burma*, ed. A. Huxley, 43–60. Bangkok: White Orchid, 1996.

Prathip Phentako. "Phraratchawong boran" [The Ancient Royal Palace]. In *Boranasathan nai jangwat phranakhon si ayutthaya* [Monuments in Ayutthaya Province], Vol. 1, 211–37. Bangkok: Fine Arts Department and James H. W. Thompson Foundation, 2008.

Reynolds, Craig. J. "Paradigms of the Premodern State." In *Seditious Histories: Contesting Thai and Southeast Asian Pasts*, ed. Craig J. Reynolds, 31–52. Seattle: University of Washington Press, 2006.

Reynolds, Frank E., and Mani B. Reynolds, tr. and ed. *Three Worlds according to King Ruang: A Thai Buddhist Cosmology*. Berkeley, University of California Press, 1982.

Royal Institute. *Kotmai tra sam duang: chabap ratchabanditsathan* [Three Seals Code: Royal Institute Edition]. Two vols. Bangkok: Royal Institute, 2007.

Royal Institute. *Kotmai tra sam duang: phra thammanun* [Three Seals Code: Phra Thammanun]. Bangkok: Royal Institute, 2010.

Royal Institute. *Kotmai tra sam duang: phra thammasat lae lak inthaphat* [Three Seals Code: Thammasat and Tenets of Indra]. Bangkok: Royal Institute, 2015.

Saichol Satyanurak. *Phutthasasana kap naeo khit thang kanmueang nai ratchasamai phrabatsomdet phraphutthayyotfa julalok (pho. so. 2325–2352)* [Buddhism and Political Thought in the Reign of King Rama I, 1782–1809]. Bangkok: Sinlapa Watthanatham, 2003.

Sanderson, Alexis. "Vajrayāna: Origin and Function." In *Buddhism into the Year 2000: International Conference Proceedings*, 87–102. Bangkok and Los Angeles: Dhammakaya Foundation, 1994.

———. "The Śaiva Religion among the Khmers." *Bulletin de L'École française d'Extrême-Orient* 90–91 (2003–4): 349–46.

Saranukrom watthanatham thai [Thai Cultural Encyclopaedia]. Bangkok: Siam Commercial Bank, 1994.

Sarup Ritchu. "Legal Manuscripts from Southern Thailand." In *Thai Law: Buddhist Law. Essays on the Legal History of Thailand, Laos and Burma*, ed. A. Huxley, 61–72. Bangkok: White Orchid, 1996.

Seni Pramoj, MR. *Pathakatha rueang kotmai samai si ayutthaya* [A Lecture on Law in the Ayutthaya Era], delivered April 8, 1957. Bangkok: Committee for the Ayutthaya Memorial, 1957.

Skilling, Peter. "King, *Sangha* and Brahmans: Ideology, Ritual and Power in Pre-modern Siam." In *Buddhism, Power and Political Order*, ed. Ian Harriss, 182–215. London: Routledge, 2007.

Stuart-Fox, Martin, and Paul Reeve. "Symbolism in City Planning in Cambodia from Angkor to Phnom Penh." *Journal of the Siam Society* 99 (2011): 105–38.

Sujit Wongthes. "Naga sangwat wannakam ratchasamnak ayutthaya suep nang nak jak nakhon thom" [Making Love to the Naga: Ayutthaya Court Literature Descended from the Naga Princess of Angkor]. *Matichon sutsapda*, October 19, 2012.

Tamra baep thamniyom nai ratchasamnak: latthi thamniyom tang tang phak thi 15 [Manual of Court Ceremonies: Collected Customs Part 15]. Printed to celebrate the seventieth birthday of Khunying Samsanguan Aphaironnarit. Bangkok: Sophon Phipanthanakon, 1923.

Tamra chang chabap ratchakan thi 1 [Manual of Elephants, First Reign Edition]. Committee for Memorial Books and Records for Celebration of the King's Age Equaling that of King Rama I in 2000. Bangkok: Ruansin, 2002.

Tamra phraratchaphithi kao [Manual of Old Royal Ceremonies]. Printed by Phrachaoborommawongthue Kromluang Phromworanuk. Bangkok: Sophon Phiphanthanathon, 1923.

Terwiel, Barend J. "The Oldest Law Texts in Mainland Southeast Asia: Some Preliminary Remarks." *Tai Culture* 6, nos. 1 & 2 (2001): 269–72.

Than Tun. *The Royal Orders of Burma*. Ten vols. Kyoto: Center for Southeast Asian Studies, 1983–90.

Thapanan Nipithakul. "Les sources du droit et du pouvoir politique au travers des anciens textes thaïlandais." Doctoral thesis, Université Toulouse 1 Capitole, 2004.

Thep Sarikabut. *Horasat nai wannakhadi* [Astrology in Literature]. Bangkok: Sinlapa Bannakhan, 1963.

Tri Amatayakul. *The Official Guide to Ayutthaya and Bang Pa-in*. Bangkok: Fine Arts Department, 1972.

Tun Aung Chain, tr. *Chronicle of Ayutthaya: A Translation of the Yodaya Yazawin*. Yangon: Myanmar Historical Commission, 2005.

Van Vliet's Siam, ed. Chris Baker, Dhiravat na Pombejra, Alfons van der Kraan, and David *Wyatt*. Chiang Mai: Silkworm Books, 2005.

Vickery, Michael. "The 2/K.125 Fragment, a Lost Chronicle of Ayutthaya." *Journal of the Siam Society* 65, no. 1 (1977): 1–80.

———. "A Guide through Some Recent Sukhothai Historiography." *Journal of the Siam Society* 66, no. 2 (1978): 182–247.

———. "Prolegomena to Methods for Using the Ayutthayan Laws as Historical Source Material." *Journal of the Siam Society* 72 (1984): 37–58.

———. "The Constitution of Ayutthaya: An Investigation into the Three Seals Code." In *Thai Law: Buddhist Law. Essays on the Legal History of Thailand, Laos and Burma*, ed. A. Huxley, 133–210. Bangkok: White Orchid, 1996.

Visanu Kreu-ngam. "Kotken kan suep ratchasombat khong thai" [Thai Law of Succession]. *Warasan ratchabanditsathan* [Journal of the Royal Institute] 31, no. 2 (2012): 1–32.

Wales, H. G. Quaritch. *Siamese State Ceremonies: Their History and Function*. London: Bernard Quartich, 1931.

Winai Pongsripian. "Khwam samkhan khong 'Kotmai tra sam duang: waen song sangkhom thai'" [The Importance of "The Three Seals Code: Mirror of Thai Society"]. In *Kotmai tra sam duang: waen song sangkhom thai* [Three Seals Code: Mirror of Thai Society], ed. Winai Pongsripian, Vol. 1, 1–32. Bangkok: Thailand Research Fund, 2004.

Winai Pongsripian, ed. *Kot monthianban chabap chaloemprakiat* [Palace Law, Royal Anniversary Version]. Published in commemoration of King Rama I on the two-hundredth anniversary of the Three Seals Code and of King Rama IX on the sixtieth anniversary of his reign, two volumes. Bangkok: Thailand Research Fund, 2005.

Winai Pongsripian, ed. *Kamsuam samut: sut yot kamsuansin* (Ocean Lament: Ultimate of the Lament Genre). Bangkok: Thailand Research Fund, 2010.

Winai Pongsripian. "Phraratcha phongsawadan krung si ayutthaya chabap ho phra samut wachirayan (chabap plik mai lek tabian 222 2/k 104)" [The Wachirayan Library Edition of the Royal Chronicles of Ayutthaya (no. 222 2/k 104)]. In *100 ekkasan samkhan sapsara prawatisat thai* [100 Important Documents, the Essence of Thai History], no. 13, 49–167. Bangkok: Thailand Research Fund, 2012.

Wood, W. A. R. *A History of Siam*. Bangkok: Chalermnit, 1994 [1924].

Woraphon Phuphongphan. "Kan borihan ratchakan krom wang sueksa jak phra-aiyakan tamnaeng na phonlaruen nai kotmai tra sam duang" [The Administration of the Palace Studied from the Civil List in the Three Seals Law]. *Warasan ruam botkhwam prawatisat* [Journal of the Historical Society] 27 (2005): 37–77.

———. "Phaplak sathaban kasat nai kot monthianban" [Image of the Monarchy in the Palace Law]. In *Kot monthianban chabap chaloemphrakiat phon ngan wijai* [Palace Law, Royal Anniversary Edition, Research Results], ed. Winai Pongsripian, 165–258. Published in commemoration of King Rama I on the two-hundredth anniversary of the Three Seals Code and of King Rama IX on the sixtieth anniversary of his reign, Bangkok: Thailand Research Fund, 2005.

———. *Sathaban kasat nai kot monthianban* [Kingship in the Palace Law]. Bangkok: Silpakorn University, 2012.

Wyatt, David K. "The *Thai 'Palatine Law'* and Malacca." In *Studies in Thai History*, ed. D. K. Wyatt, 82–89. Chiang Mai: Silkworm Books, 1994 [earlier version in *Journal of the Siam Society* 55, no. 2 (1967): 279–86].

Yelle, Robert. *Semiotics of Religion: Signs of the Sacred in History*. London: Bloomsbury, 2013.

Zhou Daguan. *A Record of Cambodia: The Land and its People*, trans. and with an intro. and notes by Peter Harris. Chiang Mai: Silkworm Books. 2007.

www.ingramcontent.com/pod-product-compliance
Ingram Content Group UK Ltd.
Pitfield, Milton Keynes, MK11 3LW, UK
UKHW012250060225
454777UK00008B/717